MW01007435

LLOYD D. NEWELL

LET HIM
ASK *of* GOD

DAILY WISDOM FROM
THE LIFE AND TEACHINGS
OF JOSEPH SMITH

DESERET
BOOK

SALT LAKE CITY, UTAH

Library of Congress Cataloging-in-Publication Data

Newell, Lloyd D.
    Let him ask of God : daily wisdom from the life and teach-
ings of Joseph Smith / Lloyd D. Newell.
        p.   cm.
    ISBN 978-1-60641-001-1 (hardbound : alk. paper)
    1. The Church of Jesus Christ of Latter-day Saints—Sacred
books—Quotations.   2. Devotional calendars—The Church
of Jesus Christ of Latter-day Saints.   3. Mormon Church—
Sacred books—Quotations.   4. Devotional calendars—
Mormon Church.   5. Smith, Joseph, 1805–1844.—I.Title.
    BX8621.N49 2008
    242'.2—dc22   2008024940

Printed in the United States of America
Inland Graphics, Menomonee Falls, WI

10   9   8   7   6   5   4   3   2   1

Preface

From my earliest years, I have always believed and never doubted that Joseph Smith was a prophet of God. Whenever I've had questions about his life or wondered about the truthfulness of his teachings and prophetic mission, I would consider the Book of Mormon, the Doctrine and Covenants, the Church he established, and the great rolling forth of the gospel of Jesus Christ he restored. Almost immediately, I would feel the quiet confidence and peaceful reassurance that Joseph Smith was the Lord's anointed prophet, the preeminent revealer of Christ and the plan of salvation in these last days. This book has served to deepen and expand that testimony; it has reaffirmed in powerful and profound ways my love and admiration for the Prophet. I add my voice in chorus with so many others on both sides of the veil in "praise to the man who communed with Jehovah."

In the preparation of this volume, I gratefully

acknowledge the encouragement and expertise of Jana Erickson, Janna Devore, Suzanne Brady, and Rachael Ward of Deseret Book. As always, I'm deeply thankful for my wife and children, who have supported me in this project; for my parents, who taught me to follow the prophets; and for many others who have helped me along the way.

JANUARY

Our only confidence can be in God;
our only wisdom obtained from Him.
JOSEPH SMITH

This being the beginning of a new year, my heart is filled with gratitude to God that He has preserved my life, and the lives of my family, while another year has passed away.

JOSEPH SMITH
HISTORY OF THE CHURCH, 2:352

In Kirtland, Ohio, on the cold morning of January 1, 1836, Joseph Smith reflected on the bounteous blessings bestowed upon him by the Lord, "We have been sustained and upheld in the midst of a wicked and perverse generation, although exposed to all the afflictions, temptations, and misery that are incident to human life; for this I feel to humble myself in dust and ashes, as it were, before the Lord" (*History of the Church*, 2:352). Gratitude is always part of a great soul. Joseph Smith was a man of character and strength, a man of goodness and compassion, a man of thankfulness and humility. He knew he was wholly dependent upon the Lord and that if he was grateful and obedient the Lord would sustain and magnify him in his divine commission (D&C 59:21). The Prophet Joseph repeatedly expressed thanksgiving to God throughout his life. We emulate the Prophet by being people of character and devotion whose hearts are filled with gratitude to God.

*When you climb up a ladder, you must begin at the bottom,
and ascend step by step, until you arrive at the top; and so it is
with the principles of the gospel—you must begin with the first,
and go on until you learn all the principles of exaltation.*

JOSEPH SMITH
HISTORY OF THE CHURCH, 6:306–7

First things first: we begin on the bottom step of the gospel ladder; with faithfulness, hope, and charity, we move ever upward, always forward into eternity. The life and teachings of the Prophet Joseph exemplify this eternal truth: if we humbly consecrate our desires, attitudes, and actions to becoming true disciples of the Lord Jesus Christ, line upon line, little by little, we will progress into eternity. Referring to the principles of exaltation, the Prophet taught, "But it will be a great while after you have passed through the veil before you will have learned them. It is not all to be comprehended in this world; it will be a great work to learn our salvation and exaltation even beyond the grave" (*History of the Church,* 6:307). As we continue to learn and progress, and as we follow more fully our Heavenly Father's great plan of mercy and happiness, we will be filled with the charity and joy that leads faithful followers of Jesus Christ to "the peace of God, which passeth all understanding" (Philippians 4:7).

I teach the people correct principles and they govern themselves.

JOSEPH SMITH
JOURNAL OF DISCOURSES 10:57–58

When the Prophet Joseph was asked by a visitor to Nauvoo how he was able to govern such a large group of people, he responded with the true order of the kingdom of God: we are given correct principles and the agency to choose whether or not to follow them. Such is the Lord's way. Just as the devil cannot coerce us into wickedness, the Lord will not force us into righteousness. We are agents unto ourselves and are free to choose good or evil, life or death, liberty or captivity (Helaman 14:30–31). It is all volitional—a free choice with accompanying consequences (D&C 130:20–21). In all the commands of God, we are free to choose for ourselves (Moses 3:17). Obedience leads to freedom; submission leads to ultimate victory. The Prophet Joseph and each of his successors teach true principles that—if we exercise our agency to humbly follow—will lead us to "peace in this world, and eternal life in the world to come" (D&C 59:23).

JANUARY 4

*I step forth into the field to tell you what
the Lord is doing, and what you must do to enjoy the
smiles of your Savior in these last days.*

JOSEPH SMITH
HISTORY OF THE CHURCH, 1:313

On this day in 1833, by commandment of the Lord,
Joseph Smith wrote to a New York newspaper editor,
provided information about the rise of the Church,
and rebuked the wicked and apathetic: "I think that it
is high time for a Christian world to awake out of
sleep, and cry mightily to that God, day and night,
whose anger we have justly incurred" (*History of the
Church,* 1:313). The Prophet clearly and boldly put forth
a witness and a warning that in order to "enjoy the
Holy Spirit of God to a fulness and escape the judgments of God, which are almost ready to burst upon
the nations of the earth," all people must repent and
be baptized, and receive the Holy Ghost (ibid., 1:314).
If we wish to enjoy the smiles of the Savior and be
clasped everlastingly in the arms of Jesus (Mormon
5:11) we must heed the counsel of the prophets: exercise faith and repent, be humble and obedient, endure
to the end in righteousness.

*The Great Parent of the universe looks upon the
whole of the human family with a fatherly care and paternal
regard; He views them as His offspring.*

JOSEPH SMITH
HISTORY OF THE CHURCH, 4:595

God is a loving Father, whose children are literally in His image and likeness (Genesis 1:26–27). Our spirits, which are in the likeness of our physical bodies (D&C 77:2), were begotten of Him in a pre-earth estate. Absent the doctrine of premortal existence, the God of the sectarian creeds becomes a metaphorical father whose creations are *ex nihilo,* meaning "out of nothing." When the meridian apostles died, the knowledge of God was taken with them. The heavens were sealed, prophets were forgotten, and God became an abstract, incomprehensible being. The Prophet Joseph revealed God anew as a personal, approachable, Heavenly Father. Latter-day prophets stand with Joseph Smith in declaring: "All human beings—male and female—are created in the image of God. Each is a beloved spirit son or daughter of heavenly parents, and, as such, each has a divine nature and destiny" ("The Family: A Proclamation to the World," *Ensign,* November 1995, 102).

God has tried you. You are a good people;
therefore I love you with all my heart. . . . You have stood
by me in the hour of trouble, and I am willing to
sacrifice my life for your preservation.

JOSEPH SMITH
HISTORY OF THE CHURCH, 6:500

Joseph Smith and his followers knew much of trials
and tribulation since the earliest days of the Church.
God tried and then refined the Prophet Joseph and
his faithful followers in the furnace of affliction.
Joseph also understood the bitterness of betrayal and
the sting of apostasy because of so many who turned
against him. But the disaffection of some made him
ever more loving and loyal to those who stood with
him. Although his responsibilities and burdens were
incredibly great, he did not bear them alone. Countless followers stood next to him, gathered to Zion to
uphold him, joined in faith and fellowship with the
Saints of God to follow the chosen seer and build up
the kingdom of God on earth. Joseph was ever faithful
to the loyal Saints. Indeed, he would give his life for
his friends.

God hath not revealed anything to Joseph, but what He will make known unto the Twelve, and even the least Saint may know all things as fast as he is able to bear them.

JOSEPH SMITH
HISTORY OF THE CHURCH, 3:380

We are to cultivate the spirit of revelation and the spirit of testimony. The principles of the gospel and the mysteries of godliness are not reserved for only a select few. If we are meek and teachable, if we seek the Spirit of the Lord in all diligence, God will make known to us His truths. Joseph Smith was eager for Latter-day Saints and others to receive all the light and wisdom they could; he spent his life tirelessly teaching what God had so liberally revealed to him. The Prophet Joseph had an abundant mentality and generosity of spirit that created within him a desire to share the eternal verities of the kingdom. We also are to search, ponder, and pray to receive more gospel light; we are to work on our problems and then counsel with the Lord and seek the ratifying seal of the Holy Spirit on the conclusions we reach; we are to nurture within us the spirit of revelation and testimony by seeking to know with all our hearts the everlasting truths proclaimed by the prophets.

*When a seal is put upon the father and mother, it secures
their posterity, so that they cannot be lost, but will be saved by
virtue of the covenant of their father and mother.*

JOSEPH SMITH
HISTORY OF THE CHURCH, 5:530

We are blessed by the covenants we make and keep.
When a father and mother have entered into gospel ordinances and kept their covenants in righteousness they
will be blessed both here and hereafter; they can be
assured of not only their own eternal reward but that of
their offspring as well. Parents, like the parents of rebellious Alma the younger and so many others, who do not
give up on their wayward children but keep their
covenants and trust God and His promises, will secure
their posterity for eternity. The story of Alma is not an
isolated miracle—whether in this life or the next. Such is
the power of covenants; such is the good news of the
gospel; such is the redemptive work of the Savior. He
starts with the center core of the gospel covenant—where
faithful parents sealed for time and all eternity in the new
and everlasting covenant of marriage live.

*Words and language are inadequate to express the gratitude that
I owe to God for having given me so honorable a parentage.*

JOSEPH SMITH
HISTORY OF THE CHURCH, 5:126

The Prophet Joseph said of his father, "He was a great and a good man. . . . He was of noble stature and possessed a high, and holy, and exalted, and virtuous mind. . . . I love my father and his memory" (*History of the Church,* 5:125–26). Just a few months following Joseph Smith Sr.'s death, the Lord revealed that the Prophet's father was in His presence and declared, "Blessed and holy is he, for he is mine" (D&C 124:19). Joseph's mother, Lucy Mack Smith, who gave birth to eleven children, was also beloved by the Prophet. "My mother is also one of the noblest and the best of all women," he said (*History of the Church,* 5:126). Both his parents played vital roles in establishing the kingdom of God upon the earth; they shared in the Prophet's sorrow and sufferings. How fitting it is that God would have His prophet born to parents of love and devotion, of goodness and strength. We honor the parents of the Prophet.

*How good and glorious it has seemed unto me, to find
pure and holy friends, who are faithful, just, and true, and
whose hearts fail not; and whose knees are confirmed
and do not falter while they wait upon the Lord.*

JOSEPH SMITH
HISTORY OF THE CHURCH, 5:107

The Prophet Joseph wrote these words after being visited by some of his friends while in hiding during the Nauvoo period of intense persecution. His enemies had again sought his life. Imagine the feelings of his heart as he expressed why these people were his friends: "These love the God that I serve; they love the truths that I promulgate; they love those virtuous, and those holy doctrines that I cherish in my bosom with the warmest feelings of my heart, and with that zeal which cannot be denied. I love friendship and truth; I love virtue and law; I love the God of Abraham, of Isaac, and of Jacob; and they are my brethren, and I shall live; and because I live they shall live also" (*History of the Church,* 5:108–9). As he prayed for his friends, the still small voice whispered to his soul, "These, that share your toils with such faithful hearts, shall reign with you in the kingdom of their God" (*History of the Church,* 5:109). What a glorious reward of faithful friendship!

He had been a humble farmer lad—divine authority sat so becomingly upon him that men looked at him with reverent awe. He had been unlearned in the great things of art and science—he walked with God until human knowledge was to his eyes an open book.

GEORGE Q. CANNON
LIFE OF JOSEPH SMITH, 19

George Q. Cannon, who was born on this day in Liverpool, England, in 1827, arrived in Nauvoo as a young man in the spring of 1843. He recognized instantly who Joseph Smith was and said that he could have known him among ten thousand. The Prophet stood out from all the men he had ever seen. In his biography of the Prophet Joseph, Cannon wrote: "Whether engaging in manly sport, during hours of relaxation, or proclaiming words of wisdom in pulpit or grove, he was ever the leader. His magnetism was masterful, and his heroic qualities won universal admiration. Where he moved all classes were forced to recognize in him the man of power. Strangers journeying to see him from a distance, knew him the moment their eyes beheld his person. . . . The Prophet's life was exalted and unselfish. His death was a sealing martyrdom, following after that which was completed upon Calvary for the redemption of a world" (*Life of Joseph Smith, the Prophet*, 20–21).

I do not dwell upon your faults, and you shall not upon mine. Charity, which is love, covereth a multitude of sins, and I have often covered up all the faults among you . . . We should cultivate a meek, quiet, and peaceable spirit.

JOSEPH SMITH
HISTORY OF THE CHURCH, 5:517

The natural man, who dwells on the faults and foibles of others, has always been an enemy to God. A true disciple of the Master seeks to become "a saint through the atonement of Christ the Lord, and becometh as a child, submissive, meek, humble, patient, full of love, willing to submit to all things which the Lord seeth fit to inflict upon him, even as a child doth submit to his father" (Mosiah 3:19). The childlike spirit of charity is calming, harmonious, and humble; it is also courageous and powerful. The Prophet Joseph continually exhorted the Saints to cultivate the virtues of goodness and love: "As you increase in innocence and virtue, as you increase in goodness, let your hearts expand, let them be enlarged towards others; you must be long-suffering, and bear with the faults and errors of mankind" (*History of the Church,* 4:606). All of us, as imperfect and developing people, need patience and love and forgiveness from the Lord, and for ourselves and each other.

It is my meditation all the day, and more than my meat and drink, to know how I shall make the Saints of God comprehend the visions that roll like an overflowing surge before my mind. Oh! how I would delight to bring before you things which you never thought of!

JOSEPH SMITH
HISTORY OF THE CHURCH, 5:362

The Prophet Joseph was known for his big-hearted approach to life. His feelings, like the revelations from heaven, would overflow at times because of his deep affection for the Saints, his humility and empathy, and his magnanimity of heart. During a funeral discourse in April 1843, he testified of the resurrection and bore witness to the unfolding gospel plan: "All your losses will be made up to you in the resurrection, provided you continue faithful. By the vision of the Almighty I have seen it. . . . Hosanna to Almighty God, that rays of light begin to burst forth upon us even now. I cannot find words in which to express myself. I am not learned, but I have as good feelings as any man. O that I had the language of the archangel to express my feelings once to my friends! But I never expect to in this life. When others rejoice, I rejoice; when they mourn, I mourn" (*History of the Church*, 5:362). His abundant life and mission was to open the windows of heaven.

If any of you lack wisdom, let him ask of God, that giveth to all men liberally, and upbraideth not; and it shall be given him.

JAMES 1:5

According to Elder Bruce R. McConkie, James 1:5 "has had a greater impact and a more far reaching effect upon mankind than any other single sentence ever recorded by any prophet in any age" (*Doctrinal New Testament Commentary*, 3:246–47). Joseph Smith said, "Never did any passage of scripture come with more power to the heart of man than this did at this time to mine. It seemed to enter with great force into every feeling of my heart. I reflected on it again and again, knowing that if any person needed wisdom from God, I did. . . . I at length came to the determination to 'ask of God,' concluding that if he gave wisdom to them that lacked wisdom, and would give liberally, and not upbraid, I might venture" (JS–H 1:12–13). We too can take the words of James to heart and act with faith. The Lord does not upbraid or find fault with our feeble but honest inquiries; rather, He rewards us liberally for coming unto Him.

*Until we have perfect love we are liable to fall
and when we have a testimony that our names are sealed in the
Lamb's book of life we have perfect love and then it is
impossible for false Christs to deceive us.*

JOSEPH SMITH
TEACHINGS, 9

A safeguard against deception is to be filled with a pure love of God and all mankind. This love can become so perfect and so in tune with the spirit of the Lord that our hearts become sanctified and steady in the cause of Christ. Perfect love casts away all fear and doubt (1 John 4:18), all anxiety and animosity; perfect love creates within us unwavering faith and reassuring hope. Those with this love have their names written in the book of life, the record kept in heaven that records the names of the faithful—those who will inherit eternal life (D&C 76:68; 132:19). The book of life names the righteous Saints who have overcome the world and progressed along the pathway to perfection while they are in mortality. The names of the wicked will be blotted out from this divine record (Revelation 13:8; 22:19). It is perfect love that purifies our heart, makes unshakeable our testimony, and gives us place in the celestial world (D&C 88:2).

The greatest event that has ever occurred in the world,
since the resurrection of the Son of God from the tomb and
his ascension on high, was the coming of the Father
and of the Son to that boy Joseph Smith.

JOSEPH F. SMITH
GOSPEL DOCTRINE, 495

Joseph F. Smith, nephew of the Prophet and sixth President of the Church, was the last latter-day prophet to have personally known Joseph Smith. He said of his unshakeable testimony of the Prophet and the First Vision: "Having accepted this truth, I find it easy to accept of every other truth that he enunciated and declared during his mission of fourteen years in the world. He never taught a doctrine that was not true. He never practiced a doctrine that he was not commanded to practice. He never advocated error. He was not deceived. He saw; he heard; he did as he was commanded to do; and therefore, God is responsible for the work accomplished by Joseph Smith—not Joseph Smith. The Lord is responsible for it, and not man" (*Gospel Doctrine*, 495–96) The First Vision opened the windows of heavenly light to lay the foundation of the Lord's kingdom in this last and greatest dispensation.

Search your hearts, and see if you are like God. I have searched mine, and feel to repent of all my sins.

JOSEPH SMITH
TEACHINGS, 216

The apostle Paul declared, "All have sinned, and come short of the glory of God" (Romans 3:23). John taught, "If we say that we have no sin, we deceive ourselves, and the truth is not in us" (1 John 1:8). Save Jesus only, no person born into this world lives without sin. Neither the mightiest prophet nor the greatest disciple is able to navigate through mortality on a sinless, perfect course. Thus, in our present condition, unaided, we cannot make it back to where God and Christ dwell. Through the process of time, we are to become perfect, like Them. That understanding fills us with a sense of divine discontent and inspires us to truly examine ourselves (2 Corinthians 13:5), to sincerely confess our weakness and sin, and to earnestly turn more fully to Him who did live the law of God perfectly, even the Lord Jesus Christ. He is mighty to save, redeem, and exalt on high.

What unspeakable delight, and what transports of
joy swelled my bosom, when I took by the hand, on that night,
my beloved Emma—she that was my wife, even the wife
of my youth, and the choice of my heart.

JOSEPH SMITH
HISTORY OF THE CHURCH, 5:107

On this day in 1827, Joseph and Emma were married in South Bainbridge, New York. Years later, while hiding from the tormentors who sought his life, Joseph Smith recorded a most poignant expression of love. He longed to be free to associate with his beloved wife and family, but until the persecutions ceased, he could see them only secretly and briefly. After such a visit by Emma, he recorded: "Many were the reverberations of my mind when I contemplated for a moment the many scenes we had been called to pass through, the fatigues and the toils, the sorrows and sufferings, and the joys and consolations, from time to time, which had strewed our paths and crowned our board. Oh what a commingling of thought filled my mind for the moment, again she is here, . . . undaunted, firm, and unwavering— unchangeable, affectionate Emma!" (*History of the Church,* 5:107). Deep love and shared heartache had bonded Joseph and Emma in a strong, unshakeable union.

The Church of Jesus Christ of Latter-day Saints was founded upon direct revelation, as the true Church of God has ever been, according to the Scriptures (Amos iii:7, and Acts i:2).

JOSEPH SMITH
HISTORY OF THE CHURCH, 6:9

The Lord has done His work in all dispensations through the instrumentality of prophets. Revelation has come through men who are called as prophets to hold the priesthood keys and administer His kingdom. The Lord has not abandoned His servants, His Church, or His people; He continues to dispense divine guidance to those who are called to lead His church. They are called of God, not of man, to be teachers and leaders in building the kingdom of God on earth, in testifying of Christ, in sharing the good news of the gospel. Joseph Smith, writing to a newspaper editor in September 1843, affirmed this truth: "Through the will and blessings of God, I have been an instrument in His hands, thus far, to move forward the cause of Zion" (*History of the Church,* 6:9). We, too, can do our part to move forward the cause of Zion.

*[Joseph] possessed a noble boldness and independence of character;
his manner was easy and familiar; his rebuke terrible as the lion;
his benevolence unbounded as the ocean. . . . Even his most bitter
enemies were generally overcome, if he could once get their ears.*

PARLEY P. PRATT
AUTOBIOGRAPHY OF PARLEY P. PRATT, 45

Joseph Smith was known for his innate goodness, his
love for all people, and his radiant personality. Many
are the accounts of those who associated with him and
became steadfast friends. Of course, there were many
so filled with jealousy, hatred, and suspicion of Joseph
that they were committed to his destruction. But
those who knew him best, his family and loved ones,
his loyal followers who had occasion to interact with
him regularly, knew his heart, his motives, and his mission. They trusted him with their lives, they sat
humbly at his feet while he opened the heavens, and
they followed him faithfully to the end. Parley P. Pratt
was one who knew Joseph well. From his baptism in
Seneca Lake in September of 1830 to his assassination
in Arkansas in May of 1857, Parley P. Pratt testified of
the mission of the Prophet, of the truthfulness of the
Book of Mormon, and of the restoration of the gospel.

*Our only confidence can be in God; our only wisdom
obtained from Him: and He alone must be our protector
and safeguard, spiritually and temporally, or we fall.*

JOSEPH SMITH
HISTORY OF THE CHURCH, 5:65

Both the times and people change. It seems in our topsy-turvy world that there isn't much we can count on. We live in a day when many disparage belief, a day when doubt and cynicism are sometimes valued above conviction. But when we choose to hope despite our doubts, when we decide to trust God in spite of questions, we begin to feel power in the present and faith in the future. Confidence in God and His higher purposes creates in us a sense of sweet assurance and positive expectancy (Isaiah 55:8–9); it helps us to discover a higher power and purpose in life. Everlasting things like love, truth, and faith are real and good because they speak to our hearts and can be depended upon to stand the test of time. They have been tried in the furnace of skepticism and doubt and have come out strong. Love, truth, and faith stand the test of time and will not fade with new fashions and old lies. Our confidence and trust must be in God, our Father and protector.

*That man who rises up to condemn others, finding fault with the
Church, saying that they are out of the way, while he himself is
righteous, then know assuredly, that that man is in the high road
to apostasy; and if he does not repent, will apostatize, as God lives.*

JOSEPH SMITH
HISTORY OF THE CHURCH, 3:385

Joseph Smith gave us "one of the *Keys* of the mysteries
of the Kingdom. It is an eternal principle, that has
existed with God from all eternity" (*History of the Church,*
3:385). It is that those who let pride and envy enter their
hearts and thereby begin to criticize and lose confidence
in their Church leaders are on the road to apostasy.
Often, some think they are wiser and better informed
than the authorized leaders; they believe they are living
a higher law; they see only the weaknesses and humanness of others instead of their own shortcomings; they
unrelentingly hold fast to a noble grievance that hard-
ens the heart; they are blinded by their need for ascen-
dancy. Such has been the case in all dispensations. The
proud and hard-hearted see no need to follow "the weak
and simple" (D&C 1:23), no need to hearken unto the
counsel of those imperfect, mortal leaders who are
called by God to preside over us. A humble heart and
repentant attitude will keep us in the path of safety.

*False prophets always arise to oppose the true
prophets and they will prophesy so very near the truth that
they will deceive almost the very chosen ones.*

JOSEPH SMITH
HISTORY OF THE CHURCH, 6:364

The conviction, born of the Holy Ghost, of millions of
believers confirms that Joseph Smith was a true prophet
of God. Jesus, knowing our day, warned: "And many false
prophets shall arise, and shall deceive many. . . . For in
those days there shall also arise false Christs, and false
prophets, and shall show great signs and wonders, inso-
much, that, if possible, they shall deceive the very elect,
who are the elect according to the covenant" (Joseph
Smith–Matthew 1:9, 22). On another occasion the Lord
said, "Beware of false prophets, which come to you in
sheep's clothing, but inwardly they are ravening wolves"
(Matthew 7:15). We who have entered the covenant of
Christ must beware false Christs and false prophets.
They may appear pious, seem inspired, or teach very close
to the truth. They may teach an easy, feel-good philoso-
phy that appeals to the carnal man (Helaman 13:24–30).
But we must know and follow Christ and His true
prophets.

One dies and is buried, having never heard the Gospel of reconciliation; to the other the message of salvation is sent, he hears and embraces it, and is made the heir of eternal life. Shall the one become the partaker of glory and the other be consigned to . . . perdition?

JOSEPH SMITH
HISTORY OF THE CHURCH, 4:425–26

Fortunately our ancestors will have the opportunity to receive and accept the saving ordinances as we identify them and complete these sacred ordinances for them by proxy," said President James E. Faust. "In the great vision in the Kirtland Temple, Elijah the prophet appeared to the Prophet Joseph Smith and Oliver Cowdery and committed the keys of temple work and the sealing power into Joseph Smith's hands. This fulfilled Malachi's prophecy that Elijah would be sent 'to turn the hearts of the fathers to the children, and the children to the fathers . . .' (D&C 110:14–15). . . . I testify that God is a just God, and He will not give privileges to us and withhold them from our forebears. But we will need to do the baptisms, the endowments, and the sealings for them by proxy here on earth in order for us and them to be linked together for eternity" (*Ensign,* November 2003, 54–56).

*It is a time-honored adage that love begets love. Let us
pour forth love—show forth our kindness unto all mankind,
and the Lord will reward us with everlasting increase.*

JOSEPH SMITH
HISTORY OF THE CHURCH, 5:517

Joseph Smith's love for the people grew out of his service to them. His entire life was motivated by love—working alongside the believers to build the Church, sacrificing to lift the Saints and fulfill the Lord's expectations, gaining access to the heavens so that revelations would pour out from on high, and ultimately giving his life for the cause of Zion. Love is a power that can transform us and others. And love is one of life's sweetest miracles. Love creates more love, which has a synergistic effect that ripples through the generations. Have you noticed that love *for* a person generates more love *within* that person? And that love works a mighty change. When there is love, hope replaces discouragement and faith removes fear. When there is love, there is more kindness in the home and forgiveness in the heart. Love is the essence of the gospel and in the hearts of all true disciples of the Lord.

JANUARY 26

Search the scriptures. . . . When men receive their instruction from Him that made them, they know how He will save them.

JOSEPH SMITH
TEACHINGS, 11–12

We receive instructions for our lives by seeking the spirit of revelation. Inspiration and direction are given as we are humble and obedient, as we sincerely pray and fast, as we willingly serve others. Also, feasting upon the words of eternal life found in the scriptures will help us find answers to our prayers and guidance for our lives. Alma and the sons of Mosiah were united in a brotherhood of strong faith because of their discipleship: "Now these sons of Mosiah were with Alma at the time the angel first appeared unto him; therefore Alma did rejoice exceedingly to see his brethren; and what added more to his joy, they were still his brethren in the Lord; yea, and they had waxed strong in the knowledge of the truth; for they were men of a sound understanding and they had searched the scriptures diligently, that they might know the word of God" (Alma 17:2). The things of godliness remain unknown to the lazy and proud; they are known to those who pray and search the scriptures.

Men must become harmless, before the brute creation;
and when men lose their vicious dispositions and cease to destroy
the animal race, the lion and the lamb can dwell together, and
the sucking child can play with the serpent in safety.

JOSEPH SMITH
HISTORY OF THE CHURCH, 2:71

To bring about peace on earth and the anticipated millennial reign of Jesus Christ, the Prophet Joseph taught that benevolence must extend to all of God's creations. We are to subdue the sensual susceptibilities of the flesh and seek for things more exalted, more refined. As Joseph led Zion's Camp from Kirtland to Missouri, he admonished the camp to not kill three rattlesnakes in their path. "Let them alone—don't hurt them! How will the serpent ever lose his venom, while the servants of God possess the same disposition, and continue to make war upon it?" the Prophet asked his men. "I exhorted the brethren not to kill a serpent, bird, or an animal of any kind during our journey unless it became necessary in order to preserve ourselves from hunger" (*History of the Church,* 2:71–72). Upon the Lord's return, when the earth is taken back to its paradisiacal state, "the enmity of man, and the enmity of beasts, yea, the enmity of all flesh, shall cease from before my face" (D&C 101:26).

*Remember, brethren, that He has called you unto holiness; and need
we say, to be like Him in purity? How wise, how holy; how chaste,
and how perfect, then, you ought to conduct yourselves in His sight;
and remember, too, that His eyes are continually upon you.*

JOSEPH SMITH
HISTORY OF THE CHURCH, 2:13

We who have entered the covenant of Christ have
been called unto holiness, called to be examples of the
believers, "in word, in conversation, in charity, in spirit,
in faith, in purity" (1 Timothy 4:12). The example of
our Christian living will convey a far greater message
than will all the preaching and pontificating in the
world. To lift others and inspire them in the direction
of gospel light, we must stand on higher ground. No
self-righteousness or holier-than-thou attitudes can
be found in those who sincerely seek to emulate Jesus.
True followers of the Master strive daily to do as He
would do. What does it mean to be "called unto holiness"? It is to follow the Savior's "more excellent way"
(Ether 12:11), which will make a profound difference
in our lives and in the lives of our family members,
friends, and all with whom we associate.

I do not want you to think that I am very righteous, for I am not. God judges men according to the use they make of the light which He gives them.

JOSEPH SMITH
HISTORY OF THE CHURCH, 5:401

We have never believed in prophetic infallibility or that the prophet is perfect. We know that he is called by God and that the Lord works through him (Amos 3:7), and we know he, like each of us, is human. President Gordon B. Hinckley said, "We recognize that our forebears were human. They doubtless made mistakes. Some of them acknowledged making mistakes. But the mistakes were minor when compared with the marvelous work which they accomplished. To highlight mistakes and gloss over the greater good is to draw a caricature. Caricatures are amusing, but they are often ugly and dishonest. . . . There was only one perfect man who ever walked the earth. The Lord has used imperfect people in the process of building his perfect society. If some of them occasionally stumbled, or if their characters may have been slightly flawed in one way or another, the wonder is the greater that they accomplished so much" (*Ensign*, April 1986, 5).

*Iniquity of any kind cannot be sustained in the Church,
and it will not fare well where I am; for I am determined
while I do lead the Church, to lead it right.*

JOSEPH SMITH
HISTORY OF THE CHURCH, 5:411

Joseph Smith's stewardship was to restore the true Church of Jesus Christ with its priesthood keys and ordinances, and to gather Zion from the four quarters of the earth (1 Nephi 22:25). He was a remarkable leader; he was homespun and down-to-earth yet transcendent as he opened the heavens to the people. He was known for his gregarious nature, his jovial personality, his good humor and love for all people. But he was also earnest and single-minded in his devotion to the Lord and His latter-day kingdom. He understood that he was the one most responsible, most accountable, for the success of this marvelous work and wonder with which he had been entrusted by God. Joseph Smith was determined to do all he could do to build the kingdom of God on the earth. And just as "the Lord cannot look upon sin with the least degree of allowance" (D&C 1:31), neither can his prophet ignore iniquity.

We are full of selfishness; the devil flatters us that we are very righteous, when we are feeding on the faults of others.

JOSEPH SMITH
HISTORY OF THE CHURCH, 5:24

Among the great deceptions of life is thinking we are righteous while we find fault with others. Joseph Smith said, "All the religious world is boasting of righteousness: it is the doctrine of the devil to retard the human mind, and hinder our progress, by filling us with self-righteousness" (*History of the Church,* 5:24). The pride that comes from faultfinding hinders our spiritual growth and stifles associations with others within and outside the Church. In our day, President Gordon B. Hinckley counseled, "We live in a society that feeds on criticism. Faultfinding is the substance of columnists and commentators, and there is too much of this among our own people. It is so easy to find fault, and to resist doing so requires much of discipline. . . . The enemy of truth would divide us and cultivate within us attitudes of criticism which, if permitted to prevail, will only deter us in the pursuit of our great divinely given goal. We cannot afford to permit it to happen" (*Ensign,* May 1982, 46).

FEBRUARY

—

To get salvation we must not only
do some things, but everything which
God has commanded.
JOSEPH SMITH

*If you would have God have mercy on you,
have mercy on one another.*

JOSEPH SMITH
HISTORY OF THE CHURCH, 5:24

The Lord taught us to forgive "seventy times seven" (Matthew 18:21–22). He is not saying that we should enumerate sins against us up to 490 but that we should extend mercy to others without limit. The parable of the unmerciful servant teaches that as God forgives us of the immeasurable debt we owe to Him, so we should forgive all others the debts incurred when others sin against us. After the king forgave his servant's large debt, he found that same servant had then demanded payment and refused to forgive the small debt of a fellow servant. The lord said, "O thou wicked servant, I forgave thee all that debt, because thou desiredst me: Shouldest not thou also have had compassion on thy fellowservant, even as I had pity on thee? And his lord was wroth, and delivered him to the tormentors, till he should pay all that was due unto him. So likewise shall my heavenly Father do also unto you, if ye from your hearts forgive not every one his brother their trespasses" (Matthew 18:32–35).

From 1820 on, Joseph Smith was steadily
attacked in a pattern of accusations—followed by
eventual vindications. The pattern continues.

NEAL A. MAXWELL
ENSIGN, NOVEMBER 2003, 99

Speaking of the Prophet Joseph, Elder Neal A. Maxwell said: "Just as prophesied, fools deride him, hell rages against him, and his name is 'both good and evil spoken of' (Joseph Smith–History 1:33). This swirl needlessly preoccupies a few who seem to prefer chewing on old bones in the outer courtyard instead of coming inside to the resplendent, revelatory banquet, thus diverting them from giving due attention to Joseph's mission as 'a choice seer' (see 2 Nephi 3:6–7)" (*Ensign,* November 2003, 99). Joseph Smith was attacked, accused, and reviled throughout his life. It continues today. Those who refuse to acknowledge his remarkable life and prophetic mission thus miss out on the understanding and joy that could be theirs. The Prophet never claimed he was perfect. But he was a good and great man, the Lord's anointed, called of God to begin a marvelous work of gospel restoration. Truth always eventually wins out. And the truth of the mission and character of the Prophet will triumph.

*Just at this moment of great alarm, I saw a pillar of
light exactly over my head, above the brightness of the sun,
which descended gradually until it fell upon me.*

JOSEPH SMITH–HISTORY 1:16

The forces of good and evil had their eyes upon that
early spring day in 1820. Joseph recounts: "I kneeled
down and began to offer up the desires of my heart to
God. I had scarcely done so, when immediately I was
seized upon by some power which entirely overcame
me, and had such an astonishing influence over me as
to bind my tongue. . . . Thick darkness gathered
around me, and it seemed to me for a time as if I were
doomed to sudden destruction. But, exerting all my
powers to call upon God to deliver me out of the
power of this enemy which had seized upon me, and
at the very moment when I was ready to sink into
despair and abandon myself to destruction . . . , I saw a
pillar of light exactly over my head" (Joseph
Smith–History 1:15–16). In that moment, all darkness
and despair dispersed, a glorious pillar of light ushered
in the greatest event to occur in this world since the
resurrection of Jesus Christ.

When the light rested upon me I saw two Personages, whose brightness and glory defy all description, standing above me in the air. One of them spake unto me, calling me by name and said, pointing to the other—This is My Beloved Son. Hear Him!

JOSEPH SMITH–HISTORY 1:17

The appearance of the Father and the Son to the boy Joseph ended the long reign of dark apostasy and ushered in the dispensation of the fulness of times. It manifested God's love for His children and His desire to bestow unnumbered blessings upon us. It is confirmation that God knows us by name, and He has a plan for us. And it helps us to understand who God is and who we are. Speaking of the supernal glory of that vision, President Gordon B. Hinckley said: "Much has been written, much will be written, in an effort to explain it away. The finite mind cannot comprehend it. But the testimony of the Holy Spirit, experienced by countless numbers of people all through the years since it happened, bears witness that it is true, that it happened as Joseph Smith said it happened, that it was as real as the sunrise over Palmyra, that it is an essential foundation stone, a cornerstone, without which the Church could not be 'fitly framed together'" (*Ensign,* November 1984, 52).

*The doctrine of baptizing children, or sprinkling them,
or they must welter in hell, is a doctrine not true, not supported
in Holy Writ, and is not consistent with the character of God.
All children are redeemed by the blood of Jesus Christ.*

JOSEPH SMITH
TEACHINGS, 197

While preaching to a congregation in Philadelphia on this day in 1840, the Prophet Joseph taught one of the most comforting doctrines ever revealed: children who die that have not reached the age of accountability will go to the celestial kingdom of God. The Lord earlier had revealed the important doctrines of salvation for the dead and salvation of little children: "All who have died without a knowledge of this gospel, who would have received it if they had been permitted to tarry, shall be heirs of the celestial kingdom of God; also all that shall die henceforth without a knowledge of it, who would have received it with all their hearts, shall be heirs of that kingdom; . . . All children who die before they arrive at the years of accountability are saved in the celestial kingdom of heaven" (D&C 137:7–8, 10). Except for those whose mental abilities prevent them from reaching the age of accountability (D&C 29:50), the age of accountability is eight (D&C 68:25). How blessed we are to have the light of revealed knowledge.

Happiness is the object and design of our existence;
and will be the end thereof, if we pursue the path that leads to it;
and this path is virtue, uprightness, faithfulness, holiness,
and keeping all the commandments of God.

JOSEPH SMITH
HISTORY OF THE CHURCH, 5:134–35

Despite the challenges and sorrows of mortality, we are here that we might have joy (2 Nephi 2:25). Life can be hard, but it also can be filled with moments of unspeakable happiness and joy unbounded. And just as the fall of Adam brought mortality and death into the world, so also did Jesus Christ bring immortality and eternal life. In the same way, it is heartache and difficulty that allow us to appreciate contentment here and the promise of lasting peace hereafter. Without opposition, without the winters of discontent in our lives, we would not be able to fully appreciate and savor the springs of hope that always come to those who hold on with faith. We can have deep happiness only if we have experienced its opposite. Real happiness is also promised to those who walk the sure path: righteousness, humility, and obedience. Life is not meant to be dreary and sad, although we will have these seasons. With the gospel as our anchor, life is designed to be joyful, happy, and good.

Joseph Smith the Prophet preached
with such power as had not there ever before been
witnessed in this nineteenth century.

EDWARD STEVENSON
IN *JOSEPH SMITH,* 334

Edward Stevenson, a pioneer, missionary, and later a member of the First Council of Seventy, was present when Joseph Smith preached a sermon in a schoolhouse in Pontiac, Michigan, in 1834. Stevenson recalled: "With uplifted hand [Joseph] said: 'I am a witness that there is a God, for I saw Him in open day, while praying in a silent grove, in the spring of 1820.' He further testified that God, the Eternal Father, pointing to a separate personage, in the likeness of Himself, said: 'This is my Beloved Son, hear ye Him.' Oh, how these words thrilled my entire system, and filled me with joy unspeakable to behold one who, like Paul the apostle of olden time, could with boldness testify that he had been in the presence of Jesus Christ!" (in *Joseph Smith,* 334–35). Edward Stevenson was loyal to the Prophet and his restored Church throughout his life.

No description of models for us to follow would be complete without including Joseph Smith. … When but 14 years of age, this courageous young man entered a grove of trees, which later would be called sacred, and received an answer to his sincere prayer.

THOMAS S. MONSON
ENSIGN, OCTOBER 2007, 8

The Prophet Joseph was ridiculed relentlessly for his testimony. He said, "Though I was hated and persecuted for saying that I had seen a vision, yet it was true. … I had seen a vision; I knew it, and I knew that God knew it, and I could not deny it, neither dared I do it" (Joseph Smith–History, 1:25). President Thomas S. Monson said of the unrelenting persecution that followed the Prophet: "Step by step, facing opposition at nearly every turn and yet always guided by the hand of the Lord, Joseph organized The Church of Jesus Christ of Latter-day Saints. He proved courageous in all that he did. Toward the end of his life, as he was led away with his brother Hyrum to Carthage Jail, he bravely faced what he undoubtedly knew lay ahead for him, and he sealed his testimony with his blood. As we face life's tests, may we ever emulate that undaunted courage epitomized by the Prophet Joseph Smith" (*Ensign,* October 2007, 7).

I could pray in my heart that all my brethren were like unto my beloved brother Hyrum, who possesses the mildness of a lamb, and the integrity of a Job, and in short, the meekness and humility of Christ; and I love him with that love that is stronger than death.

JOSEPH SMITH
HISTORY OF THE CHURCH, 2:338

Hyrum Smith was born on this day in 1800 in Tunbridge, Vermont, to Joseph Smith Sr. and Lucy Mack Smith. Hyrum was one of the original six members of the Church, one of the Eight Witness to the Book of Mormon, a counselor in the First Presidency, and Patriarch to the Church. He died as a martyr with his brother Joseph in Carthage Jail on June 27, 1844. "In life they were not divided, and in death they were not separated!" (D&C 135:3). Though five years older than the Prophet, Hyrum was ever devoted and deferential to his brother Joseph. Throughout Hyrum's life, he watched over his younger brother as tenderly as if the Prophet had been his own son. Joseph treasured the brotherly affection and fidelity of his faithful brother. The Lord also spoke of His love for Hyrum: "Blessed is my servant Hyrum Smith; for I, the Lord, love him because of the integrity of his heart, and because he loveth that which is right before me, saith the Lord" (D&C 124:15).

*The Prophet Joseph Smith faced temptation. Can you
imagine the ridicule, the scorn, the mocking that must have been
heaped upon him as he declared that he had seen a vision?*

THOMAS S. MONSON
ENSIGN, MAY 2005, 112–13

President Thomas S. Monson has reminded us that
we must withstand temptation; for we will surely meet
it. President Monson used the Prophet Joseph as an
example of one who faced temptation and remained
steadfast and immovable in the faith: "I suppose it
became almost unbearable for the boy. He no doubt
knew that it would be easier to retract his statements
concerning the vision and just get on with a normal life.
He did not, however, give in. These are his words: 'I
had actually seen a light, and in the midst of that light I
saw two Personages, and they did in reality speak to me;
and though I was hated and persecuted for saying that
I had seen a vision, yet it was true. . . . I had seen a
vision; I knew it, and I knew that God knew it, and I
could not deny it.' Joseph taught courage by example.
He faced temptation and withstood it" (*Ensign,* May
2005, 113). We too must resist the temptations of the
world and stay true to the truth.

Many of the sects cry out, "Oh, I have the testimony of Jesus; . . . but there are to be no prophets or revelators in the last days." Stop, sir! The Revelator says that the testimony of Jesus is the spirit of prophecy; so by your own mouth you are condemned.

JOSEPH SMITH
HISTORY OF THE CHURCH, 5:427

The spirit of prophecy and revelation is integral to building faith and a testimony that Jesus is the Christ, that His true church has been restored, and that a prophet of God again lives on the earth today. John the Revelator taught that the testimony of Jesus is the spirit of prophecy (Revelation 19:10). The apostle Paul observed: "No man can say that Jesus is the Lord, but by the Holy Ghost" (1 Corinthians 12:3). And Moses yearned for the spirit of prophecy to be upon the people of his day, "Would God that all the Lord's people were prophets, and that the Lord would put his spirit upon them!" (Numbers 11:29). Those with testimonies of Jesus Christ born by the spirit of prophecy stand as prophetic witnesses of Christ and His redeeming grace. How blessed we are to have apostles and prophets on the earth who hold the keys of the priesthood to guide the Church today and who know by the spirit of revelation that Jesus is the Christ.

If you will not accuse me, I will not accuse you.
If you will throw a cloak of charity over my sins, I will over
yours—for charity covereth a multitude of sins.

JOSEPH SMITH
HISTORY OF THE CHURCH, 4:445

The Prophet Joseph spoke out against a pharisaical, hypocritical approach to gospel living as he taught the Saints to not follow the example of the adversaries of righteousness in accusing one another: "If you do not accuse each other, God will not accuse you. If you have no accuser you will enter heaven, and if you will follow the revelations and instructions which God gives you through me, I will take you into heaven as my back load" (*History of the Church,* 4:445). Over and over the Prophet taught the people to not look for evil in others, to resist faultfinding and criticism, to turn away from accusations and evil speaking. Instead, he encouraged charity, forbearance, and patience with the faults and foibles of others so that we too can have claim upon the Savior's mercy. "With what measure ye mete, it shall be measured to you again" (Matthew 7:2).

*We should gather all the good and true
principles in the world and treasure them up, or we
shall not come out true "Mormons."*

JOSEPH SMITH
HISTORY OF THE CHURCH, 5:517

Prophets have always acknowledged with respect and appreciation the good people and principles diffused across the earth. We embrace truth and righteousness wherever it is found. We also "claim the privilege of worshiping Almighty God according to the dictates of our own conscience, and allow all men the same privilege, let them worship how, where, or what they may" (Articles of Faith 1:11). As members and missionaries, that is our message. President Gordon B. Hinckley said, "Let me say that we appreciate the truth in all churches and the good which they do. We say to the people, in effect, you bring with you all the good that you have, and then let us see if we can add to it. That is the spirit of this work. That is the essence of our missionary service" (*Ensign,* August 1998, 72). We can treasure true principles even as we join hands with the good people of the world to promote righteous causes and the common welfare.

Great things shall be accomplished by you from this hour;
and you shall begin to feel the whisperings of the Spirit of God;
. . . and you shall be endowed with power from on high.

JOSEPH SMITH

HISTORY OF THE CHURCH, 2:182

The first members of the Quorum of Twelve Apostles in this dispensation were called on this historic day in 1835. In 1829, under the direction of Joseph Smith, the Three Witnesses were asked to search out the Twelve (D&C 18:37–39). Within six years, the Book of Mormon was published, the Church and First Presidency were organized, and then the momentous organizing of the Quorum of Twelve Apostles took place. How the Prophet Joseph and the Saints must have anticipated this day; how the heavens must have rejoiced in this significant event. On this long-awaited day, Oliver Cowdery gave the new apostles their formal apostolic charge, and the Prophet counseled and instructed them in their special callings. Among the foremost admonitions given by the Prophet was that they would feel the whisperings of the Spirit in guiding their efforts. We too can accomplish great things as we listen to the voice of the Lord.

*If you know anything calculated to disturb the peace
or injure the feelings of your brother or sister, hold your
tongues, and the least harm will be done.*

JOSEPH SMITH
HISTORY OF THE CHURCH, 5:140

Speaking to the Relief Society in Nauvoo, the Prophet
exhorted them to not gossip or speak evil of others, to
be long-suffering with the foibles of others. He knew
all too well the sting of criticism and faultfinding.
Some, he said, would even find fault in the Savior: "No
man lives without fault. Do you think that even Jesus, if
He were here, would be without fault in your eyes? His
enemies said all manner of evil against Him—they all
watched for iniquity in Him" (*History of the Church,*
5:140). We find what we're looking for, and it's so easy
to find fault and criticize others. But when we do, we
may be revealing more about ourselves than those we
criticize. In other words, sometimes our judgment of
others stems from the worst that is in us rather than
what we assume is the worst in them. We don't know
the full story on anyone's life, so we are always better
off to hold our tongues, withhold judgment, and simply
send forth love and compassion.

*Every law, every commandment, every promise, every truth,
and every point touching the destiny of man . . . where the purity
of the scriptures remains unsullied . . . , go to show the perfection
of the theory [of different degrees of glory in the future life].*

JOSEPH SMITH
HISTORY OF THE CHURCH, 1:252

It was after the Prophet Joseph had translated John
5:29 that Doctrine and Covenants 76 was given on
this day in 1832. In this remarkable vision, Joseph
Smith and Sidney Rigdon saw the Savior on the right
hand of God, they saw events in the premortal life,
and saw the three degrees of glory. About his transcendent vision of the glories, Joseph Smith observed:
"Nothing could be more pleasing to the Saints upon
the order of the kingdom of the Lord, than the light
which burst upon the world through the foregoing
vision. . . . The sublimity of the ideas; the purity of the
language; the scope for action; the continued duration
for completion, in order that the heirs of salvation may
confess the Lord and bow the knee; the rewards for
faithfulness, and the punishments for sins, are so much
beyond the narrow-mindedness of men, that every
honest man is constrained to exclaim: '*It came from God*'"
(*History of the Church,* 1:252–53).

The devil said he would save them all, and laid his plans before the grand council, who gave their vote in favor of Jesus Christ. So the devil rose up in rebellion against God, and was cast down, with all who put up their heads for him.

JOSEPH SMITH
HISTORY OF THE CHURCH, 6:314

In the war in heaven there were two opposing forces—one offered in humility and in favor of agency; the other given in self-aggrandizement and opposed to agency. When Christ lived on earth, He taught: "I came down from heaven, not to do mine own will, but the will of him that sent me. . . . And this is the will of him that sent me, that every one which seeth the Son, and believeth on him, may have everlasting life" (John 6:38, 40). Jesus wanted the honor and glory to be given to the Father; and He understood that we must be free to choose. Satan rebelled against the Father's plan, seeking the glory for himself: "And I will redeem all mankind, that one soul shall not be lost, and surely I will do it; wherefore give me thine honor" (Moses 4:1). All of us here on earth followed the Savior, standing up in favor of the Father's plan and the agency of mankind (Abraham 3:26–28).

Thanks be to God, when the hour arrived to
usher in the dispensation of the fulness of times, there was
Joseph Smith, the mighty prophet of latter days.

BRUCE R. MCCONKIE
ENSIGN, NOVEMBER 1975, 15

One must acknowledge that Joseph Smith was no ordinary man. His life story is an epic of faith, a legacy of testimony in the face of overwhelming difficulties. He was called of God and raised up to accomplish a marvelous work and wonder as he ushered in the dispensation of the fulness of times. President Gordon B. Hinckley said of the Prophet: "He was born in poverty. He was reared in adversity. He was driven from place to place, falsely accused, and illegally imprisoned. He was murdered at the age of 38. Yet in the brief space of 20 years preceding his death, he accomplished what none other has accomplished in an entire lifetime" (*Ensign,* December 2005, 4). We understand that Joseph was human; like each of us, he was not perfect. We do not worship him. We honor him, respect him, appreciate him, and love him. Yes, Joseph Smith was no more than a man, but he was no less than a prophet of God.

*I told the brethren that the Book of Mormon was the
most correct of any book on earth, and the keystone of our
religion, and a man would get nearer to God by abiding
by its precepts, than by any other book.*

JOSEPH SMITH
HISTORY OF THE CHURCH, 4:461

Keeping in mind the tens of millions of books that
have been published over the years, it is a bold statement to assert that one book is the most correct of any
other book on earth. But that is the promise of the
Prophet Joseph. It is a declaration to which millions
can also attest—millions who have put Moroni's
promise to the test (Moroni 10:4–5). The Book of
Mormon is also the most powerful book on the earth
because it changes lives for the better. Those who read
the Book of Mormon often and apply its teachings
will enjoy heaven's inspiration and guidance along
life's challenging path. They will understand more
clearly the forces of good and evil and the pitfalls of
pride and wickedness. They will enjoy greater contentment in the home and joy in the heart. And they
will come to know the Savior, His atonement, and the
great plan of happiness in a deeper, more intimate way
(Alma 42:8).

*Nothing is so much calculated to lead people to forsake sin as
to take them by the hand, and watch over them with tenderness.
When persons manifest the least kindness and love to me,
O what power it has over my mind.*

JOSEPH SMITH
HISTORY OF THE CHURCH, 5:23–24

Kindness and love are the beginning, the end, and the middle of true gospel living. If there is a quality that defines us best as members of the Church it should be that we love the Lord with all our hearts, and we love our neighbors as ourselves (Matthew 22:36–40). Kindness and love can transform our hearts even as they work mighty miracles in the hearts of others (*Ensign,* November 2007, 30–31). Elder Joseph B. Wirthlin said, "At the final day the Savior will not ask about the nature of our callings. He will not inquire about our material possessions or fame. He will ask if we ministered to the sick, gave food and drink to the hungry, visited those in prison, or gave succor to the weak (see Matthew 25:31–40). When we reach out to assist the least of Heavenly Father's children, we do it unto Him. That is the essence of the gospel of Jesus Christ" (*Ensign,* November 2007, 30).

*To get salvation we must not only do some things,
but everything which God has commanded.*

JOSEPH SMITH
HISTORY OF THE CHURCH, 6:223

On this day in 1844, four months before his martyrdom, the Prophet Joseph gave a discourse in Nauvoo on the subject of obedience to God and standing fast by true principles: "Men may preach and practice everything except those things which God commanded us to do, and will be damned at last. We may tithe mint and rue, and all manner of herbs, and still not obey the commandments of God [see Luke 11:42]. The object with me is to obey and teach others to obey God in just what He tells us to do. It mattereth not whether the principle is popular or unpopular, I will always maintain a true principle, even if I stand alone in it" (*History of the Church*, 6:223). To gain salvation we must reject the clarion call of the world and the worldly and put first things first: follow true principles and obey God.

*I am going to inquire after God; for I want you all
to know Him, and to be familiar with Him. . . . You
will then know that I am His servant.*

JOSEPH SMITH
HISTORY OF THE CHURCH, 6:305

The Restoration begins with the First Vision. The humble prayer of Joseph Smith, a fourteen-year-old boy in the early spring of 1820, parted the veil of silence and mist of darkness that had covered the earth for centuries. The occasion was of such vast significance that God the Father and His Son, Jesus Christ, appeared to young Joseph. He became a first-hand witness of the reality of God and His Son, and both Joseph and the world would never again be the same. From the early days of the First Vision to the end of his mortal life, Joseph testified of the nature, character, and attributes of God. His witness was unlike any other. His mission was to reveal God anew and testify of His matchless love and inexhaustible gospel. As we study and ponder the scriptures given us through the Prophet Joseph we will come to know that he was no ordinary man. Indeed, he was God's chosen servant in restoring gospel truth to the world.

I love that man better who swears a stream as long as my arm, yet deals justice to his neighbors and mercifully deals his substance to the poor, than the long, smooth-faced hypocrite.

JOSEPH SMITH
HISTORY OF THE CHURCH, 5:401

The Savior's frequent stinging rebukes directed to the hypocrites resound down the centuries: "Woe unto you, scribes and Pharisees, hypocrites! for ye pay tithe of mint and anise and cummin, and have omitted the weightier matters of the law, judgment, mercy, and faith: these ought ye to have done, and not to leave the other undone. . . . for ye make clean the outside of the cup and of the platter, but within they are full of extortion and excess. . . . Woe unto you, scribes and Pharisees, hypocrites! for ye are like unto whited sepulchres, which indeed appear beautiful outward, but are within full of dead men's bones, and of all uncleanness" (Matthew 23:23, 25, 27). Some things matter more than others. Although we're all far from perfect, true disciples of the Master strive to live lives of integrity, of humility and compassion. Without compartmentalizing or rationalizing, they try to live the gospel of Jesus Christ in its fulness.

*[Joseph Smith] was the revealing conduit. Through
him, it has been estimated, more marvelous pages of scripture
passed than through any other human in history.*

HOWARD W. HUNTER
ENSIGN, SEPTEMBER 1994, 63

It is remarkable to think of the miraculous outpouring of the revealed word of God that came through
Joseph Smith. We have the Book of Mormon, the
Doctrine and Covenants, the Pearl of Great Price, and
innumerable sermons and other messages wherein the
Prophet Joseph gives divine direction. The Prophet
communed with Jehovah and other heavenly messengers, he was tutored from on high and given keys of
authority, and he was raised up as a choice seer to
reveal the everlasting gospel to all the earth. He did
not do all this as a scholar with time to write, or a professor with time to ponder, or a person with free time
to relax. All this was done in the space of a few years,
amidst intense persecution and turmoil, and while he
was trying to provide for his growing family and lead
an emerging church. There is no other way to explain
it: he was truly a mighty instrument in the hands of
God.

*It is not wisdom that we should have all knowledge
at once presented before us; but that we should have a
little at a time; then we can comprehend it.*

JOSEPH SMITH
HISTORY OF THE CHURCH, 5:387

The kingdom of God, and every member of that kingdom, grows little by little. Elder Bruce R. McConkie testified, "We believe that Joseph Smith, Jun., was the mighty prophet of the restoration; that by the grace and condescension of God (the young prophet having been prepared from eternity for his mission) he received line upon line, precept upon precept, key, power, and authority upon key, power, and authority, until all things were restored, and every power and grace was had again that would enable men to be saved and exalted in the kingdom of the [Father]" (Conference Report, October 1954, 124). Even the Savior "received not of the fulness at first, but continued from grace to grace, until he received a fulness" (D&C 93:13; see also Luke 2:52). Each of us is a work in progress. Little by little, as we are humble and obedient, we receive more light and truth, "and he that receiveth light, and continueth in God, receiveth more light" (D&C 50:24).

You must be innocent, or you cannot come
up before God: if we would come before God, we
must keep ourselves pure, as He is pure.

JOSEPH SMITH
HISTORY OF THE CHURCH, 4:605

Life is a process of repentance and forgiveness that draws us ever closer to God. By repenting of our sins and forsaking them we develop more of the attributes of godliness. But, wherever there is a desire for righteousness, wherever there is one person striving with heart and soul to repent and become more like God, the adversary will always resist and put up a fight. The powers of evil will mock innocence, deride purity, and disdain wholesomeness. As the Prophet said, "The devil has great power to deceive; he will so transform things as to make one gape at those who are doing the will of God. . . . iniquity must be purged out from the midst of the Saints; then the veil will be rent, and the blessings of heaven will flow down—they will roll down like the Mississippi river" (*History of the Church,* 4:605).

*A Word of Wisdom, . . . showing forth the order and
will of God in the temporal salvation of all saints in the last
days—Given for a principle with promise, adapted to the
capacity of the weak and the weakest of all saints.*

DOCTRINE AND COVENANTS 89:1–3

The first three verses of Doctrine and Covenants 89
are an inspired introduction and description of what
came to be known as the Word of Wisdom. On this day
in 1833 the Prophet received this revelation in response
to a question about the use of tobacco by some members
of the Church. The Word of Wisdom later became
binding upon the Saints in the early twentieth century,
manifesting the Lord's mercy in giving the Saints an
opportunity to be taught a divine health code. The Word
of Wisdom is a bulwark against enslavement to harmful
and addictive substances, a safeguard against evil designs,
and a reminder that the body is a temple—a sacred, price-
less possession that must be protected. The spirit of this
law teaches the principle of self-mastery and promises
that we will be blessed spiritually, mentally, and physically
by obeying this code of health (D&C 89:18–21). The
Word of Wisdom also provides additional evidence of
the revelatory leadership of the Prophet Joseph.

As we remember and honor the Prophet Joseph Smith,
my heart reaches out to him in gratitude. He was a good, honest,
humble, intelligent, and courageous young man with a
heart of gold and an unshaken faith in God.

DIETER F. UCHTDORF
ENSIGN, MAY 2005, 38

D o you ever wonder what would have happened if
Joseph hadn't bothered, hadn't felt the necessity, hadn't
been willing to exercise sufficient faith to pour out his
heart to God in a grove of trees one early spring day?
President Dieter F. Uchtdorf said of the Prophet
Joseph: "Through his work and sacrifice, I now have a
true understanding of our Heavenly Father and His
Son, our Redeemer and Savior, Jesus Christ, and I can
feel the power of the Holy Ghost and know of
Heavenly Father's plan for us, His children. For me,
these are truly the fruits of the First Vision. I am grateful that early in my life I was blessed with a simple faith
that Joseph Smith was a prophet of God, that he saw
God the Father and His Son, Jesus Christ, in a vision.
He translated the Book of Mormon by the gift and
power of God. That testimony has been confirmed to
me over and over again" (*Ensign,* May 2005, 38).
Thanks be to God and His Prophet of the latter days.

MARCH

The purposes of our God are great, His
love unfathomable, His wisdom infinite,
and His power unlimited.
JOSEPH SMITH

The Standard of Truth has been erected; no unhallowed hand can stop the work from progressing.

JOSEPH SMITH
HISTORY OF THE CHURCH, 4:540

On this day in 1842, in the *Times and Seasons,* Joseph Smith published the Wentworth Letter, which presented a brief history of the Church and included what we now call the Articles of Faith. Boldly and with strong conviction and prophetic vision, the Prophet laid out the ultimate destiny of the marvelous work in which he was engaged. He wrote: "Persecutions may rage, mobs may combine, armies may assemble, calumny may defame, but the truth of God will go forth boldly, nobly, and independent, till it has penetrated every continent, visited every clime, swept every country, and sounded in every ear, till the purposes of God shall be accomplished, and the Great Jehovah shall say the work is done" (*History of the Church,* 4:540). It may have sounded outrageous for a man with a few thousand followers to make such bold claims. But we are seeing the prophecy fulfilled. Thousands today gather to the Standard of Truth. Truly, no unhallowed hand can stop the work of the Lord.

For I had seen a vision; I knew it, and I knew that God knew it, and I could not deny it, neither dared I do it; at least I knew that by so doing I would offend God, and come under condemnation.

JOSEPH SMITH–HISTORY 1:25

Joseph Smith received an answer to his humble prayer that would change his life—it would, in fact, change the world. He *knew.* He could not deny it, or reframe it, or ignore it. He gained an unshakeable testimony of God and Jesus Christ that he was true to all his life, and that testimony enabled him to live the gospel with patience and perseverance. He was undeterred by animosity and persecution, for in his words: "I had actually seen a light, and in the midst of that light I saw two Personages, and they did in reality speak to me; and though I was hated and persecuted for saying that I had seen a vision, yet it was true; and while they were persecuting me, reviling me, and speaking all manner of evil against me falsely for so saying, I was led to say in my heart: Why persecute me for telling the truth? I have actually seen a vision; and who am I that I can withstand God, or why does the world think to make me deny what I have actually seen?" (Joseph Smith–History 1:25).

It was Joseph Smith who taught me how to prize
the endearing relationships of father and mother, husband
and wife; of brother and sister, son and daughter.

PARLEY P. PRATT
AUTOBIOGRAPHY OF PARLEY P. PRATT, 361

The Lord declared through the Prophet Joseph that if a husband and wife are not sealed by the power of the priesthood and remain faithful to their covenants, "they cannot be enlarged, but remain separately and singly, without exaltation, in their saved condition, to all eternity" (D&C 132:17). Knowledge of this supernal doctrine deepens our understanding of the importance of eternal covenants, as it did for early apostle Parley P. Pratt. He said: "It was from [Joseph] that I learned that the wife of my bosom might be secured to me for time and all eternity. . . . I had loved before, but I knew not why. But now I loved—with a pureness—an intensity of elevated, exalted feeling, which would lift my soul from the transitory things of this grovelling sphere and expand it as the ocean. . . . In short, I could now love with the spirit and with the understanding also" (*Autobiography of Parley P. Pratt*, 361–62). The loving and sweet unions of life can continue beyond the grave.

*In order to conduct the affairs of the Kingdom in righteousness, it
is all important that the most perfect harmony, kind feeling, good
understanding, and confidence should exist in the hearts of all.*

JOSEPH SMITH
HISTORY OF THE CHURCH, 4:165

Joseph Smith received news in 1840 that a Church
member in Kirtland was trying to destroy the Saints' confidence in their leaders. In response, Joseph wrote: "If
there are any uncharitable feelings, any lack of confidence, then pride, arrogance and envy will soon be manifested; confusion must inevitably prevail, and the authorities of the Church set at naught" (*History of the Church,*
4:165). He continued by exhorting the Saints to be
humble and obedient: "It would be gratifying to my mind
to see the Saints in Kirtland flourish, but think the time is
not yet come . . . until a different order of things be established and a different spirit manifested. When confidence is restored, when pride shall fall, and every aspir-
ing mind be clothed with humility as with a garment, and
selfishness give place to benevolence and charity, and a
united determination to live by every word which proceedeth out of the mouth of the Lord is observable, then
. . . can peace, order and love prevail" (ibid., 4:166).

*Every man who has a calling to minister to the inhabitants
of the world was ordained to that very purpose in the Grand
Council of heaven before this world was. I suppose that I
was ordained to this very office in that Grand Council.*

JOSEPH SMITH
HISTORY OF THE CHURCH, 6:364

The Prophet Joseph taught that we each have a calling
and purpose in life. Abraham was told that he was
included among the valiant spirits and was therefore chosen or foreordained before his birth to be a leader in
God's kingdom on earth (Abraham 3:22–23). Likewise,
the Lord informed Jeremiah, "Before I formed thee in
the belly I knew thee; and . . . I ordained thee a prophet
unto the nations" (Jeremiah 1:5). Alma taught that priests
belonging to a "holy order" were foreordained "according to the foreknowledge of God, on account of their
exceeding faith and good works" (Alma 13:1, 3).
Foreordination is the premortal selection of individuals
to come forth in mortality at specified times, under certain conditions, and to fulfill designated responsibilities.
Foreordained does not mean predestined or predeter-
mined. If we are true and faithful, we will have opportunities to serve, based on God's purposes and plans to bless
His children.

I soon found, however, that my telling the story
had excited a great deal of prejudice against me among
professors of religion, and was the cause of great
persecution, which continued to increase.

JOSEPH SMITH–HISTORY 1:22

How could a boy of "no consequence in the world" generate such vehement opposition? (Joseph Smith–History 1.22). Joseph recalled, "How very strange it was that an obscure boy, of a little over fourteen years of age, and one, too, who was doomed to the necessity of obtaining a scanty maintenance by his daily labor, should be thought a character of sufficient importance to attract the attention of the great ones of the most popular sects of the day, and in a manner to create in them a spirit of the most bitter persecution and reviling" (Joseph Smith–History 1:23). It is inconceivable that a young boy, a farm boy in the nineteenth century (or today), would dream of fabricating an account of a vision from God and then remain true to that vision throughout his life. Joseph suffered intense persecution, but he never wavered from testifying that he had indeed seen the Father and the Son. Ultimately, he gave his life for his testimony.

Persecution has not stopped the progress of truth,
but has only added fuel to the flame.

JOSEPH SMITH
HISTORY OF THE CHURCH, 4:540

The righteous have always been ridiculed by the worldly, whose vantage point in the great and spacious building is continuously looking down (1 Nephi 8:26–28). But the cause of truth, like a great stone cut out of a mountain (Daniel 2:34–45), will roll forth and fill the whole earth. Speaking of missionaries, the Prophet said: "Proud of the cause which they have espoused, and conscious of our innocence, and of the truth of their system, amidst calumny and reproach, have the Elders of this Church gone forth, and planted the Gospel in almost every state in the Union; it has penetrated our cities, it has spread over our villages, and has caused thousands of our intelligent, noble, and patriotic citizens to obey its divine mandates, and be governed by its sacred truths. It has also spread into England, Ireland, Scotland, and Wales, . . . there are numbers now joining in every land" (*History of the Church,* 4:540). We are today witnessing the fulfillment of prophecy: truth will continue to roll forth.

*He that arms himself with gun, sword, or pistol, except in
the defense of truth, will sometime be sorry for it. I never carry
any weapon with me bigger than my penknife. . . . God will
always protect me until my mission is fulfilled.*

JOSEPH SMITH
HISTORY OF THE CHURCH, 6:364–65

Life and death is in the Lord's hands. Our days are
appointed unto Him. The life of Joseph Smith is a vivid
testament to the protective providence of God. On so
many occasions, the Prophet faced turmoil and mal-
treatment with undaunted courage. He was unafraid of
the powers of men or the adversary, fearless in the face
of persecution. He knew who he was and whose mission he was on. We too can develop within our hearts
a feeling of faith and testimony that is stronger than any
weapon. The sword of righteousness and the shield of
faith will destroy any wicked influence or evil power.
The Lord exhorted the Prophet, "Treasure up wisdom
in your bosoms, lest the wickedness of men reveal these
things unto you by their wickedness, in a manner which
shall speak in your ears with a voice louder than that
which shall shake the earth; but if ye are prepared ye
shall not fear" (D&C 38:30). God always desires to protect and strengthen His people.

*Repentance is a thing that cannot be trifled with
every day. Daily transgression and daily repentance is not
that which is pleasing in the sight of God.*

JOSEPH SMITH
HISTORY OF THE CHURCH, 3:379

Repentance is godly sorrow; it is a change of heart, a
change of behavior. Sincere repentance means *real*
change. Remember, "He that repents and does the commandments of the Lord shall be forgiven" (D&C 1:32).
Elder Richard G. Scott has counseled: "With all the tenderness and sincerity of heart, I invite each one of you
to thoughtfully review your life. Have you deviated from
the standards that you know will bring happiness? Is
there a dark corner that needs to be cleaned out? Are
you now doing things that you know are wrong? Do you
fill your mind with unclean thoughts? When it is quiet
and you can think clearly, does your conscience tell you
to repent? For your peace now and for everlasting happiness, please repent. Open your heart to the Lord and
ask Him to help you. You will earn the blessing of forgiveness, peace, and the knowledge you have been purified and made whole. Find the courage to ask the Lord
for strength to repent, *now*" (*Ensign,* May 1995, 77).

This is the spirit of Elijah, that we redeem our dead,
and connect ourselves with our fathers which are in heaven, and
seal up our dead to come forth in the first resurrection.

JOSEPH SMITH
HISTORY OF THE CHURCH, 6:252

On this day in 1844, the Prophet addressed the Saints about Elijah's great calling: "Malachi says, 'I will send you Elijah the prophet before the coming of the great and dreadful day of the Lord: and he shall turn the heart of the fathers to the children, and the heart of the children to their fathers, lest I come and smite the earth with a curse.' Now, what I am after is the knowledge of God, and I take my own course to obtain it. . . . In the days of Noah, God destroyed the world by a flood, and He has promised to destroy it by fire in the last days: but before it should take place, Elijah should first come and turn the hearts of the fathers to the children. . . . What is this office and work of Elijah? It is one of the greatest and most important subjects that God has revealed. He should send Elijah to seal the children to the fathers, and the fathers to the children" (*History of the Church,* 6:251).

*We cannot keep all the commandments without
first knowing them, and we cannot expect to know all, or
more than we now know unless we comply with or keep
those we have already received.*

JOSEPH SMITH
HISTORY OF THE CHURCH, 5:135

The way we receive more light and truth is to give heed to the light and truth we have already received. The Lord will not reveal His secrets or make known His will to those who are proud, disobedient, intemperate, or rebellious. We must desire gospel light with all our hearts, study it out, ponder, pray, and seek the influence of the Spirit in guiding our efforts. This process is always fueled by humility and meekness, by a yearning to know the commandments and live them, by a hunger and thirst for righteousness, by a determination to "live by every word that proceedeth forth from the mouth of God" (D&C 84:44). As the Lord revealed to the Prophet Joseph: "That which is of God is light; and he that receiveth light, and continueth in God, receiveth more light; and that light groweth brighter and brighter until the perfect day" (D&C 50:24).

We must visit the fatherless and the widow in their affliction,
and we must keep ourselves unspotted from the world

JOSEPH SMITH
TEACHINGS, 76

Joseph Smith emulated the Savior's devotion to the salvation and blessing of all humankind. Those who aspire to be true followers of the Master want to do as He did, serve as He did, comfort as He did, and become even as He is. The Prophet, as did James, taught that we practice pure religion when we visit the fatherless and the widow in their affliction and keep ourselves unspotted from the world (James 1:27), "for such virtues flow from the great fountain of pure religion, strengthening our faith by adding every good quality that adorns the children of the blessed Jesus, we can pray in the season of prayer; we can love our neighbor as ourselves, and be faithful in tribulation, knowing that the reward of such is greater in the kingdom of heaven. What a consolation! What a joy! Let me live the life of the righteous, and let my reward be like his!" (*Teachings,* 76). Inexpressible joy and consolation comes to those who "live the life of the righteous."

*In His Almighty name we are determined to endure
tribulation as good soldiers unto the end.*

JOSEPH SMITH
HISTORY OF THE CHURCH, 3:297

Joseph Smith taught that the truths of the gospel will ultimately triumph: "As well might man stretch forth his puny arm to stop the Missouri river in its decreed course, or to turn it up stream, as to hinder the Almighty from pouring down knowledge from heaven upon the heads of the Latter-day Saints" (D&C 121:33). While in Liberty Jail, the Prophet affirmed that truth will always prevail: "Hell may pour forth its rage like the burning lava of mount Vesuvius, or of Etna, or of the most terrible of the burning mountains; and yet shall 'Mormonism' stand. . . . God is the author of it. He is our shield. It is by Him we received our birth. It was by His voice that we were called to a dispensation of His Gospel in the beginning of the fullness of times. It was by Him we received the Book of Mormon; and it is by Him that we remain unto this day; and by Him we shall remain" (*History of the Church,* 3:297). Let us remain steadfast and true.

MARCH 14

*That sublime occasion, the First Vision, parted the curtains
through which came the restoration to earth of the Church of
Christ. It came out of the wilderness of darkness, out of the
bleakness of ages past into the glorious dawn of a new day.*

GORDON B. HINCKLEY
ENSIGN, FEBRUARY 2001, 72

President Gordon B. Hinckley told of a time, while on
assignment at a Rochester New York Stake conference,
that he arose early in the morning with several other
priesthood leaders to visit the Sacred Grove: "No one
else was there. It was peaceful and beautiful. It had
rained during the night. . . . We knelt upon the damp
ground and prayed. We did not hear an audible voice.
We did not see a vision. But in an indefinable way we
were told in our minds, each of us, that yes, it happened
here just as Joseph said it happened. It was here that
God our Eternal Father and His Beloved Son, the resurrected Lord Jesus Christ, appeared to the 14-year-old
boy and spoke with him. Their matchless light rested
upon him, and he was instructed in what he should do"
(*Ensign,* February 2001, 72). That still, small voice will
also whisper to our hearts that Joseph was God's prophet
and the Book of Mormon is another witness of our
Savior. All this and more began with the First Vision.

MARCH 15

Trials . . . give us the knowledge necessary to understand the
minds of the ancients. For my part, I think I never could have felt
as I now do if I had not suffered the wrongs that I have suffered.
All things shall work together for good to them that love God.

JOSEPH SMITH
HISTORY OF THE CHURCH, 3:286

The Prophet Joseph administered comfort and counsel to the Saints even in the darkness of Liberty Jail. He knew that suffering would give him experience, refine his soul, deepen his understanding, and be for his good (D&C 122:7). And he maintained a robust faith in God and positive outlook despite his trials. During his Liberty Jail experience, he wrote scores of letters to family, friends, and many others. To a Mrs. Norman Bull he wrote on March 15, 1839: "Do not have any feelings of enmity towards any son or daughter of Adam. I believe I shall be let out of their hands some way or another, and shall see good days. We cannot do anything only stand still and see the salvation of God. He must do His own work, or it must fall to the ground. We must not take it in our hands to avenge our wrongs. Vengeance is mine, saith the Lord, and I will repay. I have no fears. I shall stand unto death, God being my helper" (*History of the Church,* 3:286).

*I roll the burden and responsibility of leading this church off from
my shoulders on to yours. Now, round up your shoulders and
stand under it like men; for the Lord is going to let me rest awhile.*

JOSEPH SMITH
JOSEPH SMITH, 529

In the months before his martyrdom, Joseph Smith had
forebodings that his mortal life was nearing its close. He
met with members of the Quorum of the Twelve
Apostles to instruct them and to give them the priesthood keys necessary to govern the Church and carry the
work of God forward in his absence. In March of 1844,
the Prophet explained to the Twelve that he had given
them all the keys, rights, and responsibility to lead the
kingdom. The Twelve continue to hold those keys today,
and without those keys they are not the Lord's authorized representatives. The Twelve is the bridge between
one administration and the next because collectively they
hold the keys. When Joseph died, the Twelve had the
priesthood keys and a senior apostle to carry the work
forward. It was the same when Brigham Young and then
the next prophet died, and so on to our day. We will never
be left without authorized priesthood keys or a Quorum
of Twelve Apostles to preside over the Church.

*I will organize the women under the priesthood after
the pattern of the priesthood. . . . The Church was never perfectly
organized until the women were thus organized.*

JOSEPH SMITH
JOSEPH SMITH, 451

On this date in 1842, in the Red Brick Store in Nauvoo, Illinois, Joseph Smith met with twenty women of the Church to organize the Female Relief Society. Emma Smith was called as the organization's first president. The Prophet, in turning the key to the sisters, subsequently taught the sisters of this divine organization: "This is a charitable Society, and according to your natures; it is natural for females to have feelings of charity and benevolence. You are now placed in a situation in which you can act according to those sympathies which God has planted in your bosoms. If you live up to these principles, how great and glorious will be your reward in the celestial kingdom! If you live up to your privileges, the angels cannot be restrained from being your associates" (*History of the Church,* 4:605). Today, as in the early days of the Relief Society, the women of the Church throughout the world are serving diligently and faithfully, bringing good to all around them.

One of the most pleasing scenes that can occur on earth, when a sin has been committed by one person against another, is, to forgive that sin; and then according to the sublime and perfect pattern of the Savior, pray to our Father in heaven to forgive him also.

JOSEPH SMITH
HISTORY OF THE CHURCH, 6:245

Some time after the intense persecution of the Saints in Missouri, Joseph Smith addressed the people of that state with an appeal for peace and goodwill. It was March of 1844; the Saints were settled in Nauvoo; it was only a few months before the Prophet's martyrdom. By extending the olive branch of forgiveness to those citizens, Joseph Smith demonstrated how a disciple of the Savior is a peacemaker. But at the same time he rebuked Missouri evildoers for their misdeeds against the Saints. The Prophet was ever ready to forgive, to start afresh, and to make amends with the honest, virtuous people of the state. Joseph was also modeling for the Saints what a follower of the Master should do: forgive others even as we ourselves ask for forgiveness. The Lord's command remains in force: "Forgive one another" (D&C 64:9). The Prophet ends his letter with these words: "I am the friend of all good men" (*History of the Church*, 6:247).

"Joseph, this is my Beloved; / Hear him!" Oh, how sweet the word!
Joseph's humble prayer was answered, / And he listened to the Lord.
Oh, what rapture filled his bosom, / For he saw the living God.

GEORGE MANWARING
HYMNS, NO. 26

Joseph Smith's First Prayer" is a favorite hymn that tells the transcendent story of young Joseph's theophany in a grove that would become sacred. George Manwaring (1854–1889), an English convert who emigrated to America and settled in Utah, cherished Joseph's account of the First Vision. He bore his testimony by recounting the First Vision in poetry:

> *Oh, how lovely was the morning!*
> *Radiant beamed the sun above.*
> *Bees were humming, sweet birds singing,*
> *Music ringing thru the grove,*
> *When within the shady woodland*
> *Joseph sought the God of love.* (Hymns, *no. 26*)

These words, sung by countless believers in congregations around the world, attest to the power and purity of what transpired on that "morning of a beautiful, clear day, early in the spring of eighteen hundred and twenty" (Joseph Smith–History 1:14).

There is no greater love than this, that a man lay down his life for his friends [John 15:13]. I discover hundreds and thousands of my brethren ready to sacrifice their lives for me.

JOSEPH SMITH
HISTORY OF THE CHURCH, 5:516

The Lord gave us the essence of the gospel in the meridian dispensation: "This is my commandment, That ye love one another, as I have loved you. Greater love hath no man than this, that a man lay down his life for his friends" (John 15:12–13). The Savior did just that—He gave His life for His friends. Who are His friends? The Lord said, "Ye are my friends, if ye do whatsoever I command you" (John 15:14). Think of what it means to be a friend of the Savior. True disciples of the Master are those who are obedient and meek, who strive to put off the natural man and become even as He is. When we deeply feel this love for the Savior, we wish to bless others. Such was the case early in this dispensation. Many were willing to take the place of the Prophet and offer themselves as a sacrifice so that the Prophet might continue his work in establishing the cause of Zion. This is true love and loyalty, true devotion and discipleship.

*If you have evil feelings, and speak of them to one
another, it has a tendency to do mischief.*

JOSEPH SMITH
HISTORY OF THE CHURCH, 5:140

No good comes from airing evil feelings abroad. We might temporarily feel better, we might feel justified in speaking to others, we might feel it does no harm—but we are wrong. Evil feelings and evil speaking lead only to trouble and heartache. The better and more courageous way is to follow the Savior's admonition: "If thy brother [or neighbor or ward member or coworker] shall trespass against thee, go and tell him his fault between thee and him alone: if he shall hear thee, thou hast gained thy brother" (Matthew 18:15). The first vital key is softening your heart with charity, kindheartedness, and the preparation of prayer. The next key is approaching the person with respect, humility, and sincerity "between thee and him alone." The final key is to trust the Lord and put it in His able hands. You are responsible only for what you do—not the freewill response of another. But, sooner or later, it will always come out all right with integrity, love, and kindness as your guideposts.

What is the nature and beauty of Joseph's mission? . . . When I first heard him preach, he brought heaven and earth together.

BRIGHAM YOUNG
DISCOURSES OF BRIGHAM YOUNG, 458

Joseph Smith, the untutored lad who became God's anointed prophet, was a remarkable gospel teacher. He had a hunger for revelation, a thirst to learn the mysteries of godliness, a yearning for wisdom from on high. He learned "line upon line, precept upon precept" (D&C 98:12) as heaven unfolded to him. He then would open the heavens to others. He could hold the attention of thousands for hours while he preached the truths of the restored gospel. Brigham Young described the Prophet's inspired teaching ability: "He took heaven, figuratively speaking, and brought it down to earth; and he took the earth, brought it up, and opened up, in plainness and simplicity, the things of God. . . . Did not Joseph do the same to your understandings? Would he not take the Scriptures and make them so plain and simple that everybody could understand?" (*Discourses of Brigham Young,* 458). Heaven will open to us as well as we study the words of the Prophet Joseph.

I know that the cloud will burst, and Satan's kingdom be laid in ruins, with all his black designs; and that the Saints will come forth like gold seven times tried in the fire, being made perfect through sufferings and temptations.

JOSEPH SMITH
HISTORY OF THE CHURCH, 2:353

Life gives us each our share of storms and raging tempests. Some are fierce as they churn about us with crushing intensity. Others are continuing, chronic, nagging squalls that disrupt daily life and never seem to let up. The adversary wants us to despair, to give in to doom and discouragement, to believe that life should be carefree, or at least painless, and that if our needs for happiness and contentment are not being fulfilled then we've been robbed. But hold on, hope on. Satan and his minions will ultimately fail. The faithful Saints will come out stronger and better for having weathered the storms that come; they will be refined and perfected as they resist temptation and call upon the powers of heaven in their suffering. As Jacob said to the righteous of his day, "Look unto God with firmness of mind, and pray unto him with exceeding faith, and he will console you in your afflictions, and he will plead your cause, and send down justice upon those who seek your destruction" (Jacob 3:1).

At 11 years of age, I knew Joseph Smith was a prophet of God. I didn't hear voices, see angels, or anything like that. What I felt was much more certain. My spiritual sense had been touched. I felt elation springing forth from the innermost part of my being.

GLENN L. PACE
ENSIGN, MAY 2007, 79

By the power of the Spirit we can know the truth of all things. Elder Glenn L. Pace of the Seventy taught: "Spiritual witnesses come at a young age to those who are exposed to spiritual experiences. As parents, teachers, and leaders, we are good at making certain you understand the rules and commandments. We could improve on helping you gain a testimony of the principles and doctrine. Perhaps we could pause more often and help you learn to recognize the Spirit. Once you recognize those feelings for what they are, your faith in them will increase. Soon you will find that you have developed a spiritual sixth sense which cannot be misled. . . . How does this spiritual witness feel? It is as difficult to describe as the scent of a rose or the song of a bird or the beauty of a landscape. Nevertheless, you know it when you feel it" (*Ensign*, May 2007, 78–79).

With my flesh all scarified and defaced, I preached
to the congregation as usual, and in the afternoon of the
same day baptized three individuals.

JOSEPH SMITH
HISTORY OF THE CHURCH, 1:264

On this Sabbath day in 1832 the Prophet Joseph gave a sermon after spending the night having tar and feathers painfully removed from his skin. He recorded in his journal, "My friends spent the night in scraping and removing the tar, and washing and cleansing my body, so that by morning I was ready to be clothed again" (*History of the Church*, 1:264). With an undaunted spirit, he preached to a congregation that included members of the mob that had mercilessly attacked him and Sidney Rigdon the night before. Compounding the heartache, Joseph and Emma's eleven-month-old adopted son, Joseph, died a few days later as a result of exposure during the mobbing. One can only imagine the suffering and sorrow of Joseph, his beloved wife and family, and his faithful associates. But Joseph would not give in to the mobbers or give up his divine commission. He had an unconquerable strength and conviction that would see him through this trial and others to follow.

By the power of God I translated the Book of Mormon . . . ,
in which wonderful event I stood alone, an unlearned youth,
to combat the worldly wisdom and multiplied ignorance
of eighteen centuries, with a new revelation.

JOSEPH SMITH
HISTORY OF THE CHURCH, 6:74

On this day in 1830, the first printed copies of the Book of Mormon went on sale at Grandin's bookstore in Palmyra. The book stands today as a tangible witness to the prophetic mission of Joseph Smith. It cannot easily be discounted or explained away. If the account Joseph gave us is true, then the Book of Mormon must be what it purports to be: the record of an ancient people written by ancient authors. The thought that an untutored ploughboy could create a five-hundred page forgery with intricate details of antiquity out of thin air is beyond comprehension. This was a young man with no knowledge of ancient civilizations, no training as a writer, no means to pull off a fabrication. Critics will continue to disparage the Prophet, but the Book of Mormon stands since 1830 as true and as powerful as when it was translated by the gift and power of God.

Thanks be to thy name, O Lord God of Israel, who keepest covenant and showest mercy unto thy servants who walk uprightly before thee, with all their hearts—Thou who hast commanded thy servants to build a house to thy name in this place [Kirtland].

DOCTRINE AND COVENANTS 109:1–2

The Kirtland Temple, the first temple completed in this dispensation, was dedicated on this day in 1836. The Prophet Joseph offered the prayer of dedication, which was given to him by revelation (D&C 109). This was a season of rejoicing for the Saints who had sacrificed so much. The Prophet recorded some of the remarkable events of that day: "A noise was heard like the sound of a rushing mighty wind, which filled the Temple, and all the congregation simultaneously arose, being moved upon by an invisible power; many began to speak in tongues and prophesy; others saw glorious visions; and I beheld the Temple was filled with angels, which fact I declared to the congregation. The people of the neighborhood came running together (hearing an unusual sound within, and seeing a bright light like a pillar of fire resting upon the Temple), and were astonished at what was taking place" (*History of the Church,* 2:428). Saints on both sides of the veil continue to rejoice whenever a temple is dedicated.

The servants of God teach nothing but principles of eternal life, by their works ye shall know them. A good man will speak good things and holy principles, and an evil man evil things.

JOSEPH SMITH
HISTORY OF THE CHURCH, 6:366

Among the final words of the great editor-prophet Mormon are these: "For behold, a bitter fountain cannot bring forth good water, neither can a good fountain bring forth bitter water; wherefore, a man being a servant of the devil cannot follow Christ; and if he follow Christ he cannot be a servant of the devil. Wherefore, all things which are good cometh of God; and that which is evil cometh of the devil; for the devil is an enemy unto God, and fighteth against him continually, and inviteth and enticeth to sin, and to do that which is evil continually. But behold, that which is of God inviteth and enticeth to do good continually; wherefore, every thing which inviteth and enticeth to do good, and to love God, and to serve him, is inspired of God" (Moroni 7:11–13). True servants of God teach truth, live virtuous principles, and produce good works. They are disciples of the Master and seek to become even as He is, for that which comes of God is pure and holy.

MARCH 29

*If you wish to go where God is, you must be like God,
or possess the principles which God possesses, for if we are not
drawing towards God in principle, we are going from
Him and drawing towards the devil.*

JOSEPH SMITH
TEACHINGS, 216

We cannot be apathetic or complacent when it comes
to everlasting things. Spiritual stagnation slowly, almost
imperceptibly, distances us from the things of eternity. If,
in process of time, we aren't becoming more like God,
more refined in our desires and appetites, and more
committed to the cause of Christ, we are opening our
lives to the devil's dissonance. But since we're all sinners
(Romans 3:23; 1 John 1:8), what will free us from the
stain of sin and leave us pure and spotless? Some inter-
vening and compensating power must bridge the gap.
That power is provided by the Savior in whom there was
no sin. Christ lived the law flawlessly, and therefore never
estranged Himself from God. He gave His life—a sinless
ransom, a perfect mediation—to pay the debt of sin for
all who believe on His name, repent, and come unto
Him with full purpose of heart. Through the enabling
power of His atoning sacrifice, we gain redemption and
eternal life.

*In this world, mankind are naturally selfish, ambitious
and striving to excel one above another.*

JOSEPH SMITH
TEACHINGS, 297

We are blessed to know the eternal truth that we
are spiritual sons and daughters of God and as such
have unlimited potential for good. We come from the
heavenly realm and are born into a world of sin beset
with pitfalls and temptations for the "natural man"
(Mosiah 3:19) but also full of spiritual opportunities
for growth for the divine. Being born innocent (D&C
93:38) is being born neither good nor evil but having
the potential for both. The "natural man" in us grows
as a result of sin and our rejection of the promptings
of the Spirit, whereas our divine nature is manifest
when we heed those spiritual promptings and reject
sin (Mosiah 5:2). Joseph Smith understood the weakness and susceptibility of man: "I have learned in my
travels that man is treacherous and selfish, but few
excepted" (*Teachings,* 30). We are in this fallen world
to learn to hold back the devilish and become true
Saints of God: full of selflessness, charity, and humility.

MARCH 31

By a concentration of action, and a unity of effort, we can only accomplish the great work of the last days.

JOSEPH SMITH
HISTORY OF THE CHURCH, 4:272

We move the work of the Lord forward as we work together in love and harmony. If we reach our hands out to others in the spirit of fellowship and brotherhood, we can accomplish great things with the help of the Lord. The Lord could certainly accomplish His purposes without our imperfect efforts, but He's not just building a kingdom—He's building men and women who become as He is and, as joint-heirs, inherit all that He has (Romans 8:16–17). The Prophet Joseph said, "The greatest temporal and spiritual blessings which always flow from faithfulness and concerted effort, never attended individual exertion or enterprise. The history of all past ages abundantly attests this fact" (*History of the Church*, 4:272). We are a congregation of equals who need each other—both personally and institutionally. We will not live in celestial glory alone and detached from others; and the kingdom of God cannot prosper without harmony and unity.

APRIL

Knowledge does away with
darkness, suspense and doubt; for these
cannot exist where knowledge is.

JOSEPH SMITH

Let honesty, and sobriety, and candor, and solemnity,
and virtue, and pureness, and meekness, and simplicity crown
our heads in every place; and in fine, become as little
children, without malice, guile or hypocrisy.

JOSEPH SMITH
HISTORY OF THE CHURCH, 3:296

We are the offspring of God and as such we have a divine nature and destiny. But we are born into a world filled with the alluring forces of wickedness and temptation that pull us ever downward. Our calling is to put off the worldliness and sin of the natural man and become a holy people, childlike, without enmity or evilness. The Atonement of Jesus Christ is the great act of love by which all of us may become sanctified, pure, and holy (Moroni 10:32–33). Becoming childlike is the labor of a lifetime, a process rather than a singular spiritual experience or event. The Lord taught, "Except ye be converted, and become as little children, ye shall not enter into the kingdom of heaven" (Matthew 18:3). Our unconditional surrender to God restores in us the innocence, the simplicity and pureness and meekness, the faith and unwavering trust of little children.

When finally we get that one divine thought that Joseph Smith was and is a prophet and the gospel is true, all the other seeming difficulties melt away like heavy frost before the coming of the rising sun.

HAROLD B. LEE
THE TEACHINGS OF HAROLD B. LEE, 134

We declare without equivocation that God the Father and His Son, the Lord Jesus Christ, appeared in person to the boy Joseph Smith," said President Gordon B. Hinckley. "Our whole strength rests on the validity of that vision. It either occurred or it did not occur. If it did not, then this work is a fraud. If it did, then it is the most important and wonderful work under the heavens. … Upon that unique and wonderful experience stands the validity of this Church. In all of recorded religious history there is nothing to compare with it. … Why did both the Father and the Son come to a boy, a mere lad? For one thing, they came to usher in the greatest gospel dispensation of all time, when all of previous dispensations should be gathered and brought together in one. … The instrument in this work of God was a boy whose mind was not cluttered by the philosophies of men. That mind was fresh and without schooling in the traditions of the day" (*Ensign,* November 2002, 80).

*The veil was taken from our minds, and the eyes
of our understanding were opened.*

DOCTRINE AND COVENANTS 110:1

On this day in 1836 in the recently dedicated Kirtland Temple, Joseph Smith and Oliver Cowdery retired to the west pulpit behind lowered curtains and bowed in solemn prayer. As they rose from prayer, the Savior appeared to them and proclaimed His approval of the temple: "Behold, I have accepted this house, and my name shall be here; and I will manifest myself to my people in mercy in this house" (D&C 110:7). After this extraordinary manifestation closed, Joseph and Oliver saw three separate visions in which ancient prophets from Old Testament dispensations appeared to them to restore priesthood keys necessary for the continuance of the latter-day work of the Lord (D&C 110). On this extraordinary day of great significance, the Prophet was given keys and authority to gather modern Israel and to seal families together for time and all eternity.

Be thankful for the privilege we enjoy this day of meeting so many of the Saints, and for the warmth and brightness of the heavens over our heads; and it truly makes the countenances of this great multitude to look cheerful and gladdens the hearts of all present.

JOSEPH SMITH
HISTORY OF THE CHURCH, 5:327

General conferences of the Church are a time to worship the Lord and feast upon the words of eternal life, to transact Church business and sustain officers, and to sound the voice of warning. They are a time of renewal and reflection, a time to hear the certain and inspired words of our leaders that will help prepare us for the battles of life ahead (1 Corinthians 14:8–9). We have a responsibility to pray for our leaders, to open our hearts to the Spirit of the Lord. At the 1843 April conference, the Prophet made three requests: "The first is, that all who have faith will exercise it and pray the Lord to calm the wind . . . the next is that I may have your prayers that the Lord will strengthen my lungs, so that I may be able to make you all hear; and the third is, that you will pray for the Holy Ghost to rest upon me, so as to enable me to declare those things that are true" (*History of the Church*, 5:339).

Who, among all the Saints in these last days can consider himself as good as our Lord? Who is as perfect? Who is as pure? . . . He never transgressed or broke a commandment or law of heaven—no deceit was in His mouth, neither was guile found in His heart.

JOSEPH SMITH
TEACHINGS, 67

Jesus Christ "was in all points tempted like as we are, yet without sin" (Hebrews 4:15). He "did no sin, neither was guile found in his mouth" (1 Peter 2:22). Thus, Jesus, the great High Priest of our profession, "needeth not offer sacrifice for his own sins, for he knew no sins" (JST, Hebrews 7:26). For this reason the Master could speak of His own righteousness and observe that "the prince of darkness, who is of this world, cometh, but hath no power over me" (JST, John 14:30). Because Christ was tempted and yet remained perfect, He knows how to succor and strengthen us, and He knows that perfection is pending. "The perfection that the Savior envisions for us is much more than errorless performance," taught Elder Russell M. Nelson. "It is the eternal expectation as expressed by the Lord in his great intercessory prayer to his Father— that we might be made perfect and be able to dwell with them in the eternities ahead" (*Ensign,* November 1995, 87). Jesus is our perfect mentor, model, and mediator.

Thou shalt be called a seer, a translator, a prophet, an apostle of Jesus Christ, an elder of the church through the will of God the Father, and the grace of your Lord Jesus Christ.

DOCTRINE AND COVENANTS 21:1

On this momentous day in 1830 in a log farm home belonging to Peter Whitmer in Fayette, New York, the Church of Jesus Christ was organized anew in this dispensation. On that long-awaited day, the Lord gave members of the new church the law of prophets: "Wherefore, meaning the church, thou shalt give heed unto all his words and commandments which he shall give unto you as he receiveth them, walking in all holiness before me; for his word ye shall receive, as if from mine own mouth, in all patience and faith. For by doing these things the gates of hell shall not prevail against you; yea, and the Lord God will disperse the powers of darkness from before you, and cause the heavens to shake for your good, and his name's glory" (D&C 21:4–6). The Lord does His work through prophets (Amos 3:7), and Joseph Smith is the one whom God "inspired to move the cause of Zion in mighty power for good" in this final dispensation (D&C 21:7).

APRIL 7

*Pray that the Lord may strengthen my lungs, stay the winds,
and let the prayers of the Saints to heaven appear . . . for the
effectual prayers of the righteous avail much.*

JOSEPH SMITH
HISTORY OF THE CHURCH, 6:303

On this day in 1844, during what would be his last
general conference, the Prophet Joseph delivered the
monumental King Follett discourse. Thousands of
Latter-day Saints gathered to hear him teach and testify.
On this occasion, he taught that man has an immortal
soul and can become like God, that the dead go to the
world of spirits and are absent for only a moment, and
that the greatest responsibility resting on the Saints is to
seek after their dead. During the course of this lengthy
and famous sermon, the Prophet discussed more than a
hundred different doctrinal topics, and he paid tribute to
King Follett, a member of the Church who had died in
an accident. As the Prophet spoke, four men recorded or
made notes, giving us a reasonably accurate version of the
sermon (*History of the Church*, 6:302–17). This extraordinary discourse, filled with many of the unique doctrines
of the Restoration, is further witness of the prophetic
mantle and revelatory gifts resting upon the Prophet.

*The whole of America is Zion itself from north to south,
and is described by the Prophets, who declare that it is the Zion
where the mountain of the Lord should be, and that it
should be in the center of the land.*

JOSEPH SMITH
HISTORY OF THE CHURCH, 6:318–19

On this day in 1844, Joseph Smith explained that Zion includes all of North and South America, a land "choice above all other lands" (1 Nephi 2:20). This is the land where the gospel was restored in the latter-days; the land where a great flood of heavenly light was shed forth and is now being taken to the world. Zion is also the name by which the Saints of the Lord are identified; the place to which they gather. It is the place for the pure in heart (D&C 97:21)—a place where people are unified as one, where righteousness reigns, and love abounds (Moses 7:18). It is both an actual place where the Saints gather as they join The Church of Jesus Christ of Latter-day Saints, and a glorious ideal to which the Saints aspire. We are "called to labor in [the Lord's] vineyard, and to build up [His] church, and to bring forth Zion, that it may rejoice upon the hills and flourish" (D&C 39:13).

*No man can receive the Holy Ghost without receiving
revelations. The Holy Ghost is a revelator.*

JOSEPH SMITH
HISTORY OF THE CHURCH, 6:58

The mission of the Holy Ghost is to testify of the
Father and Son. If we are faithful, the Holy Ghost will
enlighten our minds and fill our hearts with understanding. The Holy Ghost can become a personal Liahona,
showing us all things we should do (2 Nephi 32:5). Elder
Joseph B. Wirthlin counseled, "Rise above the things of
the world that clamor for your attention. For example,
some of the world's music is degrading, vulgar, and inappropriate and will drown out the promptings of the Holy
Ghost. Bringing into your body substances forbidden by
the Lord in the Word of Wisdom will prevent you from
feeling and recognizing the promptings of the Holy
Ghost. The failure to live a clean and chaste life deadens
the promptings of the Spirit. Take your thoughts to
higher levels than the vulgar and immoral. . . . Shun
pornography like a deadly, contagious sin and disease. . . .
It will drive the Holy Ghost and His influence from your
life" (*Ensign,* November 1999, 41).

These were days never to be forgotten—to sit under the sound of a voice dictated by the inspiration of heaven, awakened the utmost gratitude . . . Day after day I continued, uninterrupted, to write from his mouth, as he translated with the Urim and Thummim.

OLIVER COWDERY
JOSEPH SMITH–HISTORY 1:71, FOOTNOTE

In April 1829, Oliver Cowdery, a teacher whose school term had finished, arrived at Joseph's home in Harmony, Pennsylvania, to inquire of the Prophet concerning the work of translation. Oliver prayed and received a testimony of the truthfulness of the Prophet's work and within two days went to work as scribe. Martin Harris had earlier lost the 116-page book of Lehi transcribed in 1828, and the Prophet expected that the Lord would send another scribe (D&C 5:34). That promise was fulfilled when Oliver volunteered to write while Joseph translated the Book of Mormon from April through June 1829. He personally wrote almost the entire first copy of the translation. Oliver would go on to become one of the Three Witnesses of the Book of Mormon and Joseph's companion in receiving priesthood keys of authority from heavenly messengers. When the Lord wants a work accomplished, He opens the way.

Search the revelations which we publish, and ask your Heavenly Father, in the name of His Son Jesus Christ, to manifest the truth unto you, and if you do it with an eye single to His glory nothing doubting, He will answer you by the power of His Holy Spirit.

JOSEPH SMITH
TEACHINGS, 11

And when ye shall receive these things, I would exhort you that ye would ask God, the Eternal Father, in the name of Christ, if these things are not true; and if ye shall ask with a sincere heart, with real intent, having faith in Christ, he will manifest the truth of it unto you, by the power of the Holy Ghost. And by the power of the Holy Ghost ye may know the truth of all things" (Moroni 10:4–5). "These things" can refer to any of the doctrines, practices, and principles of the gospel. Joseph taught that we can gain an unshakeable witness of the truth: "You will then know for yourselves and not for another. You will not then be dependent on man for the knowledge of God; nor will there be any room for speculation. No; for when men receive their instruction from Him that made them, they know how He will save them" (*Teachings*, 11–12).

He interested and edified, while, at the same time,
he amused and entertained his audience; and none listened
to him that were ever weary with his discourse.

PARLEY P. PRATT
AUTOBIOGRAPHY OF PARLEY P. PRATT, 45

Parley P. Pratt, an original member of the Quorum of
the Twelve Apostles (1835–1857) and one of the early
Church's most influential writers and missionaries, was
born on this day in 1807 in Burlington, New York. He
left us an eloquent description of the Prophet: "President
Joseph Smith was in person tall and well built, strong and
active; of a light complexion, light hair, blue eyes, very
little beard, and of an expression peculiar to himself, on
which the eye naturally rested with interest, and was
never weary of beholding. His countenance was ever
mild, affable, beaming with intelligence and benevolence;
mingled with a look of interest and an unconscious smile,
or cheerfulness, and entirely free from all restraint or
affectation of gravity; and there was something connected
with the serene and steady penetrating glance of his eye,
as if he would penetrate the deepest abyss of the human
heart, gaze into eternity, penetrate the heavens, and comprehend all worlds" (*Autobiography of Parley P. Pratt*, 45).

*It is contrary to the economy of God for any member
of the Church, or any one, to receive instructions for those in
authority, higher than themselves; therefore you will see the
i[m]propriety of giving heed to them.*

JOSEPH SMITH
HISTORY OF THE CHURCH, 1:338

On this date in Kirtland in 1833, Joseph Smith
wrote a letter to a Brother Carter wherein he taught a
vital gospel principle: we cannot receive instruction or
inspiration for those who are higher than us in authority. There is no higher authority than the presiding high
priest, the President of the Church—the prophet, seer,
and revelator for the entire Church. The same principle holds true at the local level. It is not the preroga-
tive of a ward member to receive inspiration for the
bishop. It is not the right of a member of a stake to
receive direction for the stake president. We each have
our areas of stewardship, our callings and responsibilities for which we are responsible and for which we are
entitled to receive divine direction. There is order in
the Lord's kingdom: we are to be humble and teachable, follow our leaders, and not steady the ark
(1 Chronicles 13:10; see also D&C 85:8) or encroach on
stewardship responsibilities that are not ours.

*I took occasion to gently reprove all present for
letting report excite them, and advised them not to suffer
themselves to be wrought upon by any report, but to
maintain an even, undaunted mind.*

JOSEPH SMITH
HISTORY OF THE CHURCH, 5:98

We live in a day of startling reports and astonishing rumors. The headlines shout doom and gloom, and sometimes our hope and confidence in everlasting things wanes in light of discouraging news and titillating stories. The father of lies would have us lose hope, give in to despair, and feel that life is too scary and precarious to go forth with faith. But if we trust God and know that He is our loving Father and that He is mindful of us, we will be empowered to go forward with faith and sweet assurance. Faith and confidence in the Lord and His purposes filters each report and rumor through a gospel lens. Faith drives out fear and uncertainty, and hope and trust chase away the countless worries that are so common and so expected in this troubled world. We may be surprised with current events, but the Lord never is. No headline or report can thwart His purposes; no rumor or story can frustrate God's plan for His faithful children and for His kingdom.

*I never told you I was perfect; but there is no
error in the revelations which I have taught. Must I,
then, be thrown away as a thing of naught?*

JOSEPH SMITH
HISTORY OF THE CHURCH, 6:366

God works through imperfect servants to accomplish His purposes. Moroni said, "Condemn me not because of mine imperfection, . . . but rather give thanks unto God that he hath made manifest unto you our imperfections, that ye may learn to be more wise than we have been" (Mormon 9:31). B. H. Roberts, who loved the Prophet dearly, said: "Joseph Smith . . . claimed for himself no special sanctity, no faultless life, no perfection of character, no inerrancy for every word spoken by him. And as he did not claim these things for himself, so can they not be claimed for him by others; for to claim perfection for him, or even unusual sanctity, would be to repudiate the revelations themselves which supply the evidence of his imperfections, whereof, in them, he is frequently reproved. . . . yet to Joseph Smith was given access to the mind of Deity, through the revelations of God to him" (*Comprehensive History*, 2:360–61).

Knowledge does away with darkness, suspense and doubt; for these cannot exist where knowledge is. . . . In knowledge there is power.

JOSEPH SMITH
HISTORY OF THE CHURCH, 5:340

Where there is knowledge there is power. God has perfect power because He has perfect knowledge. The Prophet taught, "God has more power than all other beings, because he has greater knowledge; and hence he knows how to subject all other beings to Him. He has power over all" (*History of the Church,* 5:340). Knowledge chases away fear and darkness, suspicion and cynicism. The more we study and learn, the more we pray and ponder, the deeper our understanding and commitment to the everlasting things. Those with shallow testimonies or with only a superficial knowledge of the doctrines of the gospel run the risk of being deceived and disoriented. If we humbly plant our feet deep into gospel soil, steadfastly nurture our faith with the good word of God, and unwaveringly strive to do our best to live in accordance with the Savior's words of eternal life, we will gain the sure word of knowledge, and we will be saved at the last day.

That same sociality which exists among us here will exist among us there, only it will be coupled with eternal glory, which glory we do not now enjoy.

DOCTRINE AND COVENANTS 130:2

We are given this life to prepare for eternity. And if we have lived the gospel we shall continue to live in the family unit and inherit eternal life. Elder Neal A. Maxwell said: "Attending to all family duties includes really teaching our children 'to understand the doctrine of repentance, faith in Christ the Son of the living God' (D&C 68:25). . . . When parents fail to transmit testimony and theology along with decency, those families are only one generation from serious spiritual decline, having lost their savor. The law of the harvest is nowhere more in evidence and nowhere more relentless than in family gardens! In addition to our having loving family 'sociality,' which, one day, will be 'coupled with eternal glory,' we stress again and again the available remedies of family prayers, family home evenings, and family scripture study (D&C 130:2). Moreover, personal revelation regarding parenting can provide customized guidance and reassurance!" (*Ensign*, May 1994, 89–90).

Let not any man publish his own righteousness.

JOSEPH SMITH
TEACHINGS, 194

Paul taught the Corinthians a timeless truth: "Though I speak with the tongues of men and of angels, and have not charity, I am become as sounding brass, or a tinkling cymbal" (1 Corinthians 13:1). His similes for self-vaunting—"sounding brass" and "tinkling cymbal"—are fitting. Joseph Smith described that discordant and shallow vaunting as self-righteousness, and he continually warned the Saints against it. On one occasion, after reading 1 Corinthians 13:1 in a talk to the Relief Society in April 1842, the Prophet said, "Don't be limited in your views with regard to your neighbor's virtue, but beware of self-righteousness, and be limited in the estimate of your own virtues, and not think yourselves more righteous than others" (*Teachings,* 228). On another occasion, the Prophet said, "Christ was condemned by the self-righteous Jews because He took sinners into His society" (ibid., 240). We are to be men and women of charity—filled with love, compassion, and humility.

*We shall . . . do well to discern the signs of the
times as we pass along, that the day of the Lord may not
"overtake us as a thief in the night."*

JOSEPH SMITH
HISTORY OF THE CHURCH, 3:331

We are to be vigilant in watching for the signs of
the times. The Lord declared, "Verily I say unto you,
the coming of the Lord draweth nigh, and it over-
taketh the world as a thief in the night—Therefore,
gird up your loins, that you may be the children of
light, and that day shall not overtake you as a thief"
(D&C 106:4–5). Joseph said, "I will prophesy that the
signs of the coming of the Son of Man are already
commenced. One pestilence will desolate after
another. We shall soon have war and bloodshed. The
moon will be turned into blood. I testify of these
things, and that the coming of the Son of Man is nigh,
even at your doors" (*History of the Church,* 3:390). These
are the last days before the Lord will return in glory at
some future date. We will not be caught unawares if
we are careful to discern truth from error, fact from
fiction, as we feast upon the scriptures, hearken to the
living oracles, and draw closer to the Lord.

Nothing is a greater injury to the children of men than to be under the influence of a false spirit when they think they have the Spirit of God.

JOSEPH SMITH
TEACHINGS, 205

Self-righteousness, pride, and wickedness are at the heart of falsehood and deception. President Boyd K. Packer taught, "Before I say another word about personal revelation, I must tell you so that you cannot possibly misunderstand: 'There are many spirits which are false spirits' (D&C 50:2). There can be counterfeit revelations, promptings from the devil, temptations! As long as you live, in one way or another the adversary will try to lead you astray. . . . The seventh chapter of Moroni in the Book of Mormon tells you how to test spiritual promptings. Read it carefully—over and over. By trial, and some error, you will learn to heed these promptings. If ever you receive a prompting to do something that makes you *feel* uneasy, something you know in your *mind* to be wrong and contrary to the principles of righteousness, do not respond to it!" (*Ensign*, November 1994, 61).

Take away the Book of Mormon and the revelations,
and where is our religion? We have none.

JOSEPH SMITH
HISTORY OF THE CHURCH, 2:52

During a conference of the Church held in Norton, Ohio, on this date in 1834, the Prophet declared the role of the Book of Mormon and the revelations of God. This is a vital truth of the Restoration: We have a living head—the Lord Jesus Christ, and we have a living prophet who continues to reveal to us the will of God. The heavens are not sealed; the scriptural canon is not closed; the revelatory constitution of the Church is not finished. Because of the reality of the living Christ and His living earthly spokesman, our canon is open and adaptable to changing times and circumstances. The Lord called Noah to build an ark, not Moses; He called Moses to liberate captive Israel, not Obadiah; and in our day He called Joseph Smith to usher in the dispensation of the fulness of times, not Brigham Young—each prophet for each season. The prophet gives to us today's news for today's needs. Without continuing revelation and the truths contained in the Book of Mormon, we have nothing.

*In weakness and simplicity, I declared to you
what the Lord has brought forth by the ministering of
His holy angels to me for this generation.*

JOSEPH SMITH
HISTORY OF THE CHURCH, 1:442

In 1833 Joseph Smith wrote to Moses Nickerson in Canada who had recently joined the Church, exhorting him to remember the testimony given concerning this great latter-day work. The Prophet encouraged the new convert, "I pray that the Lord may enable you to treasure these things in your mind, for I know that His Spirit will bear testimony to all who seek diligently after knowledge from Him" (*History of the Church,* 1:442). We too must remember, especially during times of doubt and difficulty, the testimony that burned in our hearts that this work is true. The Lord spoke the same truth to Oliver Cowdery: "If you desire a further witness, cast your mind upon the night that you cried unto me in your heart, that you might know concerning the truth of these things. Did I not speak peace to your mind concerning the matter? What greater witness can you have than from God?" (D&C 6:22–23). Hold true and always remember the peace, the sweet assurance, the quiet confidence of your testimony.

The only difference between the old and young dying is, one lives longer in heaven and eternal light and glory than the other, and is freed a little sooner from this miserable wicked world.

JOSEPH SMITH
TEACHINGS, 197

Joseph Smith taught the same fundamental, unchanging doctrines of the gospel that were revealed by ancient prophets. For example, Mormon, who was writing to his son Moroni after his calling to the ministry, taught that "little children are alive in Christ, . . . wherefore, I love little children with a perfect love; and they are all alike and partakers of salvation" (Moroni 8:12, 17). God's plan of salvation is a perfect plan for the destiny of His beloved children. Children who die are alive in Christ—partakers of eternal life—because the law has no claim upon them (Moroni 8:22). Sweet comfort and reassurance is given to parents to know that some children are too pure to live in this wicked world, and a loving Heavenly Father has taken them to live everlastingly with Him.

In the multitude of counsel there is safety.

JOSEPH SMITH
HISTORY OF THE CHURCH, 5:106

There is safety and protection in our councils. President Stephen L Richards said: "The genius of our Church government is government through *councils.* . . . I have had enough experience to know the value of councils. Hardly a day passes but that I see . . . God's wisdom, in creating councils: to govern his Kingdom . . . I have no hesitancy in giving you the assurance, if you will confer in council as you are expected to do, God will give you solutions to the problems that confront you" (Conference Report, October 1953, 86). We serve in councils in our marriages, in our families, in our wards and stakes. We are to be united in counseling together to solve problems, get feedback, gather information, and make decisions. We do not operate alone. No one knows everything, and no one has all the answers. We need each other. We are blessed as we work interdependently and counsel with our councils.

*The burdens which roll upon me are very great. My
persecutors allow me no rest, and I find that in the midst of
business and care the spirit is willing, but the flesh is weak.*

JOSEPH SMITH
HISTORY OF THE CHURCH, 5:516

Joseph Smith was not unaffected by the many trials
and tribulations he experienced in his short life. He
was not a dispassionate prophet or impervious to the
tremendous responsibilities he shouldered. He was, of
course, subject to the stresses and strains and weari-
ness of life. He said of himself: "Although I was called
of my Heavenly Father to lay the foundation of this
great work and kingdom in this dispensation, and testify of His revealed will to scattered Israel, I am subject to like passions as other men, like the prophets of
olden times" (*History of the Church,* 5:516). Even so, he
was a man called above all others to be the great
prophet of the latter-days, the prophet of prophets
who would stand as head of this last and greatest of
dispensations. Although not perfect, he was remarkable, exceptional, unusual, and extraordinary in every
way—especially considering the burdens he carried
and the adversities he endured throughout life.

*Outward appearance is not always a criterion by
which to judge our fellow man; but the lips betray the haughty
and overbearing imagination of the heart; by his words
and his deeds let him be judged.*

JOSEPH SMITH
HISTORY OF THE CHURCH, 3:295

So much of the world seems an illusion. We see the superficial and counterfeit lauded all around us. The fake becomes real to those who want to keep up with the world and the worldly. It's easy to appear or talk or seem a certain way; it's more difficult to reflect true character and authenticity, to walk with integrity and honesty, to not compartmentalize and rationalize away everlasting principles. Very often our lips betray our hearts. We may say all the right things, but our heart—as reflected in our actions—reveals something else about us. The Lord is not deceived by externals: He knows our hearts, our desires, our "real" self. As He taught Samuel, "Look not on his countenance, or on the height of his stature . . . for the Lord seeth not as man seeth; for man looketh on the outward appearance, but the Lord looketh on the heart" (1 Samuel 16:7). We are judged by the content of our character, by the depth of our righteousness.

We would say, beware of pride also; for well and truly hath the wise man said, that pride goeth before destruction, and a haughty spirit before a fall.

JOSEPH SMITH
HISTORY OF THE CHURCH, 3:295

Every one of us must beware the universal sin of pride. It creeps up on us subtly, quietly, insidiously, until before we know it we become puffed up within ourselves and condescending to others around us. We all know the faces of pride: a lack or absence of meekness or teachableness, conceit and envy, hard-heartedness and haughtiness, always thinking in comparisons—we're better, richer, smarter than others. Pride is enmity in action and sets us in opposition to each other and to God. The proud see themselves as above others as they follow their own will rather than God's will. It is perhaps the one sin each of us is guilty of to some degree. The universal remedy is humility. We must choose to humble ourselves and realize our dependence upon God. We must choose to humble ourselves to see the divine worth within each person. No person is better than another or more loved by God, whose understanding and love for us is perfect. We can choose to be humble.

*If I had not actually got into this work and
been called of God, I would back out. But I cannot
back out: I have no doubt of the truth.*

JOSEPH SMITH
HISTORY OF THE CHURCH, 5:336

Joseph Smith spent his life bringing forth a new dispensation of religious truth. His life was filled with
turmoil and persecution, and he noted that "the envy
and wrath of man" had been his common lot and that
"deep water" was what he was "wont to swim in"
(D&C 127:2). In April 1843, he bore witness to an
audience in Nauvoo of his calling from God. He could
not, would not, back out of his divine commission.
The Prophet was true to the end, even though his life
could have been so much easier if he'd just given up,
given in. He lived in the hope of bringing gospel truth
to the world, and he died the victim of brutal enemies
who did not understand his prophetic mission. When
one knows in the center core of the heart that Christ
is our Savior, that this Church is true, that Joseph was
God's anointed prophet, that the Book of Mormon is
the word of God, and that we have a living prophet
today, then one cannot back out or back down.

I have even known [Joseph] to retain a congregation
of willing and anxious listeners for many hours together in the
midst of cold or sunshine, rain or wind, while they were
laughing at one moment and weeping the next.

PARLEY P. PRATT
AUTOBIOGRAPHY OF PARLEY P. PRATT, 45

The Saints loved to gather and hear the Prophet preach. On one occasion, Amasa Potter recorded a miraculous event that took place during a sermon in Nauvoo: "When [the Prophet] had spoken about thirty minutes there came up a heavy wind and storm. The dust was so dense that we could not see each other any distance, and some of the people were leaving when Joseph called out to them to stop and let their prayers ascend to Almighty God that the winds may cease blowing and the rain stop falling, and it should be so. In a very few minutes the winds and rain ceased and the elements became calm as a summer's morning. . . . we could see in the distance the trees and shrubs waving in the wind, while where we were it was quiet for one hour, and during that time one of the greatest sermons that ever fell from the Prophet's lips was preached on the great subject of the dead" (in *Joseph Smith,* 494).

A fanciful and flowery and heated imagination
beware of; because the things of God are of deep import; and
time, and experience, and careful and ponderous and
solemn thoughts can only find them out.

JOSEPH SMITH
HISTORY OF THE CHURCH, 3:295

The stirrings of the Spirit and the things of godliness are serene, soothing, steady, and sure. They are not given to drama and intrigue; not produced by a fevered and flowery imagination. Only deep pondering and praying, heartfelt searching, and time and experience can find them out. The Prophet taught, "Thy mind, O man! If thou wilt lead a soul unto salvation, must stretch as high as the utmost heavens, and search into and contemplate the darkest abyss, and the broad expanse of eternity—thou must commune with God. How much more dignified and noble are the thoughts of God, than the vain imaginations of the human heart! None but fools will trifle with the souls of men" (*History of the Church,* 3:295). Leading a soul—our own or that of someone else—to salvation takes place in process of time. The sincere seeking of the truth of God is not a trifling work or a casual endeavor—it is tender, holy ground of the most important kind and with the most far-reaching effects.

MAY

*In obedience there is joy and peace
unspotted, unalloyed.*
JOSEPH SMITH

Patience is heavenly, obedience is noble, forgiveness is
merciful, and exaltation is godly; and he that holds out faithful
to the end shall in no wise lose his reward.

JOSEPH SMITH
HISTORY OF THE CHURCH, 6:427

The impatient, disobedient, unforgiving natural man
rages all about us. Men and women of Christ seek to put
off the natural man and become Saints through the
Atonement of Christ (Mosiah 3:19). These are the core
Christian virtues: meekness, compassion, and patience.
"Patience is not indifference," said Elder Neal A.
Maxwell. "Actually, it is caring very much, but being willing, nevertheless, to submit both to the Lord and to what
the scriptures call the 'process of time.' Patience is tied
very closely to faith in our Heavenly Father. Actually,
when we are unduly impatient, we are suggesting that we
know what is best—better than does God. Or, at least,
we are asserting that our timetable is better than his.
Either way we are questioning the reality of God's
omniscience, as if, as some seem to believe, God were on
some sort of postdoctoral fellowship" (*Ensign,* October
1980, 28). These core virtues lead to "peace in this world,
and eternal life in the world to come" (D&C 59:23).

I defy all the world to destroy the work of God;
and I prophesy they never will have power to kill me till
my work is accomplished, and I am ready to die.

JOSEPH SMITH
HISTORY OF THE CHURCH, 6:58

Joseph the Prophet knew he was the Lord's latter-day chosen seer, and he knew that the Lord would watch over him until his work was done. He was courageous in the midst of persecution and fearless in the face of adversity. His courage came from his daily living of these inspired words of the Lord: "Let thy bowels also be full of charity towards all men, and to the household of faith, and let virtue garnish thy thoughts unceasingly; then shall thy confidence wax strong in the presence of God; and the doctrine of the priesthood shall distil upon thy soul as the dews from heaven. The Holy Ghost shall be thy constant companion, and thy scepter an unchanging scepter of righteousness and truth; and thy dominion shall be an everlasting dominion, and without compulsory means it shall flow unto thee forever and ever" (D&C 121:45–46). If we know who we are and whose errand we are on, we have nothing to fear.

One truth revealed from heaven is worth all
the sectarian notions in existence.

JOSEPH SMITH
HISTORY OF THE CHURCH, 6:252

We seek and embrace all truth wherever it is found, but some truths matter more than others. It's interesting to know the laws of thermodynamics; it's vital to know the risen Lord and how to draw upon the powers of heaven to pray and repent. The Lord revealed:

"Truth is knowledge of things as they are, and as they were, and as they are to come" (D&C 93:24).

"The Spirit of truth is of God" (D&C 93:26).

"He that keepeth his commandments receiveth truth and light, until he is glorified in truth and knoweth all things" (D&C 93:28).

"The glory of God is intelligence, or, in other words, light and truth. Light and truth forsake that evil one" (D&C 93:36–37).

"That wicked one cometh and taketh away light and truth, through disobedience, from the children of men, . . . But I have commanded you to bring up your children in light and truth" (D&C 93:39–40).

*Men who knew Joseph best and stood closest to him in Church
leadership loved and sustained him as a prophet.*

DALLIN H. OAKS
ENSIGN, MAY 1996, 73

Like all apostles of the latter days, Elder Dallin H. Oaks has added his testimony to those who knew best and stood closest to the Prophet Joseph Smith: "His brother Hyrum chose to die at his side. John Taylor, also with him when he was murdered, said: 'I testify before God, angels, and men, that he was a good, honorable, virtuous man . . . that his private and public character was unimpeachable—and that he lived and died as a man of God' (*The Gospel Kingdom,* [1987], 355; see also D&C 135:3). Brigham Young declared: 'I do not think that a man lives on the earth that knew [Joseph Smith] any better than I did; and I am bold to say that, Jesus Christ excepted, no better man ever lived or does live upon this earth' (in *Journal of Discourses,* 9:332). Like other faithful Latter-day Saints, I have built my life on the testimony and mission of the Prophet Joseph Smith" (*Ensign,* May 1996, 73).

Thus you see . . . the willingness of our heavenly Father to forgive sins, and restore to favor all those who are willing to humble themselves before Him, and confess their sins, and forsake them, and return to Him with full purpose of heart, acting no hypocrisy.

JOSEPH SMITH
HISTORY OF THE CHURCH, 2:315

Prophets through the ages preach the same truths concerning humility and discipleship, the same messages on repentance and forgiveness, the same principles of righteousness and faithfulness. Nephi taught the people of his day, "Wherefore, my beloved brethren, I know that if ye shall follow the Son, with full purpose of heart, acting no hypocrisy and no deception before God, but with real intent, repenting of your sins, witnessing unto the Father that ye are willing to take upon you the name of Christ, by baptism . . . behold, then shall ye receive the Holy Ghost" (2 Nephi 31:13). Our Father in Heaven is willing to forgive those who forsake their sins, anxious to pour out blessings upon those who come unto Him fully, ready to restore to favor all those who humble themselves before Him. God is omnipotent and omniloving. His love is perfect in both degree and understanding. Truly, He is our Father.

*I do not calculate or intend to please your ears with superfluity of
words or oratory, or with much learning; but I calculate [intend]
to edify you with the simple truths from heaven.*

JOSEPH SMITH
HISTORY OF THE CHURCH, 6:303

The Prophet Joseph knew that the gospel was best
preached with purity of heart and simplicity of language. Grandiose and verbose pontificating is most
often meant to impress rather than illuminate, amaze
rather than enlighten. Pride is at the root of ostenta-
tious displays of learning and oratory. The Prophet
said, "And again, outward appearance is not always a
criterion by which to judge our fellow man; but the
lips betray the haughty and overbearing imagination
of the heart; by his words and his deeds let him be
judged. Flattery also is a deadly poison" (*History of the
Church,* 3:295). We must guard our words and thoughts
and actions—which flow from the heart. If we are
meek and humble, if our first desire is truly to build
the kingdom and bless and edify, then we have the
promise of the Spirit of the Lord to inspire our words
and motivate our actions.

*It was decreed in the counsels of eternity, long before
the foundations of the earth were laid, that he, Joseph Smith,
should be the man, in the last dispensation of this world,
to bring forth the word of God to the people.*

BRIGHAM YOUNG
BRIGHAM YOUNG, 343

God is at the helm of this and all previous dispensations. In all times and places, He has a plan of happiness for His children and knows who is best suited to accomplish His purposes. God called Joseph Smith Jr. in the councils of heaven to be the prophet of the last dispensation. Brigham Young, his successor, said: "[The Lord] called upon his servant Joseph Smith, Jr., when he was but a boy, to lay the foundation of his Kingdom for the last time. Why did he call upon Joseph Smith to do it? Because he was disposed to do it. Was Joseph Smith the only person on earth who could have done this work? No doubt there were many others who, under the direction of the Lord, could have done that work; but the Lord selected the one that pleased him, and that is sufficient" (*Brigham Young*, 344). We too have been given assignments and responsibilities to fulfill. Let us honor our stewardships and move the work forward.

There are those who profess to be Saints who are
too apt to murmur, and find fault, when any advice is given,
which comes in opposition to their feelings.

JOSEPH SMITH
HISTORY OF THE CHURCH, 4:45

In the Church we often find two groups of individuals:
builders and murmurers. There are those who gladly support and encourage, who willingly obey and sustain in
thought and action, who earnestly work to build the kingdom. And there are those who have a tendency to whine
and murmur, who get in the habit of faultfinding and dis-
agreeing (which can so easily turn into resentment), who
think that they know more and better than others, even
the authorized representatives of the Lord. Joseph taught
that sometimes those who profess to be Saints murmur
"even when they, themselves, ask for counsel; much more
so when counsel is given unasked for, which does not
agree with their notion of things; but brethren, we hope
for better things from the most of you; we trust that you
desire counsel, from time to time, and that you will cheerfully conform to it, whenever you receive it from a proper
source" (*History of the Church*, 4:45). Saints who are
builders are humble, obedient, and steadfast.

God was with us, and His angels went before us, and the faith of our little band was unwavering. We know that angels were our companions, for we saw them.

JOSEPH SMITH
HISTORY OF THE CHURCH, 2:73

Zion's Camp was a group of some 200 Latter-day Saints who, during May and June of 1834, marched the thousand miles from Kirtland to Missouri. They were sent by revelation to redeem Zion and help restore the Saints to their lands (D&C 103). The difficulties of the camp proved a refining process that revealed who did not possess the spirit of humility and obedience. The Prophet exhorted those who were possessed with a rebellious spirit "to humble themselves before the Lord and become united, that they might not be scourged" (*History of the Church,* 2:68). A devastating epidemic of cholera spread through the camp and fourteen members died. In early July of 1834, the camp members were honorably discharged by the Prophet. The journey revealed who was faithful and who was worthy to serve in positions of leadership. Nine of the original apostles called in this dispensation and all of the seventies had served in Zion's Camp.

Although I do wrong, I do not the wrongs that I am charged with doing; the wrong that I do is through the frailty of human nature, like other men. No man lives without fault.

JOSEPH SMITH
TEACHINGS, 258

Joseph Smith's wrongs were a result of human frailty and mortal weakness, not the willful and malicious desire to do evil to others. He, like all of us, surely made mistakes and faltered along the way to fulfilling his prophetic mission. His life was also filled with endless false accusations and mendacious charges fueled by malevolent hearts and evil desires. Those who turned against him used any suspicion and every distortion to destroy both him and the gospel he restored. How comforting to know that God's purposes cannot be thwarted by wicked intent. How reassuring to know that God judges us by our actions and by our attitudes, by our hearts and by our desires. He who knows all things, He who perfectly sees our humanness and shortcomings, also knows the desires of our heart. Only a Perfect Judge could judge us perfectly God had a plan for Joseph, despite his shortcomings and failings. God also has a plan for each of us.

Spent the day at home in reading, meditation, and prayer.

JOSEPH SMITH
HISTORY OF THE CHURCH, 2:398

Even with all the demands of building the kingdom of God on earth, Joseph Smith took time to read, rest, and rejuvenate his soul. In Kirtland in 1835 Joseph wrote, "I returned home, being much fatigued from riding in the rain. Spent the remainder of the day in reading and meditation" (*History of the Church,* 2:287). In Nauvoo in April 1842 he recorded, "I was engaged in reading, meditation, &c., mostly with my family" (*History of the Church,* 4:601). Many of us think we simply don't have time for much reading, meditating, and praying. But the example of the Prophet Joseph is worth emulating: despite all our challenges and the demands on our time, we must make time for holiness, time for rest and renewal, time for communing with the Infinite through prayer and pondering. This purposeful activity strengthens our relationships with loved ones and with God, enlarges our minds with understanding, and deepens our commitment to everlasting things.

Be ready to forgive our brother on the first intimations of repentance, and asking forgiveness; and should we even forgive our brother, or even our enemy, before he repent or ask forgiveness, our heavenly Father would be equally as merciful unto us.

JOSEPH SMITH
HISTORY OF THE CHURCH, 3:383

In instructions to the apostles and seventies departing for missions to England in 1839, Joseph Smith exhorted those sent forth to preach the gospel to be merciful and forgiving. To commend the gospel to others as a way of life, we must be willing to forgive—even our enemies. The Lord exhorted each of us: "I say unto you, that ye ought to forgive one another; for he that forgiveth not his brother his trespasses standeth condemned before the Lord; for there remaineth in him the greater sin. I, the Lord, will forgive whom I will forgive, but of you it is required to forgive all men. And ye ought to say in your hearts—let God judge between me and thee, and reward thee according to thy deeds" (D&C 64:9–11). If we want to be forgiven for our sins and shortcomings, we too must forgive and extend mercy. How reassuring to leave ultimate judgment in the Lord's loving hands.

I have learned by experience that the enemy of truth does not slumber, nor cease his exertions to bias the minds of communities against the servants of the Lord, by stirring up the indignation of men upon all matters of importance or interest.

JOSEPH SMITH
HISTORY OF THE CHURCH, 2:437

The enemy of truth never rests. The adversary of righteousness strives to stir up contention and discord in every way possible so that he can have a foothold, a generating point of strife. The father of lies wants to distort truth and make a mockery of goodness. All these nefarious efforts come from the devil and his minions, who are in fact real and never rest. We can give in to his alluring enticements, or we can be ever vigilant in standing for truth and righteousness. Truly, we are engaged in a battle for the souls of men and women—all beloved sons and daughters of heavenly parents. This is not a little skirmish or minor scuffle, but all-out war. We must not slumber or rest in our desire for that which is good and right. We on the Lord's side in this war must, without fear or hypocrisy or equivocation, make a stand for truth, for virtue, for principle, for righteousness.

God is the only supreme governor and independent being in whom all fullness and perfection dwell; who is omnipotent, omnipresent, and omniscient; without beginning of days or end of life; . . . in him every good gift and every good principle dwell.

JOSEPH SMITH
LECTURES ON FAITH, 2:2

The Prophet Joseph Smith taught the School of the Elders that God is perfect, complete, finished, whole. There is nothing lacking in either our Father in Heaven or His Beloved Son, Jesus Christ. They are not progressing in charity, compassion, kindness, or knowledge. They are perfect, now and forever. They have all power; they are everywhere by the power of the Spirit; they know all things. In them, all good things, all perfections and principles exist. Joseph began his ministry in 1820 with the theophany in the Sacred Grove, and his earthly ministry ended in 1844 as he sealed his testimony with a martyr's blood. In those twenty-four years, he revealed God and Jesus to mankind and testified of Their true character and perfections. Joseph still reveals God to us today as we study his life and teachings.

I went into the woods to inquire of the Lord, by prayer, His will concerning me, and I saw an angel [John the Baptist], and he laid his hands upon my head, and ordained me to a Priest after the order of Aaron, and to hold the keys of this Priesthood.

JOSEPH SMITH
HISTORY OF THE CHURCH, 6:249–50

On this day in 1829, after long generations of apostasy, priesthood power was restored to the earth by the resurrected John the Baptist to Joseph Smith and Oliver Cowdery. The Aaronic Priesthood is a preparatory priesthood, or appendage to the Melchizedek Priesthood. John was the last legal administrator, holding keys and authority under the Mosaic dispensation (D&C 84:26–28). Speaking of John the Baptist, Joseph taught: "If he had been an imposter, he might have gone to work beyond his bounds, and undertook to have performed ordinances which did not belong to that office and calling. . . . John did not transcend his bounds, but faithfully performed that part belonging to his office . . . and it is necessary to know who holds the keys of power, and who does not, or we may be likely to be deceived" (*History of the Church*, 6:250–51). This important event is further evidence that both John the Baptist and Joseph were not imposters.

*Whatever principle of intelligence we attain unto in
this life, it will rise with us in the resurrection. And if a person
gains more knowledge and intelligence in this life through
his diligence and obedience than another, he will have
so much the advantage in the world to come.*

DOCTRINE & COVENANTS 130:18–19

The experience of mortality is of infinite worth. We are here to learn and grow spiritually, intellectually, and in every other positive way. Spiritual attainments in mortality accompany us into eternity, as will knowledge and wisdom. As we are diligent in expanding our souls and minds to receive light and truth we will have great advantage in the world to come. We know that "The glory of God is intelligence, or, in other words, light and truth" (D&C 93:36). Former general Relief Society president Elaine L. Jack said, "As we earnestly seek light and truth, we develop clarity in our lives that reflects spiritual understanding and commitment. This clarity results as we learn from our daily experiences, our thoughtful study, and as we receive personal inspiration from the Holy Spirit. . . . Learning—converting light and truth to everyday action in living the laws of God—is what we seek" (*Ensign,* November 1994, 89). We are blessed as we seek and live with light and truth.

Fear not, but be strong in the Lord and in the power of his might.

JOSEPH SMITH
JOSEPH SMITH, 376

While incarcerated at Liberty Jail, the Prophet Joseph and his counselors in the First Presidency wrote to Church leaders admonishing them to stand strong in the faith: "What is man that the servant of God should fear him, or the son of man that he should tremble at him? Neither think it strange concerning the fiery trials with which we are tried, as though some strange thing had happened unto us. Remember that all have been partakers of like afflictions. [See 1 Peter 4:12–13.] Therefore, rejoice in our afflictions, by which you are perfected and through which the captain of our salvation was perfected also. [See Hebrews 2:10.] Let your hearts and the hearts of all the Saints be comforted with you, and let them rejoice exceedingly, for great is our reward in heaven, for so persecuted the wicked the prophets which were before us [see Matthew 5:11–12]" (*Joseph Smith*, 376). The hope and confidence of these servants of God is an additional witness that these were no ordinary men.

We shall go on from victory to victory, and from conquest to conquest; our evil passions will be subdued, our prejudices depart; we shall find no room in our bosoms for hatred.

JOSEPH SMITH
TEACHINGS, 179

We fight ourselves all the time. It's as if we have the proverbial angel on one shoulder and the devil on the other. The devil entices us to do evil, to slack off and take the easy way, to give in to temptation. The angel appeals to our best selves, encouraging us to elevate our thoughts and actions and "give heed to the word of Christ" (Alma 37:44). This life is a continuing battle between the forces of good and evil, right and wrong, light and darkness. The real victory over self takes place as line upon line we learn and grow in gospel understanding, as we resist temptation and put off the natural man, as we turn the other cheek rather than return wrong for wrong. Peter taught, "Finally, be ye all of one mind, having compassion one of another, love as brethren, be pitiful, be courteous: Not rendering evil for evil, or railing for railing: but contrariwise blessing" (1 Peter 3:8–9). Let us develop the mind of Christ (1 Corinthians 2:16) and gain the victory over self.

*Oh, he was full of joy; he was full of gladness; he was
full of love, and of every other noble attribute that makes men
great and good, and at the same time simple and innocent,
so that he could descend to the lowest condition.*

JOSEPH F. SMITH
IN *JOSEPH SMITH*, 499

Joseph F. Smith, sixth President of the Church
(1901–1918), was five years old when his father, Hyrum,
and uncle Joseph were slain at Carthage. He was the last
latter-day prophet to have personally known the Prophet.
Wilford Woodruff said that Joseph F. looked like the
Prophet Joseph and prophesied that he would one day
lead the Church. Joseph F. Smith described his beloved
uncle as full of joy and humanness: "He was brimming
over with the noblest and purest of human nature, which
often gave vent in innocent amusements—in playing ball,
in wrestling with his brothers and scuffling with them,
and enjoying himself; he was not like a man with a stake
run down his back, and with his face cast in a brazen mold
that he could not smile, that he had no joy in his heart"
(in *Joseph Smith*, 499). Those who knew the Prophet best
knew his goodness and character. And, of course, a
prophet of God would be full of joy and gladness and love
and every noble attribute!

*Stand fast, ye Saints of God, hold on a little while longer, and
the storm of life will be past, and you will be rewarded by that
God whose servants you are, and who will duly appreciate all
your toils and afflictions for Christ's sake and the Gospel's.*

JOSEPH SMITH
HISTORY OF THE CHURCH, 4:337

The Prophet Joseph taught that if we faithfully
endure to the end, "[Our] names will be handed down
to posterity as Saints of God" (*History of the Church,*
4:337). The true Saints of God have accepted His
restored gospel and entered into a covenant relationship with Christ, they hold fast to the iron rod and
strive to keep the commandments, and they are
known to the Lord. He who sees all things will not
leave us comfortless or unrewarded. His angels will
attend us and buoy us up in our time of trials; His
Spirit will whisper peace to our souls despite the vicissitudes of life; His blessings unnumbered will come as
certain as the dawn. The Lord beckons us to Him:
"Come unto me, all ye that labour and are heavy laden,
and I will give you rest. Take my yoke upon you, and
learn of me; for I am meek and lowly in heart: and ye
shall find rest unto your souls. For my yoke is easy, and
my burden is light" (Matthew 11:28–30).

During the time I was in the hands of my enemies, I must say, that although I felt great anxiety respecting my family and friends, who were so inhumanly treated and abused, . . . I felt perfectly calm and resigned to the will of my Heavenly Father.

JOSEPH SMITH
HISTORY OF THE CHURCH, 3:328–29

Shortly after the Prophet had been allowed to escape from Liberty Jail, he recalled his feelings during imprisonment: "I knew my innocence as well as that of the Saints, and that we had done nothing to deserve such treatment from the hands of our oppressors. Consequently, I could look to that God who has the lives of all men in His hands, and who had saved me frequently from the gates of death, for deliverance; and notwithstanding that every avenue of escape seemed to be entirely closed, and death stared me in the face . . . I felt an assurance that I, with my brethren and our families, should be delivered. Yes, that still small voice, which has so often whispered consolation to my soul, in the depths of sorrow and distress, bade me be of good cheer, and promised deliverance, which gave me great comfort" (*History of the Church*, 3:329). We too, in the seasons of despair and grief, can trust God and seek for the still, small voice of comfort and consolation.

We came to this earth that we might have a body and present it pure before God in the celestial kingdom. The great principle of happiness consists in having a body.

JOSEPH SMITH
TEACHINGS, 181

We are blessed to have the happiness of having a body. Along with our aches and pains and the challenges of getting older or having corporeal difficulties come the joys of having a mortal body. Our bodies allow us to feel, experience, and sense the deepest joys of living. The blessing of a body gives us opportunity to learn how to school and discipline our physical selves, to fully put off the natural man with its fleshly susceptibilities and carnal desires, and more profoundly understand the connection between spirit and body. The spirit needs the body to feel the truest joys of life and the full range of what it means to be sons and daughters of God. Joseph Smith taught, "The devil has no body, and herein is his punishment. . . . All beings who have bodies have power over those who have not. The devil has no power over us only as we permit him" (*Teachings*, 181). The body is a blessing.

May God take away enmity from between me and thee; and may all blessings be restored, and the past be forgotten forever. May humble repentance bring us both to Thee, O God.

JOSEPH SMITH
HISTORY OF THE CHURCH, 2:343

William Smith was the Prophet's younger brother and a source of considerable heartache to the Prophet. On one occasion the Prophet wrote him a lengthy letter after William had become violently enraged and treated Joseph with contempt. "[I have spoken to you] for the express purpose of endeavoring to warn, exhort, admonish, and rescue you from falling into difficulties and sorrows, which I foresaw you plunging into, by giving way to that wicked spirit, which you call your passions, which you should curb and break down, and put under your feet; which if you do not, you never can be saved, in my view, in the Kingdom of God. God requires the will of His creatures to be swallowed up in His will" (*History of the Church*, 2:342). Joseph forgave his brother even while he exhorted him to curb his passionate rebelliousness. True repentance and forgiveness are the healing balms in all relationships—even for the deepest cut of familial enmity.

*Be virtuous and pure; be men of integrity and truth;
keep the commandments of God; and then you will be able more
perfectly to understand the difference between right and wrong—
between the things of God and the things of men.*

JOSEPH SMITH
HISTORY OF THE CHURCH, 5:31

Those who sincerely strive to put off the natural man and seek the Spirit of the Lord in their lives will grow ever stronger in truth, ever brighter in gospel light. They become men and women of Christ, fully invested in becoming even as He is and engraving His image upon their countenances (Alma 5:19). Virtue and purity chase away darkness; integrity and truth cast out evil; obedience and humility safeguard against deception and pride. All of this will give us the sweet assurance that accompanies the spirit of discernment—we will know for a surety that which is of God and that which is not; we will come to understand more clearly the forces of good and evil (Moroni 7:17). We must seek for and cleave to the things that come from God.

*Seek to know God in your closets, call upon him in the fields. Follow
the directions of the Book of Mormon, and pray over, and for your
families, your cattle, your flocks, your herds, your corn, and all
things that you possess . . . and everything that you engage in.*

JOSEPH SMITH
HISTORY OF THE CHURCH, 5:31

Amulek exhorts us to "continue in prayer unto [God].
Cry unto him when ye are in your fields, yea, over all
your flocks. Cry unto him in your houses, yea, over all
your household, both morning, mid-day, and evening.
Yea, cry unto him against the power of your enemies.
Yea, cry unto him against the devil, who is an enemy to
all righteousness. . . . pour out your souls in your closets,
and your secret places, and in your wilderness. Yea, and
when you do not cry unto the Lord, let your hearts be
full, drawn out in prayer unto him continually for your
welfare, and also for the welfare of those who are around
you" (Alma 34:19–23, 26–27). Today we all may not
have crops and fields over which to pray, but surely we
have need of God's sustaining influence in all our fields
of honorable endeavor, in our families, in our own souls.
When we pray to our Heavenly Father, we should
remember who we are addressing and strive to give Him
our undivided attention.

MAY 26

Let what will come; don't deny the faith, and all will be well.

JOSEPH SMITH
HISTORY OF THE CHURCH, 6:546

Joseph Smith offered these words of counsel just days before he was martyred. It's good counsel for us today. Life gives us trials and temptations, discouragement and difficulty, but all will be well if we grasp the iron rod with humility and courage, and trust in the Lord and His purposes. Those who walk with faith, with sweet assurances of the Spirit along the way, and with the confidence and comfort the gospel brings, will be granted "peace in this world, and eternal life in the world to come" (D&C 59:23). Our testimonies will not be uprooted if they are sunk deep into gospel soil. From the Book of Mormon we have the promise: "Come unto Christ, who is the Holy One of Israel, and partake of his salvation, and the power of his redemption. Yea, come unto him, and offer your whole souls as an offering unto him, and continue in fasting and praying, and endure to the end; and as the Lord liveth ye will be saved" (Omni 1:26).

When the Lord commands, do it.

JOSEPH SMITH
HISTORY OF THE CHURCH, 2:170

God gives us everything and then asks of us so little in return. He asks us to keep His commandments, to honor His name, to be true to the faith, to keep our covenants, to follow His authorized prophets. These are not generalities and abstractions. In our day-to-day walk of life we have so many relevant choices: Will we seek to follow the Lord and His prophets, or will we become prophets unto ourselves? Will we put exclamation points or question marks after prophetic counsel? Will we surrender our will and our desires to more fully follow the Lord and His representatives? Will we do our part, with conviction and testimony, to build Zion and establish the Lord's righteousness? If we do what the Lord asks, we have nothing to fear. If we do what the Lord asks, we will be blessed as we move forward the cause of Christ and His kingdom.

*We glory in our tribulation, because we know that
God is with us, that He is our friend, and that He will save our
souls. We do not care for them that can kill the body;
they cannot harm our souls.*

JOSEPH SMITH
HISTORY OF THE CHURCH, 3:227

Those who have faith in the future have power in the present. They know that trials and setbacks will occur—for they happen to all people, but they "know that all things work together for good to them that love God" (Romans 8:28). God is always with the righteous, with those who are trying to hold back the world and be humble and faithful. He becomes a friend to us if we, as He said, "do good, yea, and hold out faithful to the end, thou shalt be saved in the kingdom of God, which is the greatest of all the gifts of God; for there is no gift greater than the gift of salvation. . . . Fear not to do good, my sons, for whatsoever ye sow, that shall ye also reap; therefore, if ye sow good ye shall also reap good for your reward. Therefore, fear not, little flock; do good; let earth and hell combine against you, for if ye are built upon my rock, they cannot prevail" (D&C 6:13, 33–34).

Without the idea of the existence of the attributes which
belong to God the minds of men could not have power to exercise
faith in him so as to lay hold upon eternal life.

JOSEPH SMITH
LECTURES ON FAITH, 4:2

We can authentically exercise the power of faith unto
eternal life when we know the attributes, character, and
perfections of God. The Prophet Joseph taught "the following things respecting the character of God: First, that
he was God before the world was created, and the same
God that he was after it was created. Secondly, that he is
merciful and gracious, slow to anger, abundant in goodness, and that he was so from everlasting, and will be to
everlasting. Thirdly, that he changes not, neither is there
variableness with him; but that he is the same from everlasting to everlasting, being the same yesterday, today, and
for ever; and that his course is one eternal round, without variation. Fourthly, that he is a God of truth and cannot lie. Fifthly, that he is no respecter of persons: but in
every nation he that fears God and works righteousness is
accepted of him. Sixthly, that he is love" (*Lectures on Faith*,
3:12–18). We feel to echo the praise of the psalmist, "From
everlasting to everlasting, thou art God" (Psalm 90:2).

In obedience there is joy and peace unspotted, unalloyed.

JOSEPH SMITH
HISTORY OF THE CHURCH, 5:135

A sense of safety and peace always accompanies those who choose to humbly obey. They gain the quiet confidence of knowing that the Lord is bound when we do what He says, without which we have no promise (D&C 82:10). The Prophet Joseph stated that those who are obedient will be blessed, "and as God has designed our happiness—and the happiness of all His creatures, he never has—He never will institute an ordinance or give a commandment to His people that is not calculated in its nature to promote that happiness which He has designed, and which will not end in the greatest amount of good and glory to those who become the recipients of his law and ordinances" (*History of the Church,* 5:135). God, who knows all things, understands what is vital for His children to experience the greatest happiness, to become more like Him, and to inherit all that He has—which is His work and glory: "to bring to pass the immortality and eternal life of man" (Moses 1:39).

*We believe that no man can administer salvation through
the gospel, to the souls of men, in the name of Jesus Christ, except
he is authorized from God, by revelation, or by being ordained
by some one whom God hath sent by revelation.*

JOSEPH SMITH
JOSEPH SMITH, 110

Light, truth, and goodness certainly exist outside
The Church of Jesus Christ of Latter-day Saints, but
there are no priesthood keys outside the Church. The
authority of the holy priesthood and its keys were
restored in 1829 to Joseph Smith and Oliver Cowdery.
The fifth Article of Faith affirms: "We believe that a
man must be called of God, by prophecy, and by the
laying on of hands by those who are in authority, to
preach the Gospel and administer in the ordinances
thereof." One of the verities of the Restoration is that
God authorized Joseph Smith through divinely
appointed ministers and that the Prophet extended
that authority to others by conferring upon them the
priesthood and its keys. We are the beneficiaries of
this unbroken chain of conferrals and ordinations
since that time to the present day. How blessed we are
that the priesthood, with all its keys and powers and
fulness, once again is on the earth.

JUNE

—

Whatever God requires is right,
no matter what it is, although we may not
see the reason thereof till long after
the events transpire.
JOSEPH SMITH

*Great preparations were making to commence
a house of the Lord; and notwithstanding the Church was poor,
yet our unity, harmony and charity abounded to strengthen
us to do the commandments of God.*

JOSEPH SMITH
HISTORY OF THE CHURCH, 1:349

Another testimony to the prophetic leadership of Joseph Smith was his ongoing desire to build houses of the Lord where the Saints were gathered. The Church hadn't been organized long when the Prophet began to teach that special houses of worship and instruction should be constructed. On this day in 1833, Joseph received the revelation in Doctrine and Covenants 95: "I gave unto you a commandment that you should build a house, in the which house I design to endow those whom I have chosen with power from on high" (D&C 95:8). The Lord gave the Saints divine directions to build a temple and exhorted them to be obedient: "It is my will that you should build a house. If you keep my commandments you shall have power to build it. If you keep not my commandments, the love of the Father shall not continue with you, therefore you shall walk in darkness" (D&C 95:11–12). Even in their poverty, the Saints followed the Prophet and built the house of the Lord.

*Having confidence in the power, wisdom, and
love of God, the Saints have been enabled to go forward
through the most adverse circumstances.*

JOSEPH SMITH
HISTORY OF THE CHURCH, 4:185

Joseph Smith and the early Saints were tested in every
way and refined in the furnace of affliction. Those with
humble conviction and true testimonies did not shrink
from following the Prophet and going forward with
faith. Joseph Smith commended the Saints of his day,
and by extension, each Saint who stays true to the faith
today: "Frequently, when to all human appearances,
nothing but death presented itself, and destruction
[seemed] inevitable, has the power of God been manifest, His glory revealed, and deliverance effected; and the
Saints, like the children of Israel, who came out of the
land of Egypt, and through the Red Sea, have sung an
anthem of praise to his holy name" (*History of the Church,*
4:185). No matter how difficult the journey, no matter
how weary our efforts, God neither slumbers nor sleeps
as He watches over us (Psalm 121:4–5). He is our loving
Father, our keeper and caretaker as we travel life's challenging pathways.

I told them I was but a man, and they must not expect me to be perfect; if they expected perfection from me, I should expect it from them; but if they would bear with my infirmities and the infirmities of the brethren, I would likewise bear with their infirmities.

JOSEPH SMITH
HISTORY OF THE CHURCH, 5:181

We have never believed in prophetic infallibility or perfection. We acknowledge the humanness—along with the great spiritual powers and prophetic callings—of the latter-day prophets. Joseph Smith, and each of his successors, did not claim to be divine nor perfect men. They are mortal men trying whole-heartedly to fulfill the divine commission given them. While they seek perfection, they do not claim perfection. This is another witness to the humility of their character and the divinity of the prophetic call. Pretenders would advance their own egos; fakers could perpetuate a fraud for a brief season before being found out; imposters would not be so truthful about their own weaknesses and humanness. Just as we should not expect perfection in each other, we must not expect it in our apostles and prophets. They are holy men called of God to "bring forth and establish the cause of Zion" (D&C 11:6).

JUNE 4

*I do not regard my own life. I am ready to be
offered a sacrifice for this people; for what can our enemies do?
Only kill the body, and their power is then at an end.
Stand firm, my friends; never flinch.*

JOSEPH SMITH
HISTORY OF THE CHURCH, 6:500

Those who live only for the here-and-now lose the hope and promise of everlasting life hereafter. We are here to live fully and joyfully in today, but ever in our hearts should be the rewards that transcend mortality and stand the test of time. The world offers us only transitory happiness. The enemies of righteousness can harm our bodies but not our souls, our convictions, our hopes, our desires for eternal life. If we stay the gospel course, remain steadfast and immovable in righteousness, and do our best each day to be true and faithful, we will receive the greatest blessings that the Father desires to bestow upon His beloved children. Nephi has given us the transcendent promise: "Wherefore, ye must press forward with a steadfastness in Christ, having a perfect brightness of hope, and a love of God and of all men. Wherefore, if ye shall press forward, feasting upon the word of Christ, and endure to the end, behold, thus saith the Father: Ye shall have eternal life" (2 Nephi 31:20).

*If I cannot persuade them my way is better; and I
will not seek to compel any man to believe as I do, only by the
force of reasoning, for truth will cut its own way.*

JOSEPH SMITH
HISTORY OF THE CHURCH, 5:499

From the earliest days of The Church of Jesus Christ
of Latter-day Saints, Joseph Smith demonstrated his
magnanimous heart as he taught the course we should
pursue when encountering differing beliefs: the power
of truth will ultimately triumph, along with gentle persuasion and love unfeigned, therefore there is no room
for religious bigotry, self-righteousness, and holier-than-
thou attitudes in the kingdom of God. The Prophet
affirmed in our eleventh Article of Faith: "We claim the
privilege of worshiping Almighty God according to the
dictates of our own conscience, and allow all men the
same privilege, let them worship how, where, or what
they may." When we seek to share our message of truth
with others and bear witness by the power of the Spirit
that the Lord lives and His Church has been restored
through a latter-day prophet, we do so with generosity
of heart, with patience and compassion, with charity and
humility. True disciples lift and accept others with love.

We thank thee, O God, for a prophet
To guide us in these latter days.
We thank thee for sending the gospel
To lighten our minds with its rays.

WILLIAM FOWLER
HYMNS, NO. 19

"We Thank Thee, O God, for a Prophet" is one of the best known and most beloved Latter-day Saint hymns. It has been translated into countless languages and sung in congregations and general conferences of the Church since it was published in 1863. It was written by Australian-born William Fowler (1830–1865), who joined the Church in 1849 in England and emigrated to America in 1863. The words resound with gratitude to the Lord:

We thank thee for every blessing
Bestowed by thy bounteous hand.
We feel it a pleasure to serve thee,
And love to obey thy command. (Hymns, no. 19)

Although William Fowler joined the Church after the martyrdom of the Prophet Joseph, this hymn of praise and thanksgiving always stirs our hearts as we think of the Prophet Joseph and each of the prophets who have followed in his footsteps.

*Like most other leaders on the frontier,
Joseph Smith did not shrink from physical confrontation,
and he had the courage of a lion.*

DALLIN H. OAKS
ENSIGN, MAY 1996, 72

Elder Dallin H. Oaks relates the following story that demonstrates the Prophet's courage, determination, and faith: "Once he was kidnapped by two men who held cocked pistols to his head and repeatedly threatened to shoot him if he moved a muscle. The Prophet endured these threats for a time and then snapped back, 'Shoot away; I have endured so much persecution and oppression that I am sick of life; why then don't you shoot, and have done with it, instead of talking so much about it?' (in *Journal of Discourses*, 2:167; see also *History of the Church*, 5:440). The Prophet Joseph Smith experienced severe opposition and persecution throughout his life, but in the midst of all of this he never wavered from his divine calling" (*Ensign*, May 1996, 72). With the courage of a lion and the faith of a disciple, Joseph refused to be intimidated by the forces of evil. He remained ever true to the faith.

*Could you gaze into heaven five minutes,
you would know more than you would by reading all
that ever was written on the subject.*

JOSEPH SMITH
TEACHINGS, 324

The heavens opened for the Prophet Joseph, and he in turn opened the heavens to the world. Beginning with his marvelous theophany in the Sacred Grove and continuing throughout his life with visitations of heavenly messengers, revelations from the Lord, and divine light shed from above, Joseph's gaze into heaven was impressive and expansive. Perhaps no prophet has been taught more directly from heaven above, no prophet has communed more intimately with deity. In addition, Joseph was a lifelong learner—studying scriptures, language, history, astronomy, and a host of other subjects throughout his life. He was taught from books and from heaven. We too can seek to "gaze into heaven" and be taught. We gaze into heaven as we ponder and pray, as we study the scriptures, as we attend the temple and serve others. Heaven opens to us as we sincerely seek to do the will of God.

*The several elders composing this church of Christ are
to meet in conference once in three months, or from time to time
as said conferences shall direct or appoint.*

DOCTRINE AND COVENANTS 20:61

The first conference of the Church in this dispensation was held in Fayette, New York, on this day in 1830. Since then we have gathered as Saints in ward, district, stake, and general conferences to sustain and be instructed by our leaders, to feast upon the words of Christ, to strengthen our testimonies of the gospel, and to fellowship with one another. Joseph Smith said of that first conference: "To find ourselves engaged in the very same order of things as observed by the holy Apostles of old; to realize the importance and solemnity of such proceedings; and to witness and feel with our own natural senses, the like glorious manifestations of the powers of the Priesthood, the gifts and blessings of the Holy Ghost, and the goodness and condescension of a merciful God unto such as obey the everlasting Gospel of our Lord Jesus Christ, combined to create within us sensations of rapturous gratitude, and inspire us with fresh zeal and energy in the cause of truth" (*History of the Church*, 1:85–86).

As for treason, I know that I have not committed any,
and they cannot prove one appearance of anything of the kind,
so you need not have any fears that any harm can happen
to us on that score. May God bless you all.

JOSEPH SMITH
JOSEPH SMITH, 531

In Carthage Jail on June 27, the morning of his martyrdom, Joseph Smith wrote his beloved wife Emma a hasty letter of love and farewell. One can only imagine the sense of foreboding and heaviness that must have permeated his heart as he knew full well that the powers of darkness were gathering in full force. But from this letter one can also sense the serene resignation, the clear conscience, the erstwhile calm and courage that were so much a part of the Prophet's character. The Prophet was at peace with his fate—which was in the hands of his God, not the mobs. Joseph Smith had given everything—his whole might, mind, and strength—to the building up of the kingdom of God on the earth. Now he was prepared to give his life.

*I honor and revere the name of Joseph Smith. I delight
to hear it; I love it. I love his doctrine.*

BRIGHAM YOUNG
BRIGHAM YOUNG, 345

Sometimes, the better acquainted we get with someone the less they are esteemed in our eyes. It is a noteworthy witness to the character and mission of the
Prophet Joseph that over the ensuing years his successor
prophet would continue to honor his name. It also says
much about Brigham Young, who was born on this date
in 1801. Certainly, for many years following the martyrdom, the Saints remembered and revered Joseph. But
over the volumes of historical records, one does not find
any hint of resentment or jealousy toward the memory
or standing of the Prophet. Brigham Young gained much
of his knowledge of Jesus Christ and the gospel through
his constant association with the Prophet: "What I have
received from the Lord, I have received by Joseph Smith"
(*Journal of Discourses,* 6:279). Brigham praised the Prophet's
name all his life and testified of his mission in restoring
the gospel to the earth. His dying words were "Joseph,
Joseph, Joseph" (Smith, *Essentials in Church History,* 459).

*[One] who portrayed the virtue of patience
was the Prophet Joseph Smith.*

THOMAS S. MONSON
ENSIGN, SEPTEMBER 2002, 4

President Thomas S. Monson has spoken of Joseph Smith as a model of patience: "After his supernal experience in the grove called Sacred, where the Father and the Son appeared to him, he was called upon to wait. At length, after Joseph suffered through over three years of derision for his beliefs, the angel Moroni appeared to him. And then more waiting and patience were required. Let us remember the counsel found in Isaiah: 'My thoughts are not your thoughts, neither are your ways my ways, saith the Lord.' [Isaiah 55:8]" (*Ensign,* September 2002, 4–5). Another testament to the principles of faithfulness and patience in the face of difficulty is found in Alma 1:25: "Now this was a great trial to those that did stand fast in the faith; nevertheless, they were steadfast and immovable in keeping the commandments of God, and they bore with patience the persecution which was heaped upon them."

I ... testify that he [Joseph Smith] was the greatest man and the greatest prophet and the greatest personage of this generation, the greatest, I feel safe in saying, since the days of the Savior.

EMMELINE B. WELLS
IN *JOSEPH SMITH*, 498

Emmeline B. Wells, fifth general president of the Relief Society, was an extraordinary leader and advocate for women. As the editor and publisher of the *Woman's Exponent*, she defended the Church against its many detractors and advocated for women's suffrage. In 1910, at age eighty-two and after serving as general secretary of the Relief Society for twenty years, she was called as general president of that organization. Sister Wells served in that calling for eleven years and was released in April 1921. She died just three weeks later. Sister Wells knew and loved the Prophet Joseph Smith: "His majesty in appearance was something wonderful. You would think that he was much taller and much larger even than he was. Perhaps many of you have noticed men who have such a bearing when they rise up and walk. This was the way with the Prophet Joseph. There are no pictures of him extant that I know of, that compare with the beauty and majesty of his presence" (in *Joseph Smith*, 498).

Let us this very day begin anew, and now say, with all our hearts, we will forsake our sins and be righteous.

JOSEPH SMITH
HISTORY OF THE CHURCH, 6:363

On this day in June of 1828, Joseph Smith allowed Martin Harris to take the 116-page translation of the book of Lehi to show his family. It was subsequently lost. Joseph worried about his eternal salvation and felt responsible because of his repeated importuning of the Lord. In his words, "I commenced humbling myself in mighty prayer before the Lord . . . that if possible I might obtain mercy at his hands and be forgiven of all that I had done" (*Joseph Smith,* 71). The Lord chastised the Prophet for fearing man more than God but assured him he could be forgiven. "Thou art Joseph, and thou wast chosen to do the work of the Lord, but because of transgression, if thou art not aware thou wilt fall. But remember, God is merciful; therefore, repent of that which thou hast done which is contrary to the commandment which I gave you, and thou art still chosen, and art again called to the work" (D&C 3:9–10).

I could explain a hundred fold more than I ever have of the glories of the kingdoms manifested to me . . . were the people prepared to receive them.

JOSEPH SMITH
HISTORY OF THE CHURCH, 5:402

Joseph Smith's mission was to declare the reality of God. Shortly before his martyrdom he was prompted by forebodings that his remaining time on earth was short, and he wished to hasten his efforts. But so many misunderstood and opposed him at every turn, he had to move deliberately, slowly, and on the Lord's timetable. He also understood that the Lord is patient and teaches His children line upon line, precept upon precept, and he must do the same. The Prophet said, "The Lord deals with this people as a tender parent with a child, communicating light and intelligence and the knowledge of his ways as they can bear it" (*History of the Church*, 5:402). Joseph's desire to reveal more divine truth was tempered by the spiritual readiness of the Saints. It is similar for us today: Are we prepared to hearken unto the counsel of our living prophet? Are we striving to live in accordance with what the prophet has revealed today so that we can receive more light and truth tomorrow?

*After all that has been said, the greatest and most
important duty is to preach the Gospel.*

JOSEPH SMITH
HISTORY OF THE CHURCH, 2:478

Joseph Smith taught that we are co-workers in spreading the gospel message: "Let the Saints remember that great things depend on their individual exertion, and that they are called to be coworkers with us and the Holy Spirit in accomplishing the great work of the last days" (*History of the Church,* 4:230). Sharing gospel truth is part of our covenant with Christ. We who have been given so much must also give—by letting our voices be heard for truth and virtue, by being a friend and good neighbor to others across the street and around the world, by doing our part—without embarrassment or inhibition—to spread gospel light in a darkening world. President Howard W. Hunter observed, "Surely taking the gospel to every kindred, tongue, and people is the single greatest responsibility we have in mortality. . . . We have been privileged to be born in these last days, as opposed to some earlier dispensation, to help take the gospel to all the earth" (*Ensign,* September 1990, 10).

I write these few lines to inform you that we feel determined in this place not to be dismayed if hell boils over all at once. We feel to hope for the best, and determined to prepare for the worst.

JOSEPH SMITH
HISTORY OF THE CHURCH, 6:485–86

Ten days before his martyrdom at Carthage, Joseph Smith wrote a letter of determination and optimism to his uncle John Smith. Joseph was not unaccustomed to difficulty and persecution. It seems his life had been boiling with hardship since the early days of the restoration of the gospel. Remember, also, that his life had been filled with visits from heavenly messengers and outpourings of revelation and divine guidance. His essential character was one of perseverance, resolve, and sanguinity in the midst of adversity. He was God's chosen instrument, called to usher in the last and greatest of all gospel dispensations: he knew both his identity and his mission, and he understood whose errand he was on. We too can weather the storms of life as we hope for the best and prepare for the worst. With strong faith and good cheer we can face life with courage and determination; with wise and steady preparation we can face any trial and withstand any temptation.

> *Let us realize that we are not to live to*
> *ourselves, but to God; by so doing the greatest blessings*
> *will rest upon us both in time and in eternity.*

JOSEPH SMITH
HISTORY OF THE CHURCH, 4:231

We are placed in this probationary state of mortality to learn to put off the natural, selfish, worldly man and become men and women of Christ. If we live for ourselves—our interests, our desires, our whims and wants—we ultimately end up empty and unfulfilled, ever longing for elusive peace and contentment. All the alluring things in this world will never fully satisfy the deep longings of the soul. We know, as Joseph the Prophet instructed, that "there is a law, irrevocably decreed in heaven before the foundations of this world, upon which all blessings are predicated—And when we obtain any blessing from God, it is by obedience to that law upon which it is predicated" (D&C 130:20–21). Indeed, great blessings of joy and peace await the obedient. We will be blessed both here and hereafter as live with "faith, hope, charity and love, with an eye single to the glory of God" (D&C 4:5).

We see that everything is being fulfilled;
and that the time shall soon come when the Son of Man
shall descend in the clouds of heaven.

JOSEPH SMITH
HISTORY OF THE CHURCH, 3:291

Scriptural prophecies help us discern the many signs of the second coming of the Lord. They include the fulness of the gospel being restored and preached in all the world for a witness to all nations (Matthew 24:15); the gathering of the faithful to the stakes of Zion (D&C 133:4); false Christs and false prophets deceiving many (Joseph Smith–Matthew 1:22); wars and rumors of wars, with nation rising against nation (vv. 28–29); earthquakes, famine, and pestilence (v. 29); an overflowing scourge and a desolating sickness covering the land (vv. 30–32); iniquity abounding (D&C 45:27); the whole earth in commotion while men's hearts fail them (D&C 45:26). The Book of Mormon teaches, "This life is the time for men to prepare to meet God; . . . the day for men to perform their labors" (Alma 34:32). Little by little, prophetic fulfillment upon prophetic fulfillment, the great day of the Lord will come in the appointed time.

[Joseph] told me I should never get discouraged, whatever difficulties might surround me. If . . . all the Rocky Mountains piled on top of me, I ought not to be discouraged but hang on, exercise faith, and keep up good courage and I should come out on the top of the heap.

GEORGE A. SMITH
IN *JOSEPH SMITH*, 235

The counsel given by the Prophet Joseph to George A. Smith is timely. We must strive to keep up hope, faith, and courage through all our difficulties. George A. Smith was born June 26, 1817, in Potsdam, New York. At age twenty-one he became the youngest man in this dispensation to be called into the Quorum of the Twelve Apostles. He was a temple builder, missionary, member of Zion's Camp, pioneer, Church historian, and counselor in the First Presidency to Brigham Young. His grandson George Albert Smith later became the eighth President of the Church. "His great devotion to the Church led the Prophet Joseph Smith to say, 'George A., I love you as I do my own life.' George replied, 'I hope Brother Joseph, that my whole life and actions will ever prove my feelings and affection toward you.' . . . George A. Smith's valiant life was a tribute to that hope" (*Encyclopedia of Latter-day Saint History*, 1114).

The entire congregation were astounded; electrified, as it were, and overwhelmed with the sense of the truth and power by which [Joseph] spoke, and the wonders which he related. A lasting impression was made; many souls were gathered into the fold.

PARLEY P. PRATT
AUTOBIOGRAPHY OF PARLEY P. PRATT, 362

The Prophet Joseph was an extraordinary preacher of righteousness who was passionate about sharing the gospel with others. Parley P. Pratt recorded an experience that occurred in 1839 in Philadelphia: "A very large church was opened for him to preach in, and about three thousand people assembled to hear him. Brother Rigdon spoke first, and dwelt on the Gospel, illustrating his doctrine by the Bible. When he was through, brother Joseph arose like a lion about to roar; and being full of the Holy Ghost, spoke in great power, bearing testimony of the visions he had seen, the ministering of angels which he had enjoyed; and how he had found the plates of the Book of Mormon, and translated them by the gift and power of God. He commenced by saying: 'If nobody else had the courage to testify of so glorious a message from Heaven, and of the finding of so glorious a record, he felt to do it in justice to the people, and leave the event with God'" (*Autobiography of Parley P. Pratt*, 362).

Whatever God requires is right, no matter what it is, although we
may not see the reason thereof till long after the events transpire.
If we seek first the kingdom of God, all good things will be added.

JOSEPH SMITH
HISTORY OF THE CHURCH, 5:135

The Prophet Joseph said, "That which is wrong
under one circumstance, may be and often is, right
under another. God said, 'Thou shalt not kill,' at
another time He said 'Thou shalt utterly destroy.' This
is the principle on which the government of heaven is
conducted—by revelation adapted to the circumstances in which the children of the kingdom are
placed" (*History of the Church,* 5:135). God knows our
individual circumstances, and if we are open to Him,
He will guide and counsel us through the Holy Ghost.
We must depend on Him and draw upon the enabling
power of the Atonement wrought by the Lawgiver, not
simply concentrate on the law. As we place our trust
and faith in God, who is omniscient and omni-loving,
we will willingly obey His word and rely on His endless and living wisdom, not on abstract principles and
unyielding rules. When we are led by the Spirit, the
law is a means to an end—coming unto Christ.

If my life is of no value to my friends it is of none to myself.

JOSEPH SMITH
HISTORY OF THE CHURCH, 6:549

On this day in 1844, a Sunday, in response to accusations of cowardice in the Prophet's leaving Nauvoo to escape his enemies, Joseph and Hyrum Smith determined to return to give themselves up to the authorities in Carthage. Joseph felt that without the sustaining support of the Saints his life was of little value. He was the great prophet of the Restoration, the chosen seer, the Lord's anointed, but if cowardice was the perception of some "friends" he could not, would not, leave his flock. It must have been the deepest cut for a man with unquestioned faith and courage, who had stood by the Saints through peril and persecution without personal regard for so many years. Joseph and Hyrum were prepared to start for the Great Basin in the Rocky Mountains, a place Joseph had prophesied the Saints would gather, but it was not for Joseph, like Moses of old, to see the promised land. His calling was to seal his testimony with his blood.

*I am going like a lamb to the slaughter, but I am
calm as a summer's morning. I have a conscience void of
offense toward God and toward all men.*

JOSEPH SMITH
HISTORY OF THE CHURCH, 6:555

As Joseph Smith left Nauvoo for Carthage on June 24, 1844, he stated with prophetic insight that he knew what lay ahead, he was not afraid, and he had a clear conscience: "If they take my life I shall die an innocent man, and my blood shall cry from the ground for vengeance, and it shall be said of me 'He was murdered in cold blood!'" (*History of the Church*, 6:555). Then and now, the forces of evil rage with enmity and hatred against Joseph Smith; suspicion and hostility concerning him rule the day. And yet millions—then and now—testify that he was indeed innocent, he was God's anointed prophet, and he died a martyr to truth. The Prophet knew that God approved of his work to restore the gospel anew in these latter-days.

Praise to his mem'ry, he died as a martyr;
Honored and blest be his ever great name!
Long shall his blood, which was shed by assassins,
Plead unto heav'n while the earth lauds his fame. (Hymns, *no. 27*)

I will try to be contented with my lot, knowing that God is my friend. In him I shall find comfort. I have given my life into his hands. I am prepared to go at his call. I desire to be with Christ.

JOSEPH SMITH
JOSEPH SMITH, 243–44

The apostle Paul, like Joseph Smith 1800 years later, was a devout disciple of Christ. Paul was not about fame and fortune, power or prestige. He consecrated his life and energies to the mission of testifying of the risen Lord and building the Church. This whole-souled commitment to the cause of Christ gave him a certain contentment and conviction that empowered him till the end of his mortal life. His First Epistle to Timothy consists of counsel to his younger colleague—and it is good counsel for us today: "But godliness with contentment is great gain. For we brought nothing into this world, and it is certain we can carry nothing out" (1 Timothy 6:6–7). Nothing brings a sense of contentment like the knowledge that God is in heaven, that we owe everything to Him, that regardless of life's challenges, we are loved by a God whose confidence in us never ceases. If God is our friend and we seek with heart and soul to do His will, we can face any challenge and conquer any fear.

I would like to see my family again.
I would to God that I could preach to the
Saints in Nauvoo once more.

JOSEPH SMITH
HISTORY OF THE CHURCH, 6:601

On this day before his martyrdom, the Prophet spent much of the day in conversation with attorneys, visitors to the jail, and with Illinois governor Thomas Ford, who promised protection to Joseph and the other prisoners. At night the Prophet "gave expression to several presentiments that he had to die" (*History of the Church,* 6:601). The *History of the Church* documents the moving events of this terrible eve: "During the evening the Patriarch Hyrum Smith read and commented upon extracts from the Book of Mormon, on the imprisonments and deliverance of the servants of God for the Gospel's sake. Joseph bore a powerful testimony to the guards of the divine authenticity of the Book of Mormon, the restoration of the Gospel, the administration of angels, and that the kingdom of God was again established upon the earth, for the sake of which he was then incarcerated in that prison, and not because he had violated any law of God or man. They retired to rest late" (6:600).

*We announce the martyrdom of Joseph Smith the Prophet,
and Hyrum Smith the Patriarch. They were shot in Carthage
jail, on the 27th of June, 1844, about five o'clock p.m., by an
armed mob—painted black—of from 150 to 200 persons.*

JOHN TAYLOR
DOCTRINE AND COVENANTS 135:1

John Taylor provided an eyewitness description of this day of infamy: "Hyrum was shot first and fell calmly, exclaiming: *I am a dead man!* Joseph leaped from the window, and was shot dead in the attempt, exclaiming: *O Lord my God!* They were both shot after they were dead, in a brutal manner, and both received four balls. John Taylor and Willard Richards, two of the Twelve, were the only persons in the room at the time; the former was wounded in a savage manner with four balls, but has since recovered; the latter, through the providence of God, escaped, without even a hole in his robe. Joseph Smith, the Prophet and Seer of the Lord, has done more, save Jesus only, for the salvation of men in this world, than any other man that ever lived in it. . . . He lived great, and he died great in the eyes of God and his people; and like most of the Lord's anointed in ancient times, has sealed his mission and his works with his own blood" (D&C 135:1–3).

*Joseph Smith, the Prophet and Seer of the Lord,
has done more, save Jesus only, for the salvation of men in
this world, than any other man that ever lived in it.*

JOHN TAYLOR
DOCTRINE AND COVENANTS 135:3

The bold statement recorded in Doctrine and Covenants 135:3 and proclaimed without apology is part of the scriptural canon of the Church; it is our doctrine and our fervent belief. The writer, John Taylor, who was with the Prophet at Carthage, testified of the divine mission of Joseph Smith: "In the short space of twenty years, he has brought forth the Book of Mormon, which he translated by the gift and power of God, and has been the means of publishing it on two continents; has sent the fulness of the everlasting gospel, which it contained, to the four quarters of the earth; has brought forth the revelations and commandments which compose this book of Doctrine and Covenants, and many other wise documents and instructions for the benefit of the children of men; gathered many thousands of the Latter-day Saints, founded a great city, and left a fame and name that cannot be slain" (D&C 135:3).

They lived for glory; they died for glory; and glory is their eternal reward. From age to age shall their names go down to posterity as gems for the sanctified.

JOHN TAYLOR
DOCTRINE AND COVENANTS 135:6

On this day in 1844, before a public funeral for their slain leaders, some ten thousand Saints viewed the bodies of Joseph and Hyrum at the Mansion House in Nauvoo. The day before, George Cannon (father of future apostle George Q. Cannon) made death masks of Joseph and Hyrum, providing historians a valuable source of information about the martyrs' facial features. John Taylor, who himself was hit with four balls at Carthage, testified of the honored greatness of Joseph and Hyrum: "The testators are now dead, and their testament is in force. . . . their names will be classed among the martyrs of religion; and the reader in every nation will be reminded that the Book of Mormon, and this book of Doctrine and Covenants of the church, cost the best blood of the nineteenth century to bring them forth for the salvation of a ruined world" (D&C 135:5–6). Their names will continue to be held in sacred remembrance by countless people through all generations of time.

*All difficulties which might and would cross our way
must be surmounted. Though the soul be tried, the heart faint,
and the hands hang down, we must not retrace our steps;
there must be decision of character.*

JOSEPH SMITH
HISTORY OF THE CHURCH, 4:570

Among the many qualities we admire about the Prophet Joseph is his undaunted courage and steadfast faith in the face of overwhelming difficulties. With good cheer and undeterred perseverance he moved the work of the Lord forward one day at a time. He would not, could not deny his First Vision or any of the other divine revelations that brought so much gospel light to a darkening world and, at the same time, unleashed the powers of the adversary. With his remarkable gifts of leadership and charismatic personality he could have enjoyed much of the world's wealth and popularity, giving in to a life of ease and priestcraft (2 Nephi 26:29; see also Alma 1:16). Instead he chose the path of persecution and pain, of suffering and sorrow, but he also proved himself worthy of all that the Father hath (D&C 18:8). His courage, strength of character, and conviction is to be admired; his indefatigable labors to establish Zion will be heralded through generations past, present, and future.

JULY

~

Those who have done wrong always have
that wrong gnawing them. . . . You cannot go
anywhere but where God can find you out.

JOSEPH SMITH
HISTORY OF THE CHURCH, 6:366

It is inconceivable that Joseph Smith, without divine help, could have written this complex and profound book. There is no way that an unlearned young frontiersman could have fabricated the great truths contained in the book.

JAMES E. FAUST
ENSIGN, JANUARY 2004, 5

On or around this day in 1829, Joseph Smith completed the translation of the Book of Mormon. This "keystone of our religion" (*Ensign,* November 1983, 9) stands as another testament of Jesus Christ and as a further witness of the prophetic mission of the Prophet Joseph. Speaking of the Book of Mormon, President James E. Faust said, "The test for understanding this sacred book is preeminently spiritual. An obsession with secular knowledge rather than spiritual understanding will make its pages difficult to unlock. . . . The book itself testifies that it is the holy word of God. References to teachings in the Old Testament and the New Testament are so numerous and overwhelming throughout the Book of Mormon that one can come to a definitive conclusion by logic that a human intellect could not have conceived of them all. But more important than logic is the confirmation by the Holy Spirit that the story of the Book of Mormon is true" (*Ensign,* January 2004, 5).

The doctrine or sealing power of Elijah is as follows:—If you have power to seal on earth and in heaven, then we should be wise. The first thing you do, go and seal on earth your sons and daughters unto yourself, and yourself unto your fathers in eternal glory.

JOSEPH SMITH
HISTORY OF THE CHURCH, 6:253

Joseph Smith taught that, through the sealing power of Elijah, families can be sealed for eternity: "The spirit, power, and calling of Elijah is, that ye have power to hold the key of the revelation, ordinances, oracles, powers and endowments of the fullness of the Melchisedek Priesthood and of the kingdom of God on the earth; and to receive, obtain, and perform all the ordinances belonging to the kingdom of God, even unto the turning of the hearts of the fathers unto the children, and the hearts of the children unto the fathers, even those who are in heaven. . . . What is this office and work of Elijah? It is one of the greatest and most important subjects that God has revealed. He should send Elijah to seal the children to the fathers, and the fathers to the children. Now was this merely confined to the living, to settle difficulties with families on earth? By no means. It was a far greater work" (*History of the Church*, 6:251–52).

The best way to obtain truth and wisdom is not to ask it from books, but to go to God in prayer, and obtain divine teaching.

JOSEPH SMITH
TEACHINGS, 191

The Lord revealed, "Truth is knowledge of things as they are, and as they were, and as they are to come; and whatsoever is more or less than this is the spirit of that wicked one who was a liar from the beginning. The Spirit of truth is of God. I am the Spirit of truth, and John bore record of me, saying: He received a fulness of truth, yea, even of all truth; and no man receiveth a fulness unless he keepeth his commandments. He that keepeth his commandments receiveth truth and light, until he is glorified in truth and knoweth all things" (D&C 93:24–28). All truth comes from God and can be found by those who earnestly seek divine teaching. A fulness of truth can come to those who keep the commandments and continue to seek after light and truth in righteousness. In feasting upon the scriptures we will find true answers to life's questions. In humble prayer and sincere pondering we will gain wisdom and direction for our lives.

JULY 4

*I am the greatest advocate of the Constitution of
the United States there is on the earth. In my feelings I am
always ready to die for the protection of the weak and
oppressed in their just rights.*

JOSEPH SMITH
HISTORY OF THE CHURCH, 6:56–57

On this day in 1838, the Saints celebrated America's
national holiday by laying the cornerstone for the Far
West Temple in Far West, Missouri. The Prophet
Joseph loved and believed in the freedoms and destiny
of the United States of America; he was a patriot and
a believer in the Constitution of the land, although the
Saints were not upheld by its precepts for many
decades. Even so, the Prophet eloquently stated: "The
Constitution of the United States is a glorious standard; it is founded in the wisdom of God. It is a heavenly banner; it is to all those who are privileged with
the sweets of its liberty, like the cooling shades and
refreshing waters of a great rock in a thirsty and weary
land. It is like a great tree under whose branches men
from every clime can be shielded from the burning rays
of the sun" (*History of the Church,* 3.304). It is no coinci-
dence that the gospel would spread forth from a land
founded and upheld on principles of liberty and justice.

The best men bring forth the best works.

JOSEPH SMITH
HISTORY OF THE CHURCH, 6:315

While "it is the nature and disposition of almost all men . . . to exercise unrighteous dominion" (D&C 121:39), Joseph Smith chose instead to lead "by persuasion, by long-suffering, by gentleness and meekness, and by love unfeigned" (D&C 121:41). We trust the Prophet because we see the fruits of his sterling character and his divine mission. The great latter-day fruit he planted and nourished would not flourish if it was not good. He was a follower of the Savior, who taught, "Ye shall know them by their fruits. Do men gather grapes of thorns, or figs of thistles? Even so every good tree bringeth forth good fruit; but a corrupt tree bringeth forth evil fruit. A good tree cannot bring forth evil fruit, neither can a corrupt tree bring forth good fruit. Every tree that bringeth not forth good fruit is hewn down, and cast into the fire. Wherefore by their fruits ye shall know them" (Matthew 7:16–20). Those who are good and righteous bring forth good and righteous fruit.

*[Joseph] said that the very step of apostasy commenced with
losing confidence in the leaders of this church and kingdom, and
that whenever you discerned that spirit you might know that it
would lead the possessor of it on the road to apostasy.*

HEBER C. KIMBALL
IN *JOSEPH SMITH*, 318

Apostasy is usually a slow, subtle, insidious, process.
It commences little by little as a person begins to lose
confidence in leaders, begins to have a "noble grievance"
with Church authorities, begins to find fault with those
who are called to preside. These seemingly small and
subtle steps create a feeling of enmity between us and
the duly appointed leaders, which hinders our own spiritual development and the effectiveness of those leaders
in their callings. Most often, enmity is produced and
fueled by pride; it continues ever onward by jealousy,
arrogance, and laziness. The spirit of apostasy is found
in the proud, self-righteous, and slothful. Many of us
know someone who has lost confidence in the leaders
of the Church—whether general or local—and who
now walks in darkness and bitterness and apostasy. Men
and women of Christ choose to be meek and charitable.
They humbly choose to overlook imperfections and follow the leaders of the Church.

JULY 7

Praise to his mem'ry,
he died as a martyr;
Honored and blest be his ever great name!

WILLIAM W. PHELPS
HYMNS, NO. 27

William W. Phelps, the author of the seminal text praising the Prophet Joseph, turned against Joseph in Missouri and signed an affidavit that led to the Prophet's arrest and brought additional suffering for the Saints. Recognizing the evil of his betrayal, Phelps wrote a letter begging the Prophet to forgive him. Joseph wrote back: "Inasmuch as long-suffering, patience, and mercy have ever characterized the dealings of our heavenly Father towards the humble and penitent, I feel disposed to copy the example, cherish the same principles, and by so doing be a savior of my fellow men. . . . Believing your confession to be real, and your repentance genuine, I shall be happy once again to give you the right hand of fellowship, and rejoice over the returning prodigal. . . . 'Come on, dear brother, since the war is past, For friends at first, are friends again at last'" (*History of the Church,* 4:163–64). The Prophet's forgiveness won Brother Phelps's unmeasured devotion to the Prophet to the end of his life.

*From this time forth, Joseph continued to receive
instructions from the Lord, and we continued to get the children
together every evening for the purpose of listening while
he gave us a relation of the same.*

LUCY MACK SMITH
HISTORY OF JOSEPH SMITH BY HIS MOTHER, 82

Lucy Mack Smith, mother of the Prophet Joseph, was
born on this day in Gilsum, New Hampshire, in 1775.
She firmly believed in her son's prophetic mission and
was a strong defender of the faith. Imagine what their
home must have been like—a family of spirituality and
faith, of goodness and humility, of hard work and industry. Mother Smith described a scene during the fall of
1823: "I presume our family presented an aspect as singular as any that ever lived upon the face of the earth—
all seated in a circle, father, mother, sons and daughters,
and giving the most profound attention to a boy, eighteen years of age, who had never read the Bible through
in his life: he seemed much less inclined to the perusal
of books than any of the rest of our children, but far
more given to meditation and deep study. . . . This
caused us greatly to rejoice, the sweetest union and happiness pervaded our house, and tranquility reigned in
our midst" (*History of Joseph Smith by His Mother,* 82–83).

It is a love of liberty which inspires my soul—civil and religious liberty to the whole of the human race. Love of liberty was diffused into my soul by grandfathers while they dandled me on their knees.

JOSEPH SMITH
HISTORY OF THE CHURCH, 5:498

On this day in 1843, while delivering a public discourse in Nauvoo, Joseph Smith confirmed his universal regard for religious liberty: "The Saints can testify whether I am willing to lay down my life for my brethren. If it has been demonstrated that I have been willing to die for a 'Mormon,' I am bold to declare before Heaven that I am just as ready to die in defending the rights of a Presbyterian, a Baptist, or a good man of any other denomination; for the same principle which would trample upon the rights of the Latter-day Saints would trample upon the rights of the Roman Catholics, or of any other denomination who may be unpopular and too weak to defend themselves" (*History of the Church,* 5:498). Love of liberty has always been part of the gospel of Jesus Christ. We believe that we are free to choose liberty or captivity, life or death (Helaman 14:30–31). True religion cannot be forced or demanded; it flows from the wellsprings of a humble and believing heart.

*I desire with all my heart to honor and respect my husband . . . ,
ever to live in his confidence and by acting in unison with him
retain the place which God has given me by his side.*

EMMA SMITH
IN PETERSON AND GAUNT, *ELECT LADIES,* 17–18

Emma Smith was born on this day in Harmony, Pennsylvania, in 1804. She stood by Joseph through all of his trials, supporting him until the end. Theirs was a remarkable love story, filled with both exquisite joy and intense heartache. In seventeen years of marriage, Joseph and Emma were blessed with eleven children, six of whom died in infancy. Emma's mother-in-law, Lucy Mack Smith, wrote of her: "I have never seen a woman in my life, who would endure every species of fatigue and hardship, from month to month, and from year to year, with that unflinching courage, zeal, and patience, which she has ever done . . . she has been tossed upon the ocean of uncertainty—she has breasted the storms of persecution, and buffeted the rage of men and devils, which would have borne down almost any other woman" (*History of Joseph Smith by His Mother,* 190–91).

*The nearer man approaches perfection, the clearer are
his views, and the greater his enjoyments, till he has overcome
the evils of his life and lost every desire for sin.*

JOSEPH SMITH
TEACHINGS, 51

By the power of the Spirit, we can experience "a
mighty change in us, or in our hearts, that we have no
more disposition to do evil, but to do good continually"
(Mosiah 5:2). This mighty change is a like a quiet explo-
sion, a powerful, gradual process that results in an educated conscience, educated desires, educated and bridled
passions. One with a change of attitude and character
will not continue in sin (JST 1 John 3:8) but will continue to grow in light and truth until the perfect day
(D&C 50:24). Joseph Smith taught, "We consider that
God has created man with a mind capable of instruction,
and a faculty that may be enlarged in proportion to the
heed and diligence given to the light communicated
from heaven to the intellect" (*Teachings,* 51). A sincere
yearning to do good and abhor evil accompanies those
who are received into the family of Jesus Christ (Mosiah
5:7; see also D&C 25:1). To become changed is but a
beginning—the journey of faith lies ahead.

The evidences at hand lead to the convincing conclusion that Joseph Smith's story is true; that the Book of Mormon is just what it claims to be—a record written by ancient men under divine inspiration, . . . and translated in this day by the gift and power of God.

JOHN A. WIDTSOE
IN *JOSEPH SMITH*, 66

When one looks at the Restoration with an honest and humble heart, one is struck with the expansive prophetic vision and remarkable life of the Prophet Joseph Smith. Even if that knowledge does not lead one to join the Church, one cannot help but be impressed with what has come of the leadership of the Prophet Joseph. This was no ordinary man. First among the evidences of his divine commission is the Book of Mormon. It is real; we can hold it in our hands and read and ponder its pages—it resounds with truthfulness. It is an ancient record that cannot be easily explained away, discounted, or ignored—it came from God. It is another testament of Jesus Christ whose purpose is to bring all people of the earth to Christ—it is the word of God. We can know of its truthfulness and the prophetic role of the Prophet Joseph for ourselves and gain an unshakeable testimony as we ask in sincerity and faith (Moroni 10:4–5).

*I have no enmity against any man. I love you
all; but I hate some of your deeds.*

JOSEPH SMITH
HISTORY OF THE CHURCH, 6:317

The principle attribute of godliness is love, as John taught: "Let us love one another: for love is of God; and every one that loveth is born of God, and knoweth God. He that loveth not knoweth not God; for God is love" (1 John 4:7–8). Our quest is to develop this kind of pure and perfect love—like God—so that we can love ourselves and other imperfect human beings and at the same time abhor sin. God loves us perfectly, even while He hates wickedness. God's love for us, His children who are sinners (Romans 5:8), is perfect; His hatred of sin is also perfect. We hate sin by refusing to take part in it, by helping others avoid it, and by condemning it without equivocation or embarrassment. Sin is to be hated, not excused or rationalized or taken lightly. True disciples of Christ bear no ill will toward others; they have no enmity or hostility toward others—they strive to love with heart and soul even while they reject evil.

I don't care what a man's character is; if he's
my friend—a true friend, I will be a friend to him, and
preach the Gospel of salvation to him, and give him
good counsel, helping him out of his difficulties.

JOSEPH SMITH
HISTORY OF THE CHURCH, 5:517

Love and loyalty are always prized by the Lord and His prophets. If we love the Lord and are loyal to Him and His gospel, we become His friends. And, in a similar way, if we love the prophet of God and are loyal to his teachings, we become a friend to truth and righteousness. The Prophet Joseph, who experienced so much of betrayal and apostasy by so-called friends, was one who greatly cherished loyalty and true friendship. He would embrace a person regardless of background or beliefs, as long as that person was a true friend, and then he would teach that friend the gospel, give him good counsel, and help him in any way he could. A true friend is loyal, selfless, steadfast, and trustworthy. Joseph was not limited in his affection, loyalty, or kindness to another if that person was a true friend. We too can be true friends to others; we can reach out in love and friendship to all people.

*The purposes of our God are great, His love unfathomable,
His wisdom infinite, and His power unlimited; therefore,
the Saints have cause to rejoice and be glad.*

JOSEPH SMITH
HISTORY OF THE CHURCH, 4:185

Hope is born of knowing we are not alone, with no one to watch over us. As the Psalmist assured: "He that keepeth thee . . . shall neither slumber nor sleep. The Lord is thy keeper" (Psalm 121:3–5). God, the Father of our souls, is in His heaven, watching over His children; His purposes and love for each of His children is great. Just knowing that our Heavenly Father is watching over us helps us to face challenges and overcome fears. If we can remember that the Lord is the keeper of our souls, we can face any fear, deal with any difficulty, and do more than we may have thought possible. The great writer Victor Hugo advised: "Have courage for the great sorrows of life, and patience for the small ones; and when you have laboriously accomplished your daily task, go to sleep in peace. God is awake" (in Evans, *Quote Book,* 139). Rejoice in the comforting assurance that "this God is our God for ever and ever: he will be our guide even unto death" (Psalm 48:14).

Those who have done wrong always have that
wrong gnawing them. . . . You cannot go anywhere
but where God can find you out.

JOSEPH SMITH
HISTORY OF THE CHURCH, 6:366

We cannot hide from God. We may be able to deceive others and live for many years with varying degrees of duplicity and hypocrisy, but God is not deceived by externals. We cannot mislead Him into thinking we are something we are not. He, who knows all things, knows all things about us. We may choose to fill our lives with activities and entertainments so as to take our minds off our sins. We may rationalize and try to forget about an omniscient Heavenly Father who lovingly watches over His children. Or, we may decide to not worry about it all because we're convinced that it'll come out all right in the end (2 Nephi 28:7–8). But always lurking, ever gnawing, is the sense that we are not true, that we are living a lie. Of course, we all make mistakes and we all need repentance. But the world is filled with too many deceivers who have tried to hide their sins and compartmentalize their behavior. If you want to be happy, be true and be good.

*Tell the people to be humble and faithful, and be sure
to keep the Spirit of the Lord and it will lead them right.
Be careful and not turn away the still small voice;
it will teach them what to do and where to go.*

JOSEPH SMITH
JOURNAL HISTORY, FEBRUARY 23, 1847

After the Prophet Joseph's death, he appeared to Brigham Young in a dream or vision. Brigham asked him if he had a message for the Brethren. Joseph told him to tell the people to be humble and faithful and to seek the Spirit. Joseph also directed Brigham to educate the Saints concerning the feelings that accompany the Holy Ghost. He said, "They can tell the Spirit of the Lord from all other spirits; it will whisper peace and joy to their souls; it will take malice, hatred, strife and all evil from their hearts; and their whole desire will be to do good, bring forth righteousness and build up the kingdom of God" (*Journal History,* February 23, 1847). We can have confidence that the Holy Ghost is speaking to us when we feel "love, joy, peace, longsuffering, gentleness, goodness, [and] faith" (Galatians 5:22), which are the fruits of the Spirit. Meekness and lowliness of heart bring the Holy Ghost, which will fills us with hope and perfect love (Moroni 8:26).

Incomparably the most Godlike man I ever saw. . . . He was incapable of lying and deceitfulness, possessing the greatest kindness and nobility of character. I felt when in his presence that he could read me through and through. I know he was all that he claimed to be.

JESSE N. SMITH
IN WIDTSOE, *JOSEPH SMITH,* 353

Those who knew the Prophet could best attest to his temperament and integrity. So often his critics take their character witnesses from people who did not know him or had turned away from the Church in bitterness. Filled with animosity, their statements cannot be relied upon for accuracy. Consider, on the other hand, the countless statements, firsthand accounts, and fervent testimonies from those who personally knew the Prophet. Bathsheba W. Smith, wife of apostle George A. Smith and later fourth general president of the Relief Society, gave this eyewitness description: "My first impressions were that he was an extraordinary man—a man of great penetration; was different from any other man I ever saw; had the most heavenly countenance, was genial, affable and kind, and looked the soul of honor and integrity" (in Widtsoe, *Joseph Smith,* 352–53). To take a statement seriously, we must consider the source and give preeminence to those who know firsthand.

*In the same way that I know Jesus is the Christ—and that
is by revelation from the Holy Spirit—I know that Joseph Smith
is and was and everlastingly shall be a prophet of God.*

JOSEPH FIELDING SMITH
ENSIGN, AUGUST 1971, 7

Joseph Fielding Smith, tenth President of the Church, was born on this day in 1876, thirty-two years after the martyrdom of Joseph and Hyrum in Carthage. No Church President served longer as an apostle, (1910–1972), nor had anyone become Church President at such an advanced age. Known for his prolific gospel writing and profound doctrinal understanding, he spent his life testifying of the risen Lord and of the prophetic mission of Joseph Smith. Speaking of the Prophet Joseph, he said: "I revere and honor his holy name. With his brother, my grandfather, Patriarch Hyrum Smith, he sealed his testimony with his blood in Carthage Jail. And I, for one, want to be an instrument in the Lord's hands of letting the ends of the earth know that salvation is again available because the Lord raised up a mighty seer in this day to reestablish his kingdom on earth" (*Ensign*, August 1971, 7). We too can boldly testify of the prophetic mission of Joseph Smith.

*There is a love from God that should be exercised toward those of
our faith, who walk uprightly, . . . but it is without prejudice; it
also gives scope to the mind, which enables us to conduct ourselves
with greater liberality towards all that are not of our faith.*

JOSEPH SMITH
HISTORY OF THE CHURCH, 3:304

To "approximate nearer to the mind of God" (*History
of the Church,* 3:304) we must be filled with compassion,
understanding, and bigheartedness. We are here as fellow citizens to learn to love and serve, to reach out in
kindness and respect, to manifest Christian virtues of
charity and benevolence. God's love for His children is
both perfect and constant. Alma expressed the desires
of his heart: "For behold, the Lord doth grant unto all
nations, of their own nation and tongue, to teach his
word, yea, in wisdom, all that he seeth fit that they
should have; therefore we see that the Lord doth counsel in wisdom, according to that which is just and true. I
know that which the Lord hath commanded me, and I
glory in it. I do not glory of myself, but I glory in that
which the Lord hath commanded me; yea, and this is my
glory, that perhaps I may be an instrument in the hands
of God to bring some soul to repentance; and this is my
joy" (Alma 29:8–9).

Knowing the threatened judgments of God, I say,
Wo unto them who are at ease in Zion; fearfulness will
speedily lay hold of the hypocrite.

JOSEPH SMITH
HISTORY OF THE CHURCH, 1:317

Prophets teach the same truths, preach the same doctrine, and proclaim the same principles. They warn against sin, self-righteousness, and slothfulness. Nephi warned: "And others will he pacify, and lull them away into carnal security, that they will say: All is well in Zion; yea, Zion prospereth, all is well—and thus the devil cheateth their souls, and leadeth them away carefully down to hell. . . . Therefore, wo be unto him that is at ease in Zion!" (2 Nephi 28:21, 24). The devil would lead us down the pathway of ease and apathy. He knows that if we relax into a state of laziness and lethargy, we are his. We must guard against evil in all its forms, being ever vigilant of the wiles of the adversary. We must beware the easiness of idleness and the pride of self-righteousness—especially knowing what we know and what is expected of us. The devil doesn't have to tempt us with wickedness or ensnare us in blatant evil—it is enough if we are lulled into apathy.

God bless our prophet dear;
May health and comfort cheer
His noble heart.

BERNARD SNOW
HYMNS, NO. 24

The words of Bernard Snow (1822–1894), written a century and a half ago, express the deepest feelings of our heart today. Our thoughts and prayers ascend repeatedly in most Latter-day Saint homes for our dear prophet. We pray for his health and well-being, for his continued inspiration and leadership. From Joseph Smith to our prophet today, we honor their names, we cherish their words, we respect their sacred callings, and we love and look to the example of their lives.

His words with fire impress
On souls that thou wilt bless
To choose in righteousness
The better part. (Hymns, *no. 24*)

These prophets and apostles of God need our sustaining love and support for they are "upheld by the confidence, faith, and prayer of the church" (D&C 107:22).

It is . . . the privilege of any officer in this
Church to obtain revelations, so far as relates to his
particular calling and duty in the Church.

JOSEPH SMITH
TEACHINGS, III

As Latter-day Saints, "We believe all that God has revealed, all that He does now reveal, and we believe that He will yet reveal many great and important things pertaining to the Kingdom of God" (Articles of Faith 1:9). The Lord told Moses, "My works are without end, and also my words, for they never cease" (Moses 1:4). The heavens are open, the canon is not closed, and the word of God for our guidance and protection is needed more than ever. Institutionally as a Church, and personally as members of that Church, we can never be without the spirit of revelation. Of course, all saving truths must flow through the authorized channels the Lord has ordained, and those who deliver them must be properly commissioned to do so. No one is to receive revelations for those who preside over them (D&C 28:1–2). We have the blessed opportunity and the sacred obligation to receive revelation for ourselves personally, for our responsibilities as parents, and for our callings in the Church.

JULY 24

Anyplace where the Saints gather is Zion, which every righteous man will build up for a place of safety for his children.

JOSEPH SMITH
JOSEPH SMITH, 186

It was on this day in 1847 that Brigham Young entered the Salt Lake Valley and began to build Zion in the West. Having been led and tutored by the Prophet Joseph for so many years, he understood that, as Joseph taught, "the building up of Zion is a cause that has interested the people of God in every age; it is the theme upon which prophets, priests and kings have dwelt with peculiar delight; they have looked forward with joyful anticipation to the day in which we live" (*History of the Church,* 4:609). The Saints of God gather to Zion—wherever they live—as they join the Church, as they become pure in heart, as they work diligently with one heart and mind to build up the cause of Zion. Zion is more than a place—it is a process, a condition, a cause, a desire, and an attitude. Let us do our part to gather to Zion and build it up for a place of peace, a sanctuary of safety, and a haven of joy.

I believe the Bible as it read when it came from the pen of the original writers. Ignorant translators, careless transcribers, or designing and corrupt priests have committed many errors.

JOSEPH SMITH
TEACHINGS, 327

The Prophet wrote: "We believe the Bible to be the word of God as far as it is translated correctly" (Articles of Faith 1:8). The Book of Mormon has no such caveat— it came by the Spirit of the Lord from one source, from one translator, and is the "most correct of any book on earth, and the keystone of our religion" (*History of the Church,* 4:461). The Bible, on the other hand, came to us through various translating means, including copying, transcribing, adding to, taking from, interpretation, as well as the many associated problems of translation from ancient tongues before it became compiled as we know it today. Many plain and precious truths have been taken from the Bible by evil designing people, or by negligence, errors, and the passage of centuries. That's why Joseph Smith set about to correct errors in the Bible with his revelatory translation of the King James Version (known as the Joseph Smith Translation). We cherish the Bible as the word of God for it testifies of Jesus Christ.

The morning breaks, the shadows flee;
Lo, Zion's standard is unfurled!
The dawning of a brighter day, . . .
Majestic rises on the world.

PARLEY P. PRATT
HYMNS, NO. 1

On this day in 1847, two days after arriving in the Salt Lake Valley, Brigham Young and several other pioneer leaders climbed a hill north of the desert valley to survey the land. From the hill's summit they determined to name it Ensign Peak. They fastened a bandanna to a cane and waved it from the hilltop and spoke of the city and temple they would build. Joseph Smith, like Moses of old, was not able to enter the promised land of peace and rest, but these faithful followers of the Prophet did. They would take Joseph's prophetic vision to the world! Imagine the joy on both sides of the veil as they celebrated their arrival in this place that the Prophet Joseph had envisioned. Think of how they must have thought of their beloved Prophet who had pierced the veil of dark apostasy on the earth and ushered in this last and greatest of dispensations. From early spring of 1820, to the pioneer arrival in 1847, continuing to today, this is truly "the dawning of a brighter day."

My heart is large enough for all men.

JOSEPH SMITH
HISTORY OF THE CHURCH, 6:459

The Prophet's love for the people grew out of his abundant heart and his service to them. He sought ever to develop the attributes of godliness; and thus charity and compassion defined his character and motivated his actions. "I love your soul," he said to a friend in 1833, "and the souls of the children of men, and pray and do all I can for the salvation of all" (*History of the Church,* 1:339). His remarkable mission of restoring truth and his indefatigable commitment to moving forward the cause of Zion was centered in his love for the people. Anything less would not have strengthened him sufficiently through a life of hardship and heartache; anything less would not have seen him through to the end. His love was not limited to his family, friends, and followers, but ranged throughout the whole human race. He was called to be God's prophet for all people in all places.

Greatness is a product of many causes. It is like the mighty flowing river, fed and made possible by thousands of mountain rivulets. Even so, with Joseph Smith. The reflection from innumerable facets of his character makes up the picture of his greatness.

JOHN A. WIDTSOE
IMPROVEMENT ERA, DECEMBER 1948, 809

Elder John A. Widtsoe, a member of the Quorum of the Twelve Apostles from 1921 to 1952, noted that Joseph Smith had four qualities that made him great: "The cornerstones of his character: 1.) He had unchanging faith and trust in God. 2.) He was in love with truth. 3.) He was humble. 4.) He loved his fellow men. These qualities always lead to real greatness. Without them there is no true greatness. Doubt did not belong to Joseph Smith's nature. His faith in God, his existence, reality, and relationship to man, was superb. He took God at his word, as in the First Vision" (*Improvement Era,* December 1948, 809). These same four cornerstones of character are worthy of aspiration for us today: are we steadfast and immovable in our faith and trust in God, do we love truth, are we humble and teachable, do we manifest love for all people? Joseph Smith was a great prophet because he was a great man, "for of the abundance of the heart his mouth speaketh" (Luke 6:45).

I am like a huge, rough stone rolling down from a high mountain.

JOSEPH SMITH
TEACHINGS, 304

Joseph Smith was remarkably self-aware: he knew he had been given a divine commission, he knew that he was imperfect, and he knew what he needed to become. He said: "The only polishing I get is when some corner gets rubbed off by coming in contact with something else, striking with accelerated force against religious bigotry, priestcraft, lawyer-craft, doctor-craft, lying editors, suborned judges and jurors, and the authority of perjured executives, backed by mobs, blasphemers, licentious and corrupt men and women—all hell knocking off a corner here and a corner there. Thus I will become a smooth and polished shaft in the quiver of the Almighty, who will give me dominion over all and every one of them, when their refuge of lies shall fail, and their hiding place shall be destroyed" (*Teachings*, 304). The Prophet's life exemplifies that hardship and heartache have the potential to make of us true disciples of Christ who will triumph over all in the end.

The kindness of a man should never be forgotten.

JOSEPH SMITH
HISTORY OF THE CHURCH, 1:444

Ingratitude can come from a combination of pride and self-absorption, apathy or forgetfulness. Gratitude is a sign of a person who is striving to become like Jesus. Christ's healing ten lepers reminds us of that eternal principle: "And as [Jesus] entered into a certain village, there met him ten men that were lepers . . . and they lifted up their voices, and said, Jesus, Master, have mercy on us. And when he saw them, he said unto them, Go shew yourselves unto the priests. And it came to pass, that, as they went, they were cleansed. And one of them, when he saw that he was healed, turned back, and with a loud voice glorified God, and fell down on his face at his feet, giving him thanks: and he was a Samaritan. And Jesus answering said, Were there not ten cleansed? but where are the nine? There are not found that returned to give glory to God, save this stranger. And he said unto him, Arise, go thy way: thy faith hath made thee whole" (Luke 17:12–19).

*If men were duly to consider themselves, and turn their
thoughts and reflections to the operations of their own minds,
they would readily discover that it is faith, and faith only,
which is the moving cause of all action in them.*

JOSEPH SMITH
LECTURES ON FAITH, 1:10

Joseph Smith taught: "Are you not dependent on your faith, or belief, for the acquisition of all knowledge, wisdom, and intelligence? Would you exert yourselves to obtain wisdom and intelligence, unless you did believe that you could obtain them? Would you have ever sown, if you had not believed that you would reap? Would you have ever planted, if you had not believed that you would gather? Would you have ever asked, unless you had believed that you would receive? Would you have ever sought unless you had believed that you would have found? Or, would you have ever knocked, unless you had believed that it would have been opened unto you? In a word, is there anything that you would have done, either physical or mental, if you had not previously believed? Are not all your exertions of every kind, dependent on your faith? Or, may we not ask, what have you, or what do you possess, which you have not obtained by reason of your faith?" (*Lectures on Faith*, 1:11).

August

~

*God requires the will of His creatures
to be swallowed up in His will.*
JOSEPH SMITH

*[Joseph Smith] was truly a seer. He was
a revelator. He was a prophet of the living God who has
spoken to his own and all future generations.*

GORDON B. HINCKLEY
ENSIGN, MAY 2005, 83

President Gordon B. Hinckley said of Joseph Smith:
"The sun rose on Joseph's life on a cold day in Vermont in 1805. It set in Illinois on a sultry afternoon in
1844. During the brief 38 and one-half years of his life,
there came through him an incomparable outpouring
of knowledge, gifts, and doctrine. Looked at objectively, there is nothing to compare with it. Subjectively,
it is the substance of the personal testimony of millions of Latter-day Saints across the earth. You and I
are honored to be among these. As a boy I loved to
hear a man who, with a rich baritone voice, sang the
words of John Taylor: "The Seer, the Seer, Joseph, the
Seer! . . . / I love to dwell on his memory dear. . . . / He
gazed on the past and the future, too, . . . / And opened
the heavenly world to view" ("The Seer, Joseph, the
Seer," *Hymns* [1948], no. 296)." (*Ensign,* May 2005, 83.)

*The building up of Zion is a cause that has interested the people of
God in every age; it is a theme upon which prophets, priests and
kings have dwelt with peculiar delight; they have looked forward
with joyful anticipation to the day in which we live.*

JOSEPH SMITH
HISTORY OF THE CHURCH, 4:609–10

On this day in 1833, Doctrine and Covenants 97
was received, which reiterated the commandment to
build a house in Zion in which the pure in heart shall
see God: "If Zion do these things she shall prosper,
and spread herself and become very glorious, very
great, and very terrible. And the nations of the earth
shall honor her, and shall say: Surely Zion is the city of
our God, and surely Zion cannot fall, neither be
moved out of her place, for God is there, and the hand
of the Lord is there" (D&C 97:18–19). From the earliest days of the nascent Church, the Lord and His
anointed prophet had great plans and purposes for
Zion, where dwell the pure in heart (D&C 97:21).
From all generations, past and present, the people of
God looked forward to the establishment of latter-day
Zion, to the spreading of the gospel message to the
nations of the earth.

AUGUST 3

Inasmuch as the Lord Almighty has preserved me until today, He will continue to preserve me, by the united faith and prayers of the Saints, until I have fully accomplished my mission in this life.

JOSEPH SMITH
HISTORY OF THE CHURCH, 5:139–40

No power of earth or hell can stop the work of the Lord from progressing. Persecution may mount, conflict may arise, from time to time some of the elect may lose their way, but the stone cut from the mountain without hands will roll forth until it fills the whole earth (Daniel 2:34–45). Joseph Smith, and all true Saints, understood that God will watch over and protect those who are on His errand. The enemies of truth may win a few battles along the way, and the clouds may seem to darken in ever-increasing intensity, but God's purposes are sure and will not fail. There are so many more accessing the powers of heaven through mighty prayer and faith in behalf of truth and uprightness than there are working to destroy righteousness. God and His followers will triumph in the end.

Joseph bore a powerful testimony to the guards of the divine authenticity of the Book of Mormon, the restoration of the Gospel, the administration of angels, and that the kingdom of God was again established upon the earth.

DAN JONES
HISTORY OF THE CHURCH, 6:600

Dan Jones, born on this day in 1810 in Halkyn, Wales, was baptized in the frigid waters of the Mississippi River on January 19, 1843. He met the Prophet Joseph three months later and became his loyal friend. He was with the Prophet in Carthage Jail the night before the Martyrdom. That evening, Joseph Smith gave his last recorded prophecy as he told Dan Jones that he would not be killed but would see Wales and fulfill his appointed mission (*History of the Church*, 6:601). The Prophet bore a powerful testimony to the guards, a testimony he would seal the next day with his blood. Dan Jones left the prison early on the morning of June 27, 1844, at the request of the Prophet, to talk to Governor Ford about the death threats against Joseph and Hyrum. Jones survived three attempts on his life during the next thirty-six hours and became one of the great missionaries of the Church, baptizing some 2,000 converts during his two missions to Wales.

*Everlasting covenant was made between three personages
before the organization of this earth . . . ; these personages . . . are
called God the first, the Creator; God the second, the Redeemer;
and God the third, the witness or Testator.*

JOSEPH SMITH
TEACHINGS, 190

When Joseph Smith outlined the beliefs of the
Latter-day Saints, he began with this first Article of
Faith: "We believe in God, the Eternal Father, and in His
Son, Jesus Christ, and in the Holy Ghost." These three
separate, distinct persons constitute the Godhead, the
supreme presidency of the universe. Joseph further
taught: "The Father has a body of flesh and bones as tangible as man's; the Son also; but the Holy Ghost has not
a body of flesh and bones, but is a personage of Spirit.
Were it not so, the Holy Ghost could not dwell in us"
(D&C 130:22). Joseph revealed God and His Son anew
to man; he taught that we must know Them in order to
become like Them and to understand ourselves; and he
revealed the mission of the Holy Ghost. No longer were
we to be confounded by the incomprehensible mystery
of God; no longer was He unknowable, disembodied,
and implausible. All of our doctrines and beliefs trace
their roots to this fundamental truth of the Godhead.

I prophesied that the Saints would continue to suffer much affliction and would be driven to the Rocky Mountains, many would apostatize, others would be put to death by our persecutors or lose their lives in consequence of exposure or disease.

JOSEPH SMITH
TEACHINGS, 255

On this day in 1842, Joseph Smith prophesied that the Saints would be driven to the Rocky Mountains and there prosper and build great cities. At that time in America, the Rockies were largely unknown, untraveled, foreign territory. With prophetic insight, Joseph saw that the Saints would suffer great hardship in their exodus to the West, but they would thrive there and become a mighty people. This is another example of what it means to be a prophet, seer, and revelator—such a bold statement during the relative calm of 1842 Nauvoo, such a remarkable prophecy to the Saints for whom the West was unfamiliar. Joseph himself would never set foot in the midst of the Rocky Mountains, but the Saints and the restored Church have flourished there and around the world. Today we marvel at this prophecy, which has come true in every detail.

Joseph conferred upon our heads all the keys and powers belonging to the Apostleship which he himself held before he was taken away, and no man or set of men can get between Joseph and the Twelve in this world or in the world to come.

BRIGHAM YOUNG
HISTORY OF THE CHURCH, 7:230

On this day in Nauvoo in 1844, a few weeks after the martyrdom of Joseph and Hyrum Smith, Brigham Young clarified a central issue: what happens now that the Prophet is dead? Brigham Young taught that before his death, Joseph Smith conferred upon the Twelve Apostles the priesthood keys and powers that the Lord had sealed upon him. Wilford Woodruff recorded what the Prophet said in March 1844: "I have had sealed upon my head every key, every power, every principle of life and salvation that God has ever given to any man who ever lived upon the face of the earth. And these principles and this Priesthood and power belong to this great and last dispensation which the God of Heaven has set His hand to establish in the earth. Now, . . . I have sealed upon your [the Twelve] heads every key, every power, and every principle which the Lord has sealed upon my head" (in *Joseph Smith*, 532).

*I do not want to cloak iniquity—all things contrary
to the will of God, should be cast from us, but don't do more
hurt than good, with your tongues—be pure in heart.*

JOSEPH SMITH
TEACHINGS, 239

We have a duty to stand for the right and let our voices speak out for virtue and uprightness. But we must strive to never give offense, never be shrill or nasty, and do our best to guard our tongues and our actions in defense of righteousness. What doth it profit us as members of the Church if we stand up for what is right but do it in a way that offends others or appears smug or self-righteous? We have a clear commission to let our voices be heard for all that is moral and virtuous and good and at the same time reach out in love and kindness and respect to all people. We should not err too heavily on the side of tolerance ("anything goes"), and we also should not err too strongly on the side of rightness ("I'm right and you're wrong"). It is a careful line we must walk. But guided by humility and the Spirit, motivated by love and a pure heart, and armed with knowledge and understanding, we can promote the cause of Christ.

AUGUST 9

*The fundamental principles of our religion are the testimony of the
Apostles and Prophets, concerning Jesus Christ, that He died, was
buried, and rose again the third day, and ascended into heaven; and all
other things which pertain to our religion are only appendages to it.*

JOSEPH SMITH
TEACHINGS, 121

Our loving Heavenly Father has a plan for His children, a program designed to maximize our development and insure our everlasting joy. That plan of salvation—the great plan of happiness—centers in the doctrine of Jesus Christ, in His atonement and resurrection from the tomb. Everything else we preach and teach, everything else we proclaim is secondary to the truth of our Savior—He is the hub of the gospel wheel. Truly, as Nephi taught, "we talk of Christ, we rejoice in Christ, we preach of Christ, we prophesy of Christ, . . . that our children may know to what source they may look for a remission of their sins" (2 Nephi 25:26). Like Jacob, we thrill in the mercy, wisdom, goodness, and greatness of the Holy One of Israel (2 Nephi 9:8–13). Joseph Smith stands as the preeminent prophetic witness of Christ to this final dispensation.

A person may profit by noticing the first intimation of the
spirit of revelation; for instance, when you feel pure intelligence
flowing into you, it may give you sudden strokes of ideas.

JOSEPH SMITH
TEACHINGS, 151

Speaking of the spirit of revelation, the Prophet Joseph taught that "by noticing [the spirit of revelation], you may find it fulfilled the same day or soon; (i.e.) those things that were presented unto your minds by the Spirit of God, will come to pass; and thus by learning the Spirit of God and understanding it, you may grow into the principle of revelation, until you become perfect in Christ Jesus" (*Teachings,* 151). Learning how to be tutored by the influence of the spirit of revelation is part of our mortal quest and among our greatest blessings. It is holy work. It is the endeavor of educating our hearts and subduing our wills so that we can be taught by the Lord. It is the course of creativity as ideas and insights come to us. It is the process of purification and prophecy and instruction as our hearts are expanded with the desire to know the purposes of God in our lives.

*Let me be resurrected with the Saints, whether I ascend to heaven
or descend to hell, or go to any other place. And if we go to hell,
we will turn the devils out of doors and make a heaven of it.*

JOSEPH SMITH
HISTORY OF THE CHURCH, 5:517

Great powers of righteousness abide in a congregation of faithful believers who love the Lord and do their best to live the gospel. And while no branch, ward, or stake is perfection on earth, these Church units can be remarkable places of fellowship, support, charity, and goodness. Many can attest to the power of a good ward, where brotherhood and sisterhood fill each hallway with love, and where kindness and compassion dwell in each heart. Unfortunately, some have known the opposite— which becomes as a hell on earth. Where the Saints of God gather ought to be the pleasantest place on earth; it ought to be place where we "are willing to bear one another's burdens, that they may be light; yea, and are willing to mourn with those that mourn; yea, and comfort those that stand in need of comfort, and to stand as witnesses of God at all times and in all things" (Mosiah 18:8–9).

AUGUST 12

*You don't know me; you never knew my heart. No man knows my
history. I cannot tell it: I shall never undertake it. I don't blame
any one for not believing my history. If I had not experienced
what I have, I could not have believed it myself.*

JOSEPH SMITH
TEACHINGS, 361

Like his Master, Jesus Christ, Joseph Smith was
called upon to endure a life of loneliness. He acknowledged both the difficulty in recounting and believing
his remarkable story. It is exceptional that he himself
said he couldn't blame any one for not believing it. He
says, in essence, "It is difficult to believe what has transpired in my life. No one can fully understand it. No
one can really know it all." He also offers a plea for
forbearance and understanding, knowing that he
would be judged as all men are judged and that all
people will eventually know Brother Joseph at last. He
said, "I never did harm any man since I was born in
the world. My voice is always for peace. I cannot lie
down until all my work is finished. I never think any
evil, nor do anything to the harm of my fellow-man.
When I am called by the trump of the archangel and
weighed in the balance, you will know me then. I add
no more" (*Teachings*, 361–62).

244

Whenever men can find out the will of God and find an administrator legally authorized from God, there is the kingdom of God; but where these are not, the kingdom of God is not.

JOSEPH SMITH
HISTORY OF THE CHURCH, 5:259

Wishful thinking and good intentions do not authorize one to administer the ordinances of the gospel. Priesthood keys and power are central to the message of the Restoration. With authorized keys and powers we have everything; without them we have nothing. Joseph Smith taught, "All the ordinances, systems, and administrations on the earth are of no use to the children of men, unless they are ordained and authorized of God; for nothing will save a man but a legal administrator; for none others will be acknowledged either by God or angels" (*History of the Church,* 5:259). To hold the priesthood and administer in the offices therein is a sacred, holy calling. An authorized administrator is one who has received the priesthood by ordination and by the laying on of hands by those in authority (Articles of Faith 1:5); he is one who is known to the Church as authorized (1 Thessalonians 5:12–13); he is one who has power in the priesthood because of personal righteousness (D&C 121:41–46).

It is impossible for a man to be saved in ignorance.

DOCTRINE AND COVENANTS 131:6

We are here to gain the understanding and wisdom of everlasting things, to learn the doctrines of the gospel, to develop the attributes of godliness. We are to reject apathy and learn our duty with all diligence (D&C 107:99–100). "That is why education—particularly spiritual education—is constantly stressed by the Lord," said Elder M. Russell Ballard. "We cannot be saved in ignorance, but the Lord can only reveal light and truth to us as we are prepared to receive it. And so it is incumbent upon each of us to do everything we can to increase our spiritual knowledge and understanding by studying the scriptures and the words of the living prophets. When we read and study the revelations, the Spirit can confirm in our hearts the truth of what we are learning; in this way, the voice of the Lord speaks to each one of us. As we ponder the teachings of the gospel and apply them in daily living, we become better prepared to receive additional light and truth" (*Ensign,* May 1998, 32).

There is baptism . . . for those to exercise
who are alive, and baptism for the dead who die
without the knowledge of the Gospel.

JOSEPH SMITH
HISTORY OF THE CHURCH, 6:365

On this day in 1840, Joseph Smith preached the funeral sermon of Seymour Brunson, a high councilor and bodyguard of the Prophet, and revealed the doctrine of baptism for the dead. Later, on January 19, 1841, Joseph Smith received Doctrine and Covenants 124, concerning the ordinance of baptism for the dead. He taught: "Ordinances instituted in the heavens before the foundation of the world, in the priesthood, for the salvation of men, are not to be altered or changed. All must be saved on the same principles. It is for the same purpose that God gathers together His people in the last days, to build unto the Lord a house to prepare them for the ordinances and endowments, washings and anointings, etc. One of the ordinances of the house of the Lord is baptism for the dead. God decreed before the foundation of the world that that ordinance should be administered in a font prepared for that purpose in the house of the Lord" (*History of the Church,* 5:423–24).

Remember thy suffering saints, O our God; and thy servants will rejoice in thy name forever.

JOSEPH SMITH
DOCTRINE AND COVENANTS 121:6

The profound response of the Lord to the Prophet Joseph's heartfelt plea for understanding and strength stands as one of the great testaments to the Lord's loving watchcare: "If thou shouldst be cast into the pit, or into the hands of murderers, and the sentence of death passed upon thee; if thou be cast into the deep; if the billowing surge conspire against thee; if fierce winds become thine enemy; if the heavens gather blackness, and all the elements combine to hedge up the way; and above all, if the very jaws of hell shall gape open the mouth wide after thee, know thou, my son, that all these things shall give thee experience, and shall be for thy good. The Son of Man hath descended below them all. Art thou greater than he? Therefore, hold on thy way, and the priesthood shall remain with thee. . . . Thy days are known, and thy years shall not be numbered less; therefore, fear not what man can do, for God shall be with you forever and ever" (D&C 122:7–9).

*This life is not all; the voice of reason, the language of
inspiration, and the Spirit of the living God, our Creator, teaches
us, as we hold the record of truth in our hands, that this is not the
case, . . . for, the heavens declare the glory of a God.*

JOSEPH SMITH
TEACHINGS, 56

Death is not the end but instead a significant point
along the never-ending pathway of life. We are born and
then we die; the cycle of life continues everlastingly. If
there were no death, there would be no life. And, just as
there is purpose in life, there is purpose in death. God
our Father knows all things and knows all things that are
best for His children. We are not here by chance, by
some random cosmic accident. We are children of a loving God who has boundless paternal interest and fatherly
affection for His children. All things denote that there is
a God who created the world. The heavens declare His
glory and His handiwork; His children recognize His
hand. The Prophet Joseph said, "A moment's reflection is
sufficient to teach every man of common intelligence,
that all these are not the mere productions of chance, nor
could they be supported by any power less than an
Almighty hand" (*Teachings,* 56). Indeed, we are "upheld
by [His] righteous, omnipotent hand" (*Hymns,* no. 85).

*Don't envy the finery and fleeting show of sinners,
for they are in a miserable situation; but as far as you can, have
mercy on them, for in a short time God will destroy them,
if they will not repent and turn unto him.*

JOSEPH SMITH
HISTORY OF THE CHURCH, 4:607

Sometimes the world paints an alluring picture filled with temptations that beckon. The wicked and wayward appear to have lives of pleasure and entertainment, but in their desire for gratification and indulgence they find, in the end, only disillusionment and heartache. In this life, and surely in the next, they are cast off and forgotten if they refuse to turn to God and repent. We, as Latter-day Saints, must hold back the world. Some secretly envy the rich and famous and wish to have one foot in Babylon and the other foot in Zion. But the double minded and halfhearted are never fully joyful, never fully at peace, in either place. James exhorted, "A double minded man is unstable in all his ways. . . . Draw nigh to God, and he will draw nigh to you. Cleanse your hands, ye sinners; and purify your hearts, ye double minded" (James 1:8; 4:8). Those with clean hands and pure hearts reject the fleeting show of sinners and cleave ever firm to the iron rod of God.

The Great Parent of the universe looks upon the whole
of the human family with a fatherly care and paternal regard;
He views them as His offspring, and without any of those
contracted feelings that influence the children of men.

JOSEPH SMITH
HISTORY OF THE CHURCH, 4:595–96

How wonderful it is to know that God, our Father, looks upon us with a "fatherly care and paternal regard." We are His offspring, and as such He wants what is best for each one of us. He also knows all His children in the global sense, but, in a manner incomprehensible to us, He knows each of us by name. He is not just a good father, He is a perfect Father—perfectly loving, perfectly understanding, perfectly aware of our challenges and heartaches. That knowledge and testimony brings us comfort and reassurance that we are not alone in this world of sorrow and tears, that God has a personal interest in each of us individually, that we can "know that all things work together for good to them that love God" (Romans 8:28).

*One of the grand fundamental principles of "Mormonism" is
to receive truth, let it come from whence it may.*

JOSEPH SMITH
HISTORY OF THE CHURCH, 5:499

We embrace all truth that is spread across the
world. President Howard W. Hunter said: "The gospel
of Jesus Christ . . . is a global faith with an all-
embracing message. . . . Its essence is universally and
eternally true. Its message is for all the world. . . . All
men and women have not only a physical lineage leading back to Adam and Eve, . . . but also a spiritual heritage leading back to God the Eternal Father. Thus, all
persons on earth are literally brothers and sisters in
the family of God. . . . In this gospel view there is no
room for a contracted, narrow, or prejudicial view. . . .
God operates among his children in all nations, and
those who seek God are entitled to further light and
knowledge, regardless of their race, nationality, or cul-
tural traditions. . . . Ours is a perennial religion based
on eternal, saving truth . . . It embraces all truth. It cir-
cumscribes all wisdom" (*Ensign,* November 1991,
18–19).

The Father and the Son, Jesus Christ, had appeared to
Joseph Smith. The morning of the dispensation of the fulness
of times had come, dispelling the darkness of the long
generations of spiritual night.

THOMAS S. MONSON
ENSIGN, AUGUST 2006, 6

President Thomas S. Monson, who was born on this
day in 1927, has testified: "Volumes have been written
concerning the life and accomplishments of Joseph
Smith, but perhaps a highlight or two will suffice: He was
visited by the angel Moroni. He translated, from the precious plates to which he was directed, the Book of
Mormon, with its new witness of Christ to all the world.
He was the instrument in the hands of the Lord through
whom came mighty revelations pertaining to the establishment of The Church of Jesus Christ of Latter-day
Saints. In the course of his ministry he was visited by
John the Baptist, Moses, Elijah, Peter, James, and John,
that the Restoration of all things might be accomplished.
He endured persecution; he suffered grievously, as did
his followers. He trusted in God. He was true to his
prophetic calling. He commenced a marvelous missionary
effort to the entire world, which today brings light and
truth to the souls of mankind." (*Ensign,* August 2006, 7).

*I never stole the value of a pin's head, or a
picayune in my life; and when you are hungry don't steal.
Come to me, and I will feed you.*

JOSEPH SMITH
HISTORY OF THE CHURCH, 6:59

The ancient law of honesty and integrity remains in
force: "Ye shall not steal, neither deal falsely, neither
lie one to another" (Leviticus 19:11) And in our latter-
day dispensation, the law continues unchanged: "Thou
shalt love thy neighbor as thyself. Thou shalt not steal;
neither commit adultery, nor kill, nor do anything like
unto it" (D&C 59:6). To steal and be dishonest in any
way is sin that indicates that we love not God or our
neighbor. To be unchaste is a lie of truthfulness and
righteousness; to kill or do anything like unto it is a lie
against the sacred value of life. True Saints are honest
in all their dealings; they are generous in their payment of tithes and offerings; they are compassionate
to those who are struggling on the fringes and wan-
dering in sin and sorrow. Jesus Christ promised the
abundant life of joy and peace to those who walk with
integrity and honesty (John 10:10).

I have suddenly been brought from a state of health, to the borders of the grave, and as suddenly restored, for which my heart swells with gratitude to my heavenly Father, and I feel renewedly to dedicate myself . . . to His service.

JOSEPH SMITH
HISTORY OF THE CHURCH, 2:493

Over several days during the summer of 1837, Joseph Smith became so ill that he was unable to raise his head from his pillow. He recorded in his journal: "I continued to grow worse and worse until my sufferings were excruciating, and although in the midst of it all I felt to rejoice in the salvation of Israel's God, yet I found it expedient to call to my assistance those means which a kind Providence had provided for the restoration of the sick, in connection with the ordinances; and Dr. Levi Richards, at my request, administered to me herbs and mild food, and nursed me with all tenderness and attention; and my heavenly Father blessed his administrations to the easing and comforting of my system, for I began to amend in a short time, and in a few days I was able to resume my usual labors" (*History of the Church*, 2:493). In the midst of suffering he was grateful; in the agony of affliction he was determined to employ all supplementary means to get well.

*God requires the will of His creatures to be
swallowed up in His will.*

JOSEPH SMITH
HISTORY OF THE CHURCH, 2:342

Elder Neal A. Maxwell said: "God's blessings, including those associated with consecration, come by unforced obedience to the laws upon which they are predicated (see D&C 130:20–21). Thus our deepest desires determine our degree of 'obedience to the unenforceable.' God seeks to have us become more consecrated by giving everything. Then, when we come home to Him, He will generously give us 'all that He hath' (see D&C 84:38). In conclusion, the submission of one's will is really the only uniquely personal thing we have to place on God's altar. The many other things we 'give' . . . are actually the things He has already given or loaned to us. However, when you and I finally submit ourselves, by letting our individual wills be swallowed up in God's will, then we are really giving something to Him! It is the only possession which is truly ours to give! Consecration thus constitutes the only unconditional surrender which is also a total victory!" (*Ensign,* November 1995, 24).

*God glorified Himself by saving all that His
hands had made, whether beasts, fowls, fishes or men;
and He will glorify Himself with them.*

JOSEPH SMITH
TEACHINGS, 291

The glory of God is to save His beloved creations. Indeed, His work and glory is to "bring to pass the immortality and eternal life of man" (Moses 1:39). All living things in every "sphere of creation" are entitled to "the enjoyment of their eternal felicity" (D&C 77:3). All of God's creations glorify His name as they fill the measure of their creation and find joy therein. All His creations denote His power and goodness. All things made by His hands have been created to beautify and enhance the world in preparation for what it will become (D&C 59:18–19). We glorify our Father by worshipping Him in reverence and devotion, by striving to live with virtue and integrity, by becoming His true sons and daughters through obedience, consecration, and discipleship.

His lofty soul comprehended the grandeur of his mission upon earth; and with divine fortitude he fulfilled the destiny which God had ordained for him before the world was.

GEORGE Q. CANNON
LIFE OF JOSEPH SMITH, 19

George Q. Cannon (1827–1901) was ordained an apostle on this day in 1860. He joined the Church in Liverpool, England, at age twelve, served in the First Presidency under four Presidents of the Church, and spent his life testifying of the Prophet Joseph. In 1888 he published a biography of the Prophet in which he provided this description: "He had eyes which seemed to read the hearts of men. His mouth was one of mingled power and sweetness. His majesty of air was natural, not studied. Though full of personal and prophetic dignity whenever occasion demanded, he could at other times unbend and be as happy and unconventional as a boy. This was one of his most striking characteristics; and it was sometimes held up to scorn by his traducers, that the chosen 'man of God' should at times mingle as a man of earth with his earthly brethren. And yet it is a false ridicule; for Savior and prophets must, like other men, eat, drink and wear apparel" (*Life of Joseph Smith*, 20).

*Mine has been the privilege of bearing witness on
continents north and south, east and west, that [Joseph Smith]
was and is a prophet of God, a mighty servant and
testifier of the Lord Jesus Christ.*

GORDON B. HINCKLEY
ENSIGN, DECEMBER 2005, 6

President Gordon B. Hinckley said: "When I was a boy
12 years of age, my father took me to a meeting of the
priesthood of the stake in which we lived. . . . At the
opening of that meeting, the first of its kind I had ever
attended, 300 or 400 men stood. They were from varied
backgrounds and many vocations, but each had in his
heart the same conviction, out of which together they
sang these great words:

> *Praise to the man who communed with Jehovah!*
> *Jesus anointed that Prophet and Seer.*
> *Blessed to open the last dispensation,*
> *Kings shall extol him, and nations revere.*
> ('*Praise to the Man,*' Hymns, no. 27)

Something happened within me as I heard those men of
faith sing. There came into my boyish heart a knowledge,
placed there by the Holy Spirit, that Joseph Smith was
indeed a prophet of the Almighty" (*Ensign,* December
2005, 6).

In all things be temperate; abstain from . . . swearing,
and from all profane language, and from everything which is
unrighteous or unholy; also from enmity, and hatred, and
covetousness, and from every unholy desire.

JOSEPH SMITH
HISTORY OF THE CHURCH, 3:233

To be temperate is to be mild, moderate of appetite or desire, and self-disciplined. The temperate are able to keep their emotions in check, they are not extreme or excessive, not given to unholy outbursts and unrestrained emotionality. The temperate strive to be self-controlled, reasonable, and appropriate in each situation. That doesn't mean the temperate don't have great fun or laugh heartily or enjoy life. They do. But they're able to keep their thoughts and tongues and actions within the limits and boundaries the Lord has set. Those who let their tempers get the best of them, who swear and profane, who give in to enmity and covetousness, lack sufficient spiritual self-discipline. To swear is not "cool," to profane is not "macho," but they are an indication of weakness that the person lacks discipline and richness of expression. We are here to tame the carnal, lazy, natural man and become men and women of Christ.

Baptism by water is but half a baptism, and is good for nothing without the other half—that is, the baptism of the Holy Ghost.

JOSEPH SMITH
HISTORY OF THE CHURCH, 5:499

The baptism of water must be accompanied by the baptism of fire. Baptism is for the remission of sins, and the baptism of fire—receiving the gift of the Holy Ghost—will bring blessings unnumbered to those who live worthy of its companionship (2 Nephi 31:12–17). These are the requirements for baptism as set forth in D&C 20:37: "All those who humble themselves before God, and desire to be baptized, and come forth with broken hearts and contrite spirits, and witness before the church that they have truly repented of all their sins, and are willing to take upon them the name of Jesus Christ, having a determination to serve him to the end, and truly manifest by their works that they have received of the Spirit of Christ unto the remission of their sins, shall be received by baptism into his church." We are promised that the Holy Ghost will guide us and "show unto [us] all things what [we] should do" (2 Nephi 32:5).

As a Church and a people it behooves us to be wise, and to seek to know the will of God, and then be willing to do it.

JOSEPH SMITH
HISTORY OF THE CHURCH, 5:65

Ignorance is not bliss when it comes to the kingdom of God. Laziness and lack of effort or understanding will not be a sufficient excuse if we are to withstand the temptations of the world, triumph over trials, and know the will of God. The Lord counseled His Twelve Apostles, "I send you forth as sheep in the midst of wolves: be ye therefore wise as serpents, and harmless as doves" (Matthew 10:16). We are to seek the spirit of revelation in humility and then have the wisdom and good judgment to follow the will of God in our lives. It's one thing to seek to know the will of God, it's another thing altogether to have the submissiveness and strength to follow through. We will be judged and held accountable not only for what we *know*, but for what we *do*.

There is no better example of an older brother's love than that exhibited in the life of Hyrum Smith for the Prophet Joseph Smith. . . . They were as united and as affectionate and as loving as mortal men could be.

HEBER J. GRANT
IMPROVEMENT ERA, AUGUST 1918, 854

On this day in 1830, in Fayette, New York, Hyrum Smith introduced Parley P. Pratt to the Prophet Joseph Smith. From Joseph's recounting of his First Vision in 1820 to dying with him at Carthage in 1844, Hyrum stood faithful and strong next to his younger brother Joseph. Consider the jealousy of older brothers toward their younger brothers: Cain, Joseph of Egypt's older siblings, Laman and Lemuel. President Heber J. Grant said of the loyalty and humility of Hyrum: "There never was one particle of the jealousy that ofttimes fills the hearts of older brothers toward younger brothers who seem to be preferred ahead of them. There was no place for jealousy in the heart of Hyrum Smith. No mortal man could have been more loyal, more true, more faithful in life or in death than was Hyrum Smith to the Prophet of the living God" (*Improvement Era,* August 1918, 854–55).

SEPTEMBER

*For a man to be great, he must not dwell on
small things, though he may enjoy them.*
JOSEPH SMITH

What do we hear in the gospel which we have received?
A voice of gladness! A voice of mercy from heaven; and a voice of
truth out of the earth; glad tidings for the dead; a voice of gladness
for the living and the dead; glad tidings of great joy.

JOSEPH SMITH
DOCTRINE AND COVENANTS 128:19

In an epistle to the Church written in September of 1842, Joseph Smith identified many heavenly messengers who had appeared to him in bringing about the restoration of the gospel. The keys of salvation, along with gospel truth and instruction, were given to the Prophet by these authorized servants of the Lord: "Glad tidings from Cumorah! Moroni, an angel from heaven, declaring the fulfilment of the prophets—the book to be revealed. A voice of the Lord in the wilderness of Fayette, Seneca county, declaring the three witnesses to bear record of the book! The voice of Michael on the banks of the Susquehanna, detecting the devil when he appeared as an angel of light! The voice of Peter, James, and John . . . , declaring themselves as possessing the keys of the kingdom, and of the dispensation of the fulness of times!" (D&C 128:20). These are indeed glad tidings of great joy!

I have felt to rejoice exceedingly in what I saw of Brother Joseph, for in his public and private career he carried with him the Spirit of the Almighty, and he manifested a greatness of soul which I had never seen in any other man.

WILFORD WOODRUFF
IN *JOSEPH SMITH*, 495–96

Wilford Woodruff, fourth President of the Church, died at age ninety-one on this day in 1898. He served more than fifty years as an apostle and nearly a decade as Church President. He was a remarkable missionary and leader, and he knew the Prophet Joseph personally. It is another testament to the character and prophetic mission of Joseph Smith that those who knew him best stood strong and faithful at his side. They knew the Prophet's soul as they associated with him over many years. You cannot fool so many for so long. Truth and authenticity and character will win out—and it did in the Prophet's case. Each of Joseph's successors—from Brigham Young to today, and countless members of the Church worldwide—stand in awe at what the Prophet accomplished. They praise his name, honor his memory, and testify of the glorious gospel he restored.

*Sectarian priests cry out concerning me, and ask,
"Why is it this babbler gains so many followers, and retains them?"
I answer, It is because I possess the principle of love. All I
can offer the world is a good heart and a good hand.*

JOSEPH SMITH
HISTORY OF THE CHURCH, 5:498

Elder Joseph B. Wirthlin tells the story of "a 14-year-old boy who had come to Nauvoo in search of his brother who lived near there. The young boy had arrived in winter with no money and no friends. When he inquired about his brother, the boy was taken to a large house that looked like a hotel. There he met a man who said, 'Come in, son, we'll take care of you.' . . . The next day it was bitter cold, but in spite of that, the boy prepared himself to walk the eight miles to where his brother was staying. When the man of the house saw this, he . . . said there would be a team coming soon and that he could ride back with them. When the boy protested, saying that he had no money, the man told him not to worry about that, that they would take care of him. Later the boy learned that the man of the house was none other than Joseph Smith, the Mormon prophet" (*Ensign,* November 2007, 29).

We feel to exhort you in the name of the Lord Jesus,
to be strong in the faith in the new and everlasting covenant,
and nothing frightened at your enemies.

JOSEPH SMITH
HISTORY OF THE CHURCH, 3:232–33

To be strong in the faith is an active, robust process that inspires us to be steadfast and immovable. Strong faith is not passive, weak-kneed, or fainthearted if we want to withstand the troubles and temptations ahead. Our strength will drive away fear, and our confidence and trust in the Lord will sustain our faith. The Prophet Joseph said, "Hold on even unto death; for 'he that seeks to save his life shall lose it; and he that loses his life for my sake, and the Gospel's, shall find it,' saith Jesus Christ [see Mark 8:35]. . . . We say unto you, brethren, be not afraid of your adversaries; contend earnestly against mobs, and the unlawful works of dissenters and of darkness. And the very God of peace shall be with you, and make a way for your escape from the adversary of your souls" (*History of the Church,* 3:233). Don't cower from the enemies of truth—stand tall; don't shrink from the adversaries of righteousness—stand strong.

Make yourselves acquainted with the commandments of the Lord,
and the laws of the state, and govern yourselves accordingly.

JOSEPH SMITH
HISTORY OF THE CHURCH, 1:341

Ignorance and forgetfulness will not stand in the day of our judgment. We are responsible to know the commandments of the Lord and keep them; we are likewise responsible to know the laws of the land and honor them. Indeed, we believe "in obeying, honoring, and sustaining the law" (Article of Faith, 1:12). The Prophet Joseph taught, "We will keep the laws of the land; we do not speak against them; we never have" (*History of the Church*, 5:257). We become acquainted with the laws of the land by staying informed, following current events and legislative actions, and sharing and learning from others. We know the commandments of God by reading the scriptures, hearkening to the counsel of our prophets in general conference, and seeking to know the will of the Lord in our lives. We are accountable with a duty to govern ourselves according to the commandments of God and the laws of the land.

We want the power of Elijah to seal those who dwell on earth to those who dwell in heaven.

JOSEPH SMITH
HISTORY OF THE CHURCH, 6:252

On this day in 1842, Joseph Smith addressed a letter to the Church containing further instructions regarding the work of redeeming the dead. Its text, now found in Doctrine and Covenants 128, read, in part: "Let us, therefore, as a church and a people, and as Latter-day Saints, offer unto the Lord an offering in righteousness; and let us present in his holy temple, when it is finished, a book containing the records of our dead, which shall be worthy of all acceptation" (v. 24). This is the Spirit of Elijah: when we give an offering in righteousness, when our hearts turn to our forebears, when we go often to the temple to do work to redeem the dead and connect ourselves to those on the other side of the veil. Temple work blesses us with roots (ancestors) and branches (descendants) that are sealed and connected everlastingly by the power of the priesthood. Heaven and earth come together and are centered in the house of the Lord, the temple.

*The Prophet Joseph is an example and a teacher of
enduring well in faith. I do not worship him, but I thank and
love him as the Lord's prophet of the Restoration.*

HENRY B. EYRING
ENSIGN, NOVEMBER 2003, 92

President Henry B. Eyring, like all apostles and
prophets of the latter-days, has an enduring testimony
of both the truthfulness and the blessings that flow
from the mission of the Prophet Joseph: "He has
helped me pray with the intent to obey. I am better
able to feast in the word and the love of God. Because
of him I feel the Holy Ghost more often in the
moments when I try to build the faith of a person in
the Lord's kingdom. And because of what I know of
the Prophet Joseph and the scriptures which were
revealed through him, I more often feel the love of
God for His children and of His for me when I reach
down to lift someone up" (*Ensign,* November 2003,
92). We can choose to follow the Prophet's example
and endure well with faith in the restored gospel of
Jesus Christ. Truly, we thank God for a prophet.

The appearing of the Father and the Son to
Joseph Smith is the foundation of this Church. Therein
lies the secret of its strength and vitality.

DAVID O. McKAY
IMPROVEMENT ERA, JANUARY 1942, 54

The Church of Jesus Christ of Latter-day Saints begins with the marvelous vision given young Joseph in a grove of trees in Palmyra, New York. From that vision we learn divine truths lost to mankind for centuries—among them the fact that God continues to have a loving interest in the welfare of His children. All who have received the witness of the Spirit concerning the mission of the Prophet can testify of the truthfulness of his discourse with God. President David O. McKay, who was born on this day in 1873, said of the First Vision: "This is true, and I bear witness to it. That one revelation answers all the queries of science regarding God and His divine personality. Don't you see what that means? What God is, is answered. His relation to His children is clear. His interest in humanity through authority delegated to man is apparent. The future of the work is assured. These and other glorious truths are clarified by that glorious First Vision" (*Improvement Era,* January 1942, 54).

The Priesthood is an everlasting principle, and
existed with God from eternity, and will to eternity,
without beginning of days or end of years.

JOSEPH SMITH
HISTORY OF THE CHURCH, 3:386

The priesthood is an everlasting principle with everlasting power. Joseph Smith taught, "The Priesthood is everlasting—without beginning of days or end of years. . . . Wherever the ordinances of the Gospel are administered, there is the Priesthood" (*History of the Church,* 3:387). It is God's power and authority delegated to man for the blessing of all the sons and daughters of God and for the upbuilding of the kingdom of God on earth. God accomplishes His work by priesthood power and authority. President Harold B. Lee said, "When we [act] in the name of the Lord, as holders of the priesthood, we are doing it in the name and in behalf of our Heavenly Father. Priesthood is the power by which our Heavenly Father works through men" (Conference Report, April 1973, 129). The power that comes through priesthood authority depends upon the righteousness of the priesthood holder (D&C 121:41–46). How grateful we should be for the power and the authority of the holy priesthood.

Although I never feel to force my doctrine upon any person; I rejoice to see prejudice give way to truth, and the traditions of men dispersed by the pure principles of the Gospel of Jesus Christ.

JOSEPH SMITH
HISTORY OF THE CHURCH, 6:213

Latter-day Saints offer the world a restored gospel of Jesus Christ that contains a fullness of everlasting truth. We offer it without price or prejudice, without force or coercion of any kind. Indeed, "we claim the privilege of worshiping Almighty God according to the dictates of our own conscience, and allow all men the same privilege, let them worship how, where, or what they may" (Articles of Faith 1:11). We, of all people and churches, believe that people are free to choose. But they can choose only if they have had a choice, an opportunity. That's why thousands of missionaries are sent out across the world, and why every member is a missionary. We seek to share our testimony of truth; we desire that all might know the joy and understanding that comes of the plan of happiness; we want everyone to hear the "glad tidings of great joy" (D&C 128:19) the gospel can bring to our hearts and homes.

Do not be discouraged on account of the greatness of the work; . . . He who scattered Israel has promised to gather them; therefore . . . He will endow you with power, wisdom, might, and intelligence, and every qualification necessary.

JOSEPH SMITH
HISTORY OF THE CHURCH, 4:128–29

This marvelous work and wonder in which we are engaged is not for the fainthearted and weak-kneed. Courage and perseverance will carry the day and move the work forward. It may seem overwhelming at times, but the kingdom shall not fail, and this work cannot be stopped. Joseph Smith stated, "We feel disposed to go forward and unite our energies for the upbuilding of the Kingdom. . . . The work which has to be accomplished in the last days is one of vast importance, and will call into action the energy, skill, talent, and ability of the Saints, so that it may roll forth with that glory and majesty described by the prophet [Daniel 2:34–35; 44–45]; and will consequently require the concentration of the Saints, to accomplish works of such magnitude and grandeur" (*History of the Church,* 4:185–86). The Lord will bless us with power, wisdom, and intelligence to become mighty instruments in His hands.

*With respect to the deaths in Zion, we feel to
mourn with those that mourn, but remember that
the God of all the earth will do right.*

JOSEPH SMITH
HISTORY OF THE CHURCH, 1:341

Our God sees the end from the beginning and everything in between. At times it may seem that all is dark and unrelenting in its difficulty. But God is our Father who will always watch over and protect His children. It often takes time and always requires patience and humility, but things will work out—they always do. If we hold on, hope on, and trust God, things will work out for the best. Our Father knows what is best for each of His children. That doesn't mean that a loving God will insulate us from heartbreak, or that there will be no skinned knees or misfortune because of His providential protection. All these things—joy and sadness, pleasure and pain, happiness and heartache—will give us experience and opportunity to educate our spirits and learn and grow. This we can know with confidence: God will always do right.

SEPTEMBER 13

Sunday, 13. — I was with my family.

JOSEPH SMITH
HISTORY OF THE CHURCH, 4:550

From this simple, oft-repeated entry in Joseph Smith's journal we get a glimpse into his caring heart and familial priorities. Because of his remarkable accomplishments and prophetic mission, it is easy to lose sight of the fact that he was a husband, father, brother, and son. He certainly had more than enough to do on any given day to build the kingdom. But he understood that building the kingdom begins at home. He had a tender regard for his loved ones; his heart yearned to be in their embrace. One gets the sense that it was with his family that he was rejuvenated to face the challenges of the day; it was with his loved ones that his spirit was strengthened and his faith fortified. Although he knew the loneliness of leadership, he was also blessed with the affection and fidelity of loved ones. Home ought to be a place of renewal and relaxation, a place where love and laughter and loyalty abounds, a place to be bolstered and reenergized to take on the trials of life.

The harder the persecution the greater the gifts of God upon his church. Yea, all things shall work together for good to them who are willing to lay down their lives for Christ's sake.

JOSEPH SMITH
JOSEPH SMITH, 231

If we trust the Lord and exercise faith in His purposes, we will be able to bear with patience the great afflictions that come our way. In a letter to the Church written from Liberty Jail, Joseph quoted Matthew 5:11–12: "'Blessed are ye when men shall revile you, and persecute you, and shall say all manner of evil against you falsely for my sake; rejoice and be exceeding glad, for great is your reward in heaven, for so persecuted they the Prophets which were before you.' Now, dear brethren," Joseph continued, "if any men ever had reason to claim this promise, we are the men; for we know that the world not only hate us, but they speak all manner of evil of us falsely, for no other reason than that we have been endeavoring to teach the fullness of the Gospel of Jesus Christ" (*Teachings*, 124). It may take time and always takes fortitude, but faith, hope, and charity will ultimately triumph over the wicked designs and evil machinations of men.

God himself, finding he was in the midst of spirits and glory, because he was more intelligent, saw proper to institute laws whereby the rest could have a privilege to advance like himself. The relationship we have with God places us in a situation to advance in knowledge.

JOSEPH SMITH
TEACHINGS, 354

Our Heavenly Father has instituted a plan whereby we can advance in knowledge, develop His attributes, and inherit His quality of life. The Prophet Joseph taught the principles of this "delicious doctrine" when he said: "[God] has power to institute laws to instruct the weaker intelligences, that they may be exalted with himself, so that they might have one glory upon another, and all that knowledge, power, glory, and intelligence, which is requisite in order to save them in the world of spirits. This is good doctrine. It tastes good. I can taste the principles of eternal life, and so can you. They are given to me by the revelations of Jesus Christ. . . . You say honey is sweet, and so do I. I can also taste the spirit of eternal life. I know it is good; and when I tell you of these things which were given me by inspiration of the Holy Spirit, you are bound to receive them as sweet, and rejoice more and more" (*Teachings,* 354–55).

*I . . . gave much instruction calculated to guard them against
self-sufficiency, self-righteousness, and self-importance . . . , and
especially teaching them to observe charity, wisdom and
fellow-feeling, with love one towards another.*

JOSEPH SMITH
HISTORY OF THE CHURCH, 3:383

Joseph Smith exhorted the Twelve to manifest love,
charity, and wisdom in all their interactions. This is
worthwhile counsel for us today. We may not all be
sent forth as missionaries, but we are each walking
manifestations of the power of the gospel in our lives.
Christ and His gospel are change agents, designed to
make bad people good and good people better. If we
aren't more humble, less proud, kinder, gentler, and
better in thought and action in meaningful ways, we
have little to commend the gospel to others as a way
of life. If, on the other hand, we are kindhearted and
loving we will open doors of friendship and build
bridges of understanding that will reverberate down
the generations. We will see no end to the good that
comes of charity and caring fellowship. Whether
around the world or in our neighborhoods, we best
represent Christ and His gospel as we walk humbly
before the Lord and love one another.

It is a false idea that the Saints will escape all the judgments,
whilst the wicked suffer; for all flesh is subject to suffer, and 'the
righteous shall hardly escape;' still many of the Saints
will escape, for the just shall live by faith.

JOSEPH SMITH
HISTORY OF THE CHURCH, 4:11

The Prophet Joseph understood that not all suffering is caused by sin. Adversity falls upon the just and the unjust, the righteous and the wicked. The Prophet taught, "Yet many of the righteous shall fall a prey to disease, to pestilence, etc., by reason of the weakness of the flesh, and yet be saved in the Kingdom of God. So that it is an unhallowed principle to say that such and such have transgressed because they have been preyed upon by disease or death, for all flesh is subject to death; and the Savior has said, 'Judge not, lest ye be judged' [Matthew 7:1]" (*History of the Church,* 4:11). We must hold off on judgments of ourselves and others, since we know not the beginning from the end, as God does. And, we must be patient in our afflictions, trust God, and know that our mortal views are at best myopic and incomplete.

*Our acts are recorded, and at a future day they will be
laid before us, and if we should fail to judge right and injure our
fellow-beings, they may there, perhaps, condemn us.*

JOSEPH SMITH
HISTORY OF THE CHURCH, 2:26

The Bible Dictionary describes a Book of Life as
"the sum total of one's thoughts and actions—the record of his life. However, the scriptures indicate that a
heavenly record is kept of the faithful, whose names
are recorded, as well as an account of their righteous
deeds (D&C 88:2; 128:7)" (Bible Dictionary, 626–27).
Each one of us has our own unique Book of Life that is
written on our hearts—it is an inventory of what we
are becoming, a record of how we are progressing on
the pathway of discipleship. Similarly, heaven main-
tains a Book of Life that documents our actions and
attitudes, our righteous desires and daily interactions.
Every day, moment by moment, we write a page in
these eternal books. In a sense, these two books are
one and the same book, each filled with a true repre-
sentation of our lives. One day these books will be laid
before us—either to our everlasting joy and happiness
or to our shame and consternation.

We ever pray for thee, our prophet dear,
That God will give to thee comfort and cheer;
As the advancing years furrow thy brow,
Still may the light within shine bright as now.

EVAN STEPHENS
HYMNS, NO. 23

Evan Stephens (1854–1930) was born in Pencader, Wales, in 1854, ten years after the martyrdom of the Prophet Joseph. He emigrated to Utah at age twelve with his parents and became a renowned conductor and prolific composer. He directed the Mormon Tabernacle Choir for twenty-six years (1890–1916) and led them to public prominence. In addition, he wrote more than eighty hymns and numerous anthems, operas, and cantatas. Although he did not know the Prophet Joseph personally, he proclaimed his name and defended the restored gospel in song throughout his life:

The voice of God again is heard.
The silence has been broken.
The curse of darkness is withdrawn.
The Lord from heav'n has spoken.
(Hymns, *no. 18*)

*Help us by the power of thy Spirit, that we may mingle
our voices . . . with acclamations of praise, singing Hosanna to God
and the Lamb! And let these, thine anointed ones, be clothed with
salvation, and thy saints shout aloud for joy.*

JOSEPH SMITH
DOCTRINE AND COVENANTS 109:79–80

Joseph Smith concluded his inspired prayer for the dedication of the Kirtland Temple with a joyous Hosanna shout. As part of every temple dedication today, we also joyously shout, "Hosanna, Hosanna, Hosanna, to God and the Lamb! Amen, Amen, and Amen." We sing these exultant words in the beloved hymn "The Spirit of God," which was written for the dedication of the Kirtland Temple (*Hymns,* no. 2). Whenever a temple is dedicated, we join in thanksgiving and joyous acclamations as we ask the Lord to accept this holy house—a place where He may visit (D&C 109:4–5). We thank the God of heaven that a house of prayer and fasting, a house of faith and learning, a house of glory and order, a house of God has been built (D&C 109:8). Knowing what we know about the plan of salvation, understanding what we do of the sacred covenants made in the Lord's holy house, our exultant voices join with those on both sides of the veil in gratitude and joyous praise.

*He called me by name, and said unto me that he was
a messenger sent from the presence of God to me, and that his
name was Moroni; that God had a work for me to do; and
that my name should be had for good and evil among
all nations, kindreds, and tongues.*

JOSEPH SMITH—HISTORY 1:33

On this day in 1823, the angel Moroni appeared to seventeen-year-old farm boy Joseph Smith and uttered what are among the most remarkable prophetic words of all time. What is the likelihood that an unknown, uneducated boy from western New York would be spoken of among all nations of the earth? Who could have imagined that from a small, nineteenth-century farmhouse would come a man and a work that would fill the whole earth? Today, there are those who boldly testify without fear or embarrassment that Joseph Smith was God's prophet—the great Prophet of the Restoration. Others proclaim him an imposter and a false prophet. It was so in Joseph's day, and it is so today. Great truth and light will always be opposed by great heresy and dissent; the voices of envy and enmity always strive to smother the voices of righteousness; the forces of evil always fight against light and truth. Moroni's prophecy is another witness of the prophetic calling of Joseph Smith.

SEPTEMBER 22

*I left the field, and went to the place where the messenger had
told me the plates were deposited; and owing to the distinctness of
the vision which I had had concerning it, I knew the
place the instant that I arrived there.*

JOSEPH SMITH–HISTORY 1:50

This is a day of great importance to The Church of
Jesus Christ of Latter-day Saints. On this day in 1823,
the angel Moroni appeared to Joseph Smith at the Hill
Cumorah and showed him the gold plates for the first
time. Moroni would then visit with Joseph on this
same date and at this location for the next four years.
Then, on this day in 1827, Joseph received the plates,
the Urim and Thummim, and the breastplate from
Moroni at the Hill Cumorah. A year later, on this day,
Moroni returned the gold plates to Joseph Smith, having taken them from the Prophet after Martin Harris
lost 116 manuscript pages of the translated record.
Also beginning on this day in 1832, the Prophet
received Doctrine and Covenants 84, a marvelous
revelation on priesthood. What transpired on this
date has eternal significance for all people of the
world.

The more sure word of prophecy means a man's knowing that he is sealed up unto eternal life, by revelation and the spirit of prophecy, through the power of the Holy Priesthood.

DOCTRINE AND COVENANTS 131:5

In an address entitled "The Ten Blessings of the Priesthood," Elder Bruce R. McConkie said: "We have power to make our calling and election sure, so that while we yet dwell in mortality, having overcome the world and been true and faithful in all things, we shall be sealed up unto eternal life and have the unconditional promise of eternal life in the presence of Him whose we are. . . . During the latter years of his ministry, in particular, the Prophet Joseph Smith pleaded fervently with the Saints to press forward in righteousness until they made their calling and election sure, until they heard the heavenly voice proclaim: 'Son, thou shalt be exalted.' (*Teachings,* p. 150) He himself became the pattern for all such attainment in this dispensation, when the voice from heaven said to him: 'I am the Lord thy God, and will be with thee even unto the end of the world, and through all eternity; for verily I seal upon you your exaltation'" (*Ensign,* November 1977, 34).

*For a man to be great, he must not dwell on small
things, though he may enjoy them.*

JOSEPH SMITH
HISTORY OF THE CHURCH, 5:298

Life is too short and too precious to fill our allotted
mortal minutes with minutiae and triviality. So many
consume their lives with petty thoughts, idle gossip, and
the mundane matters of mortality. The world crowds
upon us, beckoning us to partake of its allurements and
enticing us to spend time on things of trifling importance. Power, prestige, and possessions are what matter
on the worldly scoreboard, and the small things of mortality can crowd out thoughts of the mansions that can
await us in eternity if we are humble and obedient. The
Lord, ever encouraging us toward Zion and treasures in
heaven, admonishes us to "lay aside the things of this
world, and seek for the things of a better" (D&C 25:10).
The things that matter to the Lord are the things that
should matter to us. The Master of the universe is not
impressed by wealth or celebrity. He cares about the
integrity of our hearts, our willingness to love and to forgive, our selfless service to others, our obedience to truth.

And when thy people transgress, any of them, they may speedily repent and return unto thee, and find favor in thy sight, and be restored to the blessings which thou hast ordained to be poured out upon those who shall reverence thee.

JOSEPH SMITH
DOCTRINE AND COVENANTS 109:21

Each of us knows of righteous men and women of Christ who have fully turned their lives over to Him, who have suffered for His sake, who have served Him will full purpose of heart, and who have remained faithful to their covenants to the end of their mortal lives. They have died firm in the faith and valiant in the testimony of Jesus, but they were not perfect. They had been born of the Spirit, changed from a carnal and fallen state to a state of righteousness (Mosiah 27:25), but it could never be said that they were completely flawless or that they had never sinned or made a mistake. Rather, "Whosoever is born of God *doth not continue in sin*" (JST, 1 John 3:9; emphasis added). Having walked in the light and embraced the gospel covenant, the God-fearing and faithful cannot remain long in darkness; they repent forthwith and return to the light which brings comfort and peace and sweet assurance.

*After this vision closed, the heavens were again opened unto us;
and Moses appeared before us, and committed unto us the keys of
the gathering of Israel from the four parts of the earth, and the
leading of the ten tribes from the land of the north.*

JOSEPH SMITH
DOCTRINE AND COVENANTS 110:11

Moses, who had gathered ancient Israel, bestowed "the keys of the gathering of [modern] Israel" (D&C 110:11) upon Joseph Smith and Oliver Cowdery on April 3, 1836. Since that day, missionaries have shared the gospel message with people across the earth, and the receptive of Israel have gathered to stakes of Zion in the Lord's restored latter-day church. All who gather into the kingdom of God through baptism and faithfulness are recipients of the blessings that have come from the bestowal of keys in the Kirtland Temple. Today the Church is growing at an ever-increasing rate, as was foretold anciently: "I will take you one of a city, and two of a family, and I will bring you to Zion" (Jeremiah 3:14). The gospel fold enlarges as individuals and families come into the Church. We are not baptized as a congregation or given the gift of the Holy Ghost as a group. One by one we make a choice for Christ and His restoration of priesthood keys and power.

*It is the first principle of the Gospel to know
for a certainty the Character of God.*

JOSEPH SMITH
TEACHINGS, 345

We cannot understand our destiny if we do not understand our origin. The Prophet Joseph said, "If men do not comprehend the character of God, they do not comprehend themselves" (*Teachings,* 343). To truly come to know who we are and whose we are, we must know our Father in Heaven and Jesus Christ whom He has sent. We will know very little about our true selves and our divine nature and destiny without a true knowledge of God. If we know not God, we know not ourselves. The character, attributes, and perfections of God are known by the power of personal revelation when we humbly seek to know God and Jesus Christ. They are known through sincere pondering, prayer, and scripture study, through willingly following the prophets, through a humble desire and a trusting heart. The word of the Lord came with timeless clarity to the prophet Jeremiah: "And ye shall seek me, and find me, when ye shall search for me with all your heart" (Jeremiah 29:13).

*After the many testimonies which have been given of him,
this is the testimony, last of all, which we give of him: That he
lives! For we saw him, even on the right hand of God.*

JOSEPH SMITH
DOCTRINE AND COVENANTS 76:22–23

Joseph Smith and Sidney Rigdon were eyewitnesses of the living reality of the Father and the Son. The Lord "touched the eyes of [their] understandings" (D&C 76:19), and they saw God seated on His heavenly throne and Jesus Christ at His right hand, surrounded by the celestial inhabitants who were worshipping God and the Lamb (D&C 76:20–21). Their knowledge and faith combined as they bore testimony to the world: "He lives! For we saw him. . . . [and] by him, and through him, and of him, the worlds are and were created, and the inhabitants thereof are begotten sons and daughters unto God" (D&C 76:22–24). A testimony is an endowment of heavenly truth distilled upon the souls of humble seekers by the power of the Holy Ghost. It is a witness borne of the Spirit that Jesus is the Christ, who provided an infinite atonement for all those who come unto Him. It comes as a result of obedience and humility, of desiring with all our hearts to know the truth that "He lives!"

*Never . . . have we seen manifested . . . a more ardent
desire to do the will of God, more strenuous exertions used, or
greater sacrifices made than there have been since the Lord said,
"Let the Temple be built by the tithing of my people."*

JOSEPH SMITH
HISTORY OF THE CHURCH, 4:609

The Prophet Joseph wrote of the power of sacrifice
and unity in building the Nauvoo Temple: "It seemed
as though the spirit of enterprise, philanthropy and
obedience rested simultaneously upon old and young,
and brethren and sisters, boys and girls, and even
strangers, who were not in the Church, united with an
unprecedented liberality in the accomplishment of
this great work; nor could the widow, in many
instances, be prevented, out of her scanty pittance
from throwing in her two mites. We feel at this time
to tender to all . . . our unfeigned thanks for their
unprecedented liberality, kindness, diligence, and obedience which they have so opportunely manifested on
the present occasion. . . . When the brethren, as in this
instance, show a unity of purpose and design, our care,
labor, toil and anxiety is materially diminished, our
yoke is made easy and our burden is light" (*History of
the Church,* 4:609).

*We never can comprehend the things of God
and of heaven, but by revelation.*

JOSEPH SMITH
TEACHINGS, 292

We are instructed in heavenly things by the spirit of revelation. As Paul taught the Corinthians, "For what man knoweth the things of a man, save the spirit of man which is in him? even so the things of God knoweth no man, but the Spirit of God. Now we have received, not the spirit of the world, but the spirit which is of God; that we might know the things that are freely given to us of God. Which things also we speak, not in the words which man's wisdom teacheth, but which the Holy Ghost teacheth; comparing spiritual things with spiritual. But the natural man receiveth not the things of the Spirit of God: for they are foolishness unto him: neither can he know them, because they are spiritually discerned. But he that is spiritual judgeth all things, yet he himself is judged of no man. For who hath known the mind of the Lord, that he may instruct him? But we have the mind of Christ" (1 Corinthians 2:11–16).

OCTOBER

*Knowledge is power; and the man who has
the most knowledge has the greatest power.*

JOSEPH SMITH

This afternoon I labored on the Egyptian alphabet, in company with Brothers Oliver Cowdery and W. W. Phelps, and during the research, the principles of astronomy as understood by Father Abraham and the ancients unfolded to our understanding.

JOSEPH SMITH
HISTORY OF THE CHURCH, 2:286

A glimpse into the expansive breadth of the Prophet Joseph's mind and soul is given us in his journal account of this day in 1835. Joseph Smith recorded that while he labored on the Egyptian alphabet the principles of astronomy as understood anciently by Abraham were unfolded to him. Joseph lived the principles taught in an earlier revelation he received: "Teach ye diligently and my grace shall attend you, that you may be instructed more perfectly in theory, in principle, in doctrine, in the law of the gospel, in all things that pertain unto the kingdom of God, that are expedient for you to understand; of things both in heaven and in the earth, and under the earth; things which have been, things which are, things which must shortly come to pass; things which are at home, things which are abroad . . . and a knowledge also of countries and of kingdoms—That ye may be prepared in all things when I shall send you again to magnify the calling whereunto I have called you" (D&C 88:78–80).

Congregations throughout the world sing in their native tongues,
"We thank thee, O God, for a prophet." They are singing of him
who stands at the head of the work of the Almighty in this
the final dispensation of God's work on the earth.

GORDON B. HINCKLEY
HEROES OF THE RESTORATION, 6

President Gordon B. Hinckley, fifteenth President of
the Church, wrote of Joseph Smith: "I stand humbly in
his lengthened shadow, fifteenth in line to hold the keys
first given him in these latter days. He stands as my
leader, my model, my prophet, my seer and revelator. I
am overwhelmed. I am humbled. I am profoundly and
deeply grateful. God be thanked for His chosen servant,
whom He nurtured and taught, to whom He appeared
and spoke, who under divine direction was visited by
those who anciently held precious keys and authority,
and whose image stands before the world as an instrument in the hands of the Almighty bringing to pass the
great work of immortality and eternal life for all of the
sons and daughters of God" (*Heroes of the Restoration*, 7).
No one could understand the demands of the calling,
the sacred stewardship, and the deep appreciation for
the one who stands at the head of this final dispensation better than one who would later become a prophet.

God sees the secret springs of human action,
and knows the hearts of all living.

JOSEPH SMITH
HISTORY OF THE CHURCH, 1:317

Oliver Cowdery, later one of the Three Witness of the Book of Mormon and Assistant President of the Church, was born on this day in 1806 in Wells, Vermont. God, who understands the hearts of all His children, surely knew the desires of Oliver Cowdery. In Doctrine and Covenants 6, the Lord directed a revelation to Oliver: "Blessed art thou for what thou hast done; for thou hast inquired of me, and behold, as often as thou hast inquired thou hast received instruction of my Spirit. If it had not been so, thou wouldst not have come to the place where thou art at this time. Behold, thou knowest that thou hast inquired of me and I did enlighten thy mind; and now I tell thee these things that thou mayest know that thou hast been enlightened by the Spirit of truth; yea, I tell thee, that thou mayest know that there is none else save God that knowest thy thoughts and the intents of thy heart" (vv. 14–16).

*Do good and work righteousness with an eye single to
the glory of God, and you shall reap your reward when the Lord
recompenses every one according to his work.*

JOSEPH SMITH
HISTORY OF THE CHURCH, 2:229–30

In order to do the Lord's work and qualify to carry
forth His kingdom, we need "faith, hope, charity and
love, with an eye single to the glory of God" (D&C 4:5).
"An eye single to the glory of God" means we are meek
and submissive, desirous to do God's will, courageous
and determined to do good and work righteousness.
The Lord said, "And if your eye be single to my glory,
your whole bodies shall be filled with light, and there
shall be no darkness in you; and that body which is filled
with light comprehendeth all things" (D&C 88:67).
The Prophet Joseph observed, "We can only say, that if
an anticipation of the joys of the celestial glory, as witnessed to the hearts of the humble is not sufficient, we
will leave to yourselves the result of your own diligence;
for God ere long, will call all His servants before Him,
and there from His own hand they will receive a just
recompense and a righteous reward for all their labors"
(*History of the Church,* 2:14–15).

*Declare the first principles, and let mysteries
alone, lest ye be overthrown.*

JOSEPH SMITH
TEACHINGS, 292

Along with his many responsibilities as prophet, Joseph Smith served numerous missions throughout his life. On this day in 1833, he left Kirtland with Sidney Rigdon on a one-month proselyting mission to Ontario Province in Canada. He sent missionaries to preach to the nations of the world—a work that continues today. His counsel to these missionaries is good counsel for all who seek to share the gospel with others: "Oh, ye elders of Israel, hearken to my voice; and when you are sent into the world to preach, tell those things you are sent to tell; preach and cry aloud, 'Repent ye, for the kingdom of heaven is at hand; repent and believe the Gospel'" (*Teachings,* 292). The gospel is beautifully simple and simply beautiful. We are to teach the first principles: faith in the Lord Jesus Christ, repentance, baptism for the remission of sins, and laying on of hands for the gift of the Holy Ghost (Articles of Faith 1:4).

Thursday, 29.—*This day, Emma began to be sick with fever; consequently I kept in the house with her all day.*

Friday, 30.—*Emma is no better. I was with her all day.*

JOSEPH SMITH
HISTORY OF THE CHURCH, 5:166

These excerpts from the Prophet's journal during late September and early October of 1842, concerning the well-being of his beloved Emma, are a testament to Joseph and Emma's strong bond and a clear indication of the Prophet's care and concern for his loved ones:

"*Monday, 3.*—Emma was a little better. I was with her all day.

"*Tuesday, 4.*—Emma is very sick again. I attended with her all the day, being somewhat poorly myself.

"*Wednesday, 5.*— My dear Emma was worse. Many fears were entertained that she would not recover. . . . I was unwell, and much troubled on account of Emma's sickness. . . .

"*Thursday, 6.*—Emma is better. . . . May the Lord speedily raise her to the bosom of her family, that the heart of His servant may be comforted again. Amen. . . .

"*Friday, 7.*—Emma is somewhat better. I am cheerful and well" (*History of the Church*, 5:167–69).

Do away with lightmindedness, and be sober.

JOSEPH SMITH
HISTORY OF THE CHURCH, 6:52

The Lord has said, "Therefore, cease from all your . . .
pride and light-mindedness, and from all your wicked
doings" (D&C 88:121). We should take the things of the
kingdom of God seriously, yet we are to have cheerful,
glad hearts and countenances (D&C 59:15). Because of
the gospel we ought to smile and laugh and look on the
bright side of life, while avoiding idle thoughts and excessive or inappropriate laughter (D&C 88:69). The
Prophet Joseph counseled: "How vain and trifling have
been our spirits, our conferences, our councils, our meet-
ings, our private as well as public conversations—too low,
too mean, too vulgar, too condescending for the dignified characters of the called and chosen of God, according to the purposes of His will, from before the foundation of the world! . . . let honesty, and sobriety, and
candor, and solemnity, and virtue, and pureness, and
meekness, and simplicity crown our heads in every place"
(*History of the Church,* 3:295–96).

Thursday, 8.—At home. I attended on my father with great anxiety.
Friday, 9.—At home. Waited on my father.
Saturday, 10.—At home, and visited the house of my father,
found him failing very fast.

JOSEPH SMITH
HISTORY OF THE CHURCH, 2:289

In October of 1835, the Prophet's personal journal records a poignant entry about his gravely ill father: "*Sunday, 11.*—Waited on my father again, who was very sick. In secret prayer in the morning, the Lord said, 'My servant, thy father shall live.' I waited on him all this day with my heart raised to God in the name of Jesus Christ, that He would restore him to health, that I might be blessed with his company and advice, esteeming it one of the greatest earthly blessings to be blessed with the society of parents, whose mature years and experience render them capable of administering the most wholesome advice" (*History of the Church,* 2:289). Joseph's prayer was answered. Father Smith did recover and continued to serve as an inspired patriarch and later as an assistant counselor to the Prophet Joseph Smith. He died September 14, 1840, in Nauvoo at age sixty-nine.

We do not worship the Prophet. We worship God our Eternal Father and the risen Lord Jesus Christ. But we acknowledge the Prophet; we proclaim him; we respect him; we reverence him as an instrument in the hands of the Almighty.

GORDON B. HINCKLEY
ENSIGN, DECEMBER 2005, 4

The life story of Joseph Smith defies ordinary explanation. His life was a mixture of high adventure and solemn devotion. It was filled with the deep happiness that comes of family and loved ones, the inexpressible joy of moving the work of the Lord forward, the quiet confidence of knowing God is pleased with your efforts (D&C 124:1). He also knew much of heartache and sorrow, suffering and persecution. Ultimately, he sealed his life and testimony with his blood. Then, and now, he has been misunderstood. But he also cannot be discounted or ignored. Even if one doesn't believe him to be a prophet of God, by any standard he was truly remarkable, one of a kind, an authentic religious genius. When you come to know, by the spirit of revelation and faith, that he is God's anointed prophet, your life will never be the same. With this burning conviction, you will respect his name and wish to proclaim it to others. Indeed, we praise and honor the man who communed with the Father and the Son.

*Joseph Smith is naturally a man of strong mental powers,
and is possessed of much energy and decision of character, great
penetration, and a profound knowledge of human nature.*

JOHN M. BERNHISEL
HISTORY OF THE CHURCH, 6:468

John M. Bernhisel, a medical doctor who boarded with
Joseph and Emma Smith for nine months during 1843
and 1844, wrote Illinois governor Thomas Ford on
June 14, 1844: "[Joseph Smith] is a man of calm judgment, enlarged views, and is eminently distinguished by
his love of justice. He is kind and obliging, generous and
benevolent, sociable and cheerful, and is possessed of a
mind of a contemplative and reflective character. He is
honest, frank, fearless and independent. . . . He is a true
lover of his country, and a bright and shining example of
integrity and moral excellence. . . . As a religious teacher,
as well as a man, he is greatly beloved by this people. It is
almost superfluous to add that the numerous ridiculous
and scandalous reports in circulation respecting him have
not the least foundation in truth" (*History of the Church,*
6:468). Bernhisel remained loyal to the restored gospel
throughout his life. He later served as the first congres-
sional delegate for the Utah Territory.

*A man is his own tormentor and his own
condemner. . . .The torment of disappointment in the mind
of man is as exquisite as a lake burning with fire and
brimstone. I say, so is the torment of man.*

JOSEPH SMITH
HISTORY OF THE CHURCH, 6:314

So much of what happens in life is a result of our
own choices. We all make mistakes; we falter and fail
all across the life course. The gospel of Jesus Christ
gives us knowledge, understanding, and a pathway that
we can follow to find joy and peace in this life and
eternal life in the world to come (D&C 59:23). Christ
is our mentor, exemplar, and friend, our greatest
source of comfort, solace, and reassurance. Alma
taught, "And he shall go forth, suffering pains and
afflictions and temptations of every kind; and this that
the word might be fulfilled which saith he will take
upon him the pains and the sicknesses of his people.
And he will take upon him death, that he may loose
the bands of death which bind his people; and he will
take upon him their infirmities, that his bowels may
be filled with mercy, according to the flesh, that he
may know according to the flesh how to succor his
people according to their infirmities" (Alma 7:11–12).

Adam was made to open the way of the world.

Joseph Smith
Teachings, 12

The Latter-day Saint view of the Fall is optimistic and filled with purpose. Adam and Eve went into the Garden of Eden to fall. "Adam fell that men might be," Lehi observed, "and men are, that they might have joy" (2 Nephi 2:25). Their transgression had the approbation of God and was thus not a sin. Elder Orson F. Whitney taught: "The fall had a twofold direction— downward, yet forward. It brought man into the world and set his feet upon progression's highway" (*Cowley,* 287). We do not believe that little children are subject to "original sin" or that human beings are depraved creatures because of the Fall. Being born innocent (D&C 93:38) is being born neither good nor evil but having the potential for both. Yes, we live in a fallen world, and the Fall takes a toll on us all. But the Fall was also a great blessing, for which Adam and Eve rejoiced and praised God (Moses 5:10–12). The Fall was a forward move in the eternal plan of the Father.

*To be justified before God we must love one another:
we must overcome evil; we must visit the fatherless and
the widow in their affliction, and we must keep
ourselves unspotted from the world.*

JOSEPH SMITH
TEACHINGS, 76

Justification is a legal term that signifies the removal of punishment for past sin; being justified establishes our righteous standing before God. Elder D. Todd Christofferson taught, "Pardon comes by the grace of Him who has satisfied the demands of justice by His own suffering, 'the just for the unjust, that he might bring us to God' (1 Pet. 3:18). He removes our condemnation without removing the law. We are pardoned and placed in a condition of righteousness with Him. We become, like Him, without sin. We are sustained and protected by the law, by justice. We are, in a word, *justified.* Thus, we may appropriately speak of one who is justified as pardoned, without sin, or guiltless" (*Ensign,* June 2001, 20). Sanctification is the ongoing work of the Holy Spirit to become clean, pure, and holy. These two, justification and sanctification, "are at the center of God's gracious plan of salvation" (*Ensign,* June 2001, 18).

Let the Saints remember that great things
depend on their individual exertion, and that they are
called to be co-workers with us and the Holy Spirit in
accomplishing the great work of the last days.

JOSEPH SMITH
HISTORY OF THE CHURCH, 4:230

This 1840 exhortation from the Prophet Joseph for unity and love still applies to us today: "Let every selfish feeling be not only buried, but annihilated; and let love to God and man predominate, and reign triumphant in every mind, that [your] hearts may become like unto Enoch's of old, and comprehend all things, present, past and future, and come behind in no gift, waiting for the coming of the Lord Jesus Christ. The work in which we are unitedly engaged is one of no ordinary kind. The enemies we have to contend against are subtle . . . it behooves us to be on the alert to concentrate our energies, and that the best feelings should exist in our midst; and then, by the help of the Almighty, we shall go on from victory to victory, . . . our evil passions will be subdued, our prejudices depart; we shall find no room in our bosoms for hatred; . . . and we shall stand approved in the sight of heaven" (*History of the Church*, 4:230–31).

All your losses will be made up to you in the resurrection, provided you continue faithful. By the vision of the Almighty I have seen it.

JOSEPH SMITH
HISTORY OF THE CHURCH, 5:362

Joseph Smith knew more about disappointment, heartache, and spiritual affliction than most. He knew loss and anguish that shakes one to the core, and he understood that although these things will give us experience and be for our good (D&C 122:7), they're still painful; they hurt. How reassuring to know and never forget that if we remain faithful, if we stand strong in hope and faith, all these hardships and heartbreaks will be made up to us—we will be recompensed and restored, healed and succored, in the glorious resurrection. We must reach out to God. Thank Him in every moment that He loves us enough to permit us to undergo tutorial suffering. Open our hearts in humility and trust and patience. Follow His word, be obedient, and keep the commandments. Understand that in a coming day of peace and rest and joy, all heartache will be healed and all pain will dissolve.

OCTOBER 16

All are subjected to vanity while they travel through the crooked
paths and difficulties which surround them. Where is the man
that is free from vanity? None ever were perfect but Jesus.

JOSEPH SMITH
Teachings, 187

To the question, "And why was [Jesus] perfect?" the
Prophet answered: "Because He was the Son of God,
and had the fullness of the Spirit, and greater power
than any man" (*Teachings,* 188). We are to move toward
perfection, understanding that perfection in its fullness
comes later. Elder Russell M. Nelson said, "Let us do the
best we can and try to improve each day. When our
imperfections appear, we can keep trying to correct
them. We can be more forgiving of flaws in ourselves
and among those we love. We can be comforted and
forbearing. The Lord taught, 'Ye are not able to abide
the presence of God now . . . ; wherefore, continue in
patience until ye are perfected' (D&C 67:13). We need
not be dismayed if our earnest efforts toward perfection
now seem so arduous and endless. Perfection is pending. It can come in full only after the Resurrection and
only through the Lord. It awaits all who love him and
keep his commandments" (*Ensign,* November 1995, 86).

*Knowledge is power; and the man who has the
most knowledge has the greatest power.*

JOSEPH SMITH
HISTORY OF THE CHURCH, 5:392

The great missionary Ammon was asked a question
of King Lamoni: "Art thou sent from God?" Ammon
answered, "I am a man; and man in the beginning was
created after the image of God, and I am called by his
Holy Spirit to teach these things unto this people, that
they may be brought to a knowledge of that which is
just and true; and a portion of that Spirit dwelleth in
me, which giveth me knowledge, and also power
according to my faith and desires which are in God"
(Alma 18:33–35). Ammon then proceeded to teach the
king of the Creation and Fall and plan of redemption,
he laid before him the scriptures and spoke of the
words of the prophets, he told of his family history,
and he taught him concerning the coming of Jesus
Christ. The king believed all his words (Alma
18:36–40). Ammon had great power because he had
great knowledge and great faith. He had great power
because of his righteous desires and humble heart.

*Shall we not go on in so great a cause? Go forward
and not backward. Courage, brethren; and on, on to the victory!
Let your hearts rejoice, and be exceedingly glad.*

JOSEPH SMITH
DOCTRINE AND COVENANTS 128:22

Joseph Smith, who was so well acquainted with trial and heartache, was a man of optimism and joyful expectation. He rejoiced that the gospel restoration would roll forth and fill the earth: "Let the earth break forth into singing. Let the dead speak forth anthems of eternal praise to the King Immanuel. . . . Let the mountains shout for joy, and all ye valleys cry aloud; and all ye seas and dry lands tell the wonders of your Eternal King! And ye rivers, and brooks, and rills, flow down with gladness. Let the woods and all the trees of the field praise the Lord; and ye solid rocks weep for joy! And let the sun, moon, and the morning stars sing together, and let all the sons of God shout for joy! And let the eternal creations declare his name forever and ever! And again I say, how glorious is the voice we hear from heaven, proclaiming in our ears, glory, and salvation, and honor, and immortality, and eternal life; kingdoms, principalities, and powers!" (D&C 128:22–23).

Let us cheerfully do all things that lie in our power;
and then may we stand still, with the utmost assurance, to see
the salvation of God, and for his arm to be revealed.

JOSEPH SMITH
DOCTRINE AND COVENANTS 123:17

While incarcerated illegally in Liberty, Missouri, the Prophet Joseph offered encouragement and good cheer to the Saints. His counsel in that dark hour applies to members of the Church today. We are to trust the purposes of God, be patient, hope on, and wait to see the salvation of God. In the meantime, we can do our part by flooding the earth with the Book of Mormon, by sharing gospel truth with others, by being good neighbors and good friends, by striving in our daily walk and talk to be "an example of the believers, in word, in conversation, in charity, in spirit, in faith, in purity" (1 Timothy 4:12). Our small and sincere efforts can produce miraculous results.

*I was in their hands, as a prisoner, about six months; but not-
withstanding their determination to destroy me, . . . yet through
the mercy of God, in answer to the prayers of the Saints, I have
been preserved and delivered out of their hands.*

JOSEPH SMITH
HISTORY OF THE CHURCH, 3:328

While imprisoned in Liberty Jail and awaiting trial
on trumped up charges, Joseph was informed that he
and his companions "were sentenced to be shot, without the least shadow of the law . . . , and had the time
and place appointed for that purpose" (*History of the
Church,* 3:328). But the Lord is ever mindful of His followers. Joseph and his companions believed they were
delivered by divine intervention. Joseph echoed the
apostle Paul as he wrote shortly after his deliverance:
"Although the heathen raged, and the people imagined
vain things, yet the Lord of Hosts, the God of Jacob was
my refuge; and when I cried unto Him in the day of
trouble, He delivered me; for which I call upon my soul,
and all that is within me, to bless and praise His holy
name. For although I was 'troubled on every side, yet [I
was] not distressed; perplexed, but not in despair; persecuted, but not forsaken; cast down, but not destroyed'
[see 2 Corinthians 4:8–9]" (*History of the Church,* 3:329).

The cause of God is one common cause, in which the Saints are alike all interested; we are all members of the one common body, and all partake of the same spirit, and are baptized into one baptism and possess alike the same glorious hope.

JOSEPH SMITH
HISTORY OF THE CHURCH, 4:609

We are all in this together, and we all need each other. We have a common cause in which we ought to be anxiously engaged, and that is to build up Zion, save ourselves and our families, and once again live with God and Christ in eternal felicity. We who have entered a covenant with Christ are a congregation of equals—we exercise faith in the Father and Son and everlasting principles of truth, we rely on the merits and mercy of our Savior and Redeemer, we possess the same glorious hope of eternal life. We are brothers and sisters because we not only share the same eternal parentage, but we are all members of "the one common body, and all partake of the same spirit" (*History of the Church,* 4:609). Indeed, we are fellow-citizens in the household of God.

I called to see Cousin Joseph. He gave me a Book of Mormon, shook hands with me, and said, "Preach short sermons, make short prayers, and deliver your sermons with a prayerful heart."

GEORGE A. SMITH
IN *JOSEPH SMITH*, 332

George A. Smith was Joseph Smith's first cousin, and before he left for a mission in 1835 he visited with the Prophet for counsel and direction. Joseph advised him to not be loquacious but to teach the simple truths of the gospel with a meek and humble heart. On another occasion, the Prophet said: "I spoke and explained concerning the uselessness of preaching to the world about great judgments, but rather to preach the simple Gospel" (*History of the Church,* 4:11). Missionaries who are sent forth to teach need not preach the exciting but secondary principles of the gospel, but rather should focus on primary doctrines, the core principles and beliefs of the Church. We need not spend time on the controversial or esoteric, but concentrate our energies and teaching on fundamental truths. A sermon or prayer to be meaningful and heartfelt need not be long or impressive in language. We should focus on core doctrines and do so with a humble, prayerful heart.

*We would wish the Saints to understand that,
when they come here, they must not expect perfection, or that
all will be harmony, peace, and love; if they indulge these
ideas, they will undoubtedly be deceived.*

JOSEPH SMITH
HISTORY OF THE CHURCH, 4:272

From the early days of the Church to now, many have gathered to Zion from various parts of the world at great personal travail and sacrifice. With high hopes and great expectations, some new members of the Church gather to the kingdom of God on earth and expect that they have come to the end of their troubles and are gathering with perfected Saints. But long-time members are just like new members—imperfect people trying to overcome the world and become true Saints of God. It is a safeguard against deception to know that true believers with strong testimonies and righteous desires also are striving to put off the natural man (Mosiah 3:19). It is a sign of immaturity and lack of understanding to think that the Saints are perfect people with no problems or struggles. That's not the reality of our mortal probation. True Saints of God, all in process of becoming, gather to wards and stakes in a spirit of harmony and humility, of peace and patience, of love and longsuffering.

The servants of the Lord are required to guard against those things that are calculated to do the most evil. The little foxes spoil the vines—little evils do the most injury to the Church.

JOSEPH SMITH
TEACHINGS, 258

The forces of evil oppose every good and virtuous effort. The Prophet Joseph wisely observed, "When I do the best I can—when I am accomplishing the greatest good, then the most evils and wicked surmisings are got up against me. I would to God that you would be wise. I now counsel you, that if you know anything calculated to disturb the peace or injure the feelings of your brother or sister, hold your tongues and the least harm will be done" (*Teachings,* 259). It's often the little things, the little evils, that do the most damage. A little rumor is spread, a morsel of gossip is shared; a small sin and tiny transgression seem so insignificant and unimportant. Also, the adversary of righteousness would like us to enlarge perceived offenses and focus on the small slights and shortcomings of fellow members of the Church. These "little foxes" will surely spoil the Spirit and harden the heart.

OCTOBER 25

*There are mansions for those who obey a celestial
law, and there are other mansions for those who come short
of the law, every man in his own order.*

JOSEPH SMITH
HISTORY OF THE CHURCH, 6:365

The revelations in the Doctrine and Covenants help
us understand the nature of life after death. The Savior
taught, "In my Father's house are many mansions" (John
14:2). The Prophet Joseph explained that "mansions"
may be understood to mean "kingdoms"—those kingdoms in which we will dwell in the next life. We will
receive our just reward and will live in a degree of glory in
the life after this according to the eternal laws we have
obeyed in mortality. "For he who is not able to abide the
law of a celestial kingdom cannot abide a celestial glory"
(D&C 88:22). The same holds true for the terrestrial
and telestial kingdoms (D&C 88:23–24). As the Prophet
was laboring on his translation of the Bible in Hiram,
Ohio, he received a vision later recorded as Doctrine and
Covenants 76. This remarkable revelation sheds further
light on the plan of salvation and provides a comparison
of the three degrees of glory: the celestial, terrestrial, and
telestial kingdoms and who shall inherit each.

OCTOBER 26

*What constitutes the kingdom of God? Where there is
a prophet, a priest, or a righteous man unto whom God gives
His oracles . . . and where the oracles of God are not,
there the kingdom of God is not.*

JOSEPH SMITH
TEACHINGS, 271–72

Prefacing remarks on the subject of the kingdom of
God on earth, the Prophet Joseph said, "Now I will
give my testimony. I care not for man. I speak boldly
and faithfully and with authority" (*Teachings,* 271).
Joseph Smith was fearless in proclaiming the gospel
restored and the establishment anew of the kingdom
of God on the earth—which kingdom exists wherever
the priesthood of God is. In the meridian dispensation, Jesus set up the kingdom of God on earth, called
and ordained apostles, established His church, and
bestowed priesthood authority (Matthew 16:19; see
also John 15:16). After a great apostasy removed
priesthood keys and power from the earth, the authority to reestablish the kingdom of God on the earth was
given to the Prophet Joseph (D&C 65:2, 5–6). The
kingdom of God on the earth is the stone spoken of
by Daniel that would roll forth to fill the earth and
never be destroyed (Daniel 2:34–45).

*When the Savior shall appear we shall see him as he is.
We shall see that he is a man like ourselves.*

JOSEPH SMITH
DOCTRINE AND COVENANTS 130:1

When the resurrected Christ ascended into heaven, two angels stood by testifying to the Twelve who were with him, "Ye men of Galilee, why stand ye gazing up into heaven? this same Jesus, which is taken up from you into heaven, shall so come in like manner as ye have seen him go into heaven" (Acts 1:11). It was a flesh and bones man, with body, parts, and passions who ascended into heaven that day, a man with whom they had walked and talked, a man whom they knew well. The Prophet Joseph taught, "The Father has a body of flesh and bones as tangible as man's; the Son also" (D&C 130:22), and he further observed, "That which is without body, parts and passions is nothing. There is no other God in heaven but that God who has flesh and bones" (*Teachings*, 181). The mission of Joseph Smith was to reveal God anew to man. He opened the heavens to the world and restored the everlasting truths of the gospel.

*Salvation is nothing more nor less than to triumph over
all our enemies and put them under our feet.*

JOSEPH SMITH
TEACHINGS, 297

We gain salvation as we win the victory over our enemies. President Ezra Taft Benson said: "Let your minds be filled with the goal of being like the Lord, and you will crowd out depressing thoughts as you anxiously seek to know him and do his will. 'Let this mind be in you,' said Paul. (Philip. 2:5.) 'Look unto me in every thought,' said Jesus. (D&C 6:36.). . . . We can rise above the enemies of despair, depression, discouragement, and despondency by remembering that God provides righteous alternatives. . . . Yes, life is a test; it is a probation; and perhaps being away from our heavenly home we feel sometimes, as holy men in the past have felt, that 'they were strangers and pilgrims on the earth.' (See D&C 45:13.) . . . To lift our spirit and send us on our way rejoicing, the devil's designs . . . can be defeated in a dozen ways, namely: repentance, prayer, service, work, health, reading, blessings, fasting, friends, music, endurance, and goals" (*Ensign*, November 1974, 67).

For there are many yet on the earth among all sects, parties, and denominations, who are blinded by the subtle craftiness of men, whereby they lie in wait to deceive, and who are only kept from the truth because they know not where to find it.

JOSEPH SMITH
DOCTRINE AND COVENANTS 123:12

There are so many people who are seeking truth. They know by the Spirit of God that there is a Heavenly Father, that they are His children and were created in His image. Many look for something more than power, possessions, and prestige; they desire for more than the mundane matters of this workaday world. So many have been blinded by the enticements of the world and the vainness, frailties, and foolishness of man (2 Nephi 9:28); they have been deceived by the lies and distortions perpetrated by the dark enemies of light. They wander the earth searching for the word of God, and they know not where to find it (Amos 8:11–12). But thanks be to God—the glorious restoration of the fulness of the gospel makes available the truths that the honest in heart seek, and it provides the necessary keys, powers, and authority to establish anew the kingdom of God on the earth.

Let all the saints rejoice, therefore, and be exceedingly glad; for Israel's God is their God, and he will mete out a just recompense of reward upon the heads of all their oppressors.

JOSEPH SMITH
DOCTRINE AND COVENANTS 127:3

On this day in 1838 vigilantes attacked Haun's Mill, killing seventeen innocent men and boys and wounding fourteen more. Then as now, dark clouds of trouble may become increasingly ominous, but good will always triumph over evil. Joseph Smith, who understood the eternal order of heaven, had a heart filled with gladness and rejoicing even in the midst of persecution. On one occasion he said, "I shall triumph over my enemies: I have begun to triumph over them at home, and I shall do it abroad. All those that rise up against me will surely feel the weight of their iniquity upon their own heads. Those that speak evil of me and the Saints are ignorant or abominable characters, and full of iniquity. All the fuss, and all the stir, and all the charges got up against me are like the jack-a-lantern, which cannot be found" (*Teachings*, 258). Just as sure as the light of the Lord chases away darkness, those who oppose the work of God and persecute the righteous will receive their just reward.

*As for the perils which I am called to pass through, they
seem but a small thing to me, as the envy and wrath of man have
been my common lot all the days of my life.*

JOSEPH SMITH
DOCTRINE AND COVENANTS 127:2

Joseph Smith experienced nearly constant harassment, hounding, and persecution, yet he remained sanguine. With the confidence born of trust in the Lord, he said, "Deep water is what I am wont to swim in. It all has become a second nature to me; and I feel, like Paul, to glory in tribulation; for to this day has the God of my fathers delivered me out of them all, and will deliver me from henceforth; for behold, and lo, I shall triumph over all my enemies, for the Lord God hath spoken it" (D&C 127:2). The Prophet knew that the work of the Lord would not fail, and he knew he was an instrument in the hands of God. He declared, "Every man who has a calling to minister to the inhabitants of the world was ordained to that very purpose in the Grand Council of heaven before this world was. I suppose that I was ordained to this very office in that Grand Council" (*History of the Church,* 6:364).

NOVEMBER

~

*Faith is not only the principle
of action, but of power.*
JOSEPH SMITH

And the voice of warning shall be unto all people, by the mouths
of my disciples, whom I have chosen in these last days.

DOCTRINE AND COVENANTS 1:4

On this day in 1831, the chosen seer Joseph Smith received the "Lord's Preface" to the doctrines, covenants, and commandments given in this dispensation, now known as Doctrine and Covenants 1. The voice of warning is sounded today by the Lord's prophets and apostles: "And the arm of the Lord shall be revealed; and the day cometh that they who will not hear the voice of the Lord, neither the voice of his servants, neither give heed to the words of the prophets and apostles, shall be cut off from among the people" (D&C 1:14). When the prophets speak as moved upon by the Holy Ghost, they speak for the Lord: "What I the Lord have spoken, I have spoken, and I excuse not myself; and though the heavens and the earth pass away, my word shall not pass away, but shall all be fulfilled, whether by mine own voice or by the voice of my servants, it is the same" (D&C 1:38; see also D&C 68:2–4).

[God] never will institute an ordinance or give a commandment to His people that is not calculated in its nature to promote that happiness which He has designed.

JOSEPH SMITH
HISTORY OF THE CHURCH, 5:135

God's commandments are designed to help us become like Him. Elder Joseph B. Wirthlin said, "Because your Heavenly Father is perfect, you can have complete faith in Him. You can trust Him. You can keep His commandments by continually striving to do so. . . . God's commandments are not given to limit or punish us. They are exercises that create character and sanctify souls. If we disregard them, we become spiritually flabby and weak and without defense. If we keep them, we can become spiritual giants, strong and bold in righteousness. Do you take the time each day to review your day's events with your Heavenly Father? Do you express to Him the desires of your heart and your gratitude for the blessings He pours out upon you? Day-to-day obedience to God's commandments is indispensable, and it protects us during mortality and prepares us for the tremendous adventure that awaits us on the other side of the veil" (*Ensign,* November 1999, 40).

Many . . . dishonor themselves and the Church,
and bring persecution swiftly upon us, in consequence
of their zeal without knowledge.

JOSEPH SMITH
HISTORY OF THE CHURCH, 2:394

Some of us have a burning testimony of the gospel but at the same time hope no one asks us questions about our doctrine. We have the fervency of truth beating in our hearts but are afraid or unprepared to explain the principles of the gospel. We have the zeal but are not confident in our knowledge. This zeal causes us to sometimes keep quiet when our voices need to be heard, and it might cause us to say the wrong things or confuse rather than enlighten. Joseph Smith said, "Many, having a zeal not according to knowledge, and not understanding the pure principles of the doctrine of the Church, have, no doubt, in the heat of enthusiasm, taught and said many things which were derogatory to the genuine character and principles of the Church; and for these things we are heartily sorry, and would apologize, if apology would do any good" (*History of the Church,* 2:255). We need to gain confidence in answering questions and blessing others with our gospel understanding and testimonies.

*A religion that does not require the sacrifice
of all things never has power sufficient to produce the
faith necessary unto life and salvation.*

JOSEPH SMITH
LECTURES ON FAITH, 6:7

The principle and practice of personal sacrifice is
both a rich legacy and a mandate for us today. Joseph
Smith taught: "From the first existence of man, the
faith necessary unto the enjoyment of life and salvation never could be obtained without the sacrifice of
all earthly things. It was through this sacrifice, and this
only, that God has ordained that men should enjoy
eternal life; and it is through the medium of the
sacrifice of all earthly things that men do actually
know that they are doing the things that are well
pleasing in the sight of God. When a man has offered
in sacrifice all that he has for the truth's sake, not
even withholding his life, and believing before God
that he has been called to make this sacrifice because
he seeks to do his will, he does know, most assuredly,
that God does and will accept his sacrifice and offering, and that he has not, nor will not seek his face in
vain" (*Lectures on Faith,* 6:7).

*I bear witness to the world today that more than
a century and a half ago the iron ceiling was shattered;
the heavens were once again opened, and since that
time revelations have been continuous.*

SPENCER W. KIMBALL
ENSIGN, MAY 1977, 77

President Spencer W. Kimball, who passed away on this day in 1985, added his eloquent testimony of the Prophet Joseph: "That new day dawned when another soul with passionate yearning prayed for divine guidance. A spot of hidden solitude was found, knees were bent, a heart was humbled, pleadings were voiced, and a light brighter than the noonday sun illuminated the world— the curtain never to be closed again. A young lad . . . , Joseph Smith, of incomparable faith, broke the spell, shattered the 'heavens of iron' and reestablished communication. Heaven kissed the earth, light dissipated the darkness, and God again spoke to man, revealing anew 'his secret unto his servants the prophets' (Amos 3:7.) A new prophet was in the land and through him God set up his kingdom, never to be destroyed nor left to another people—a kingdom that will stand forever. . . . Never again will God be hidden from his children on the earth. Revelation is here to remain" (*Ensign,* May 1977, 77).

*Let us be wise in all things, and keep all the commandments
of God, that our salvation may be sure. Having our armor ready
and prepared against the time appointed and having on the whole
armor of righteousness, we may be able to stand in that trying day.*

JOSEPH SMITH
JOSEPH SMITH, 255

The Lord declares in His preface to our compilation
of modern revelation, "Prepare ye, prepare ye for that
which is to come, for the Lord is nigh" (D&C 1:12)
We do not need to live in fear of that which is to come
if we are wise, if we strive to keep the commandments
of God, if we are shielded with the armor of righteousness (D&C 38:30). "Wherefore," the Savior tells
us, "be faithful, praying always, having your lamps
trimmed and burning, and oil with you, that you may
be ready at the coming of the Bridegroom—For
behold, verily, verily, I say unto you, that I come
quickly" (D&C 33:17–18). The Lord's triumphant
return will be a great day of joy to those who are prepared and ready; it will be a terrible day of terror for
the wicked and ungodly. Let us prepare and be faithful so that we are ready for the coming of the
Bridegroom.

The love the saints had for him was inexpressible.
They would willingly have laid down their lives for him. If he
was to talk, every task would be laid aside that they might
listen to his words. He was not an ordinary man.

MARY ALICE CANNON LAMBERT
IN *JOSEPH SMITH,* 498

Mary Alice Cannon Lambert, an English convert
who emigrated to Nauvoo in 1843, lived through the
trauma of the persecutions and martyrdom of the
Prophet Joseph and journeyed with the Saints in the
westward exodus. Mary Alice recognized the Prophet
the moment she saw him and from then on never
doubted his prophetic calling: "I first saw Joseph Smith
in the Spring of 1843. When the boat in which we came
up the Mississippi River reached the landing at Nauvoo,
several of the leading brethren were there to meet the
company of saints that had come on it. Among those
brethren was the Prophet Joseph Smith. I knew him
the instant my eyes rested upon him, and at that
moment I received my testimony that he was a Prophet
of God. . . . He was not pointed out to me. I knew him
from all the other men, and, child that I was (I was only
fourteen) I knew that I saw a Prophet of God" (in
Joseph Smith, 496).

Live in strict obedience to the commandments of God, and walk humbly before Him, and He will exalt thee in His own due time.

JOSEPH SMITH
HISTORY OF THE CHURCH, 1:408

God gives laws to His children because of His love for us (John 14:21) and because He knows that those who learn humility and obedience will be blessed. Joseph Smith taught the following in 1843, later recorded in Doctrine and Covenants 130:20–21: "There is a law, irrevocably decreed in heaven before the foundations of this world, upon which all blessings are predicated—and when we obtain any blessing from God, it is by obedience to that law upon which it is predicated." On another occasion the Lord revealed to the Prophet that if we do what the Lord says and keep His commandments, we are bound by a covenant and promised the blessing (D&C 82:10). God's blessings—large and small—are given to those who keep the first law of heaven: obedience. Some blessings come soon, some come later, but they surely come to those who humbly obey.

Joseph Smith is a great man, a man of principle, a straight forward man; no saintish long-faced fellow, but quite the reverse. Indeed some stumble because he is such a straight forward, plain spoken, cheerful man, but that makes me love him the more.

JOHN NEEDHAM
IN *JOSEPH SMITH*, 498

Many are the testimonies, like that of early English convert John Needham, of those who knew well the Prophet Joseph. Their statements of his disposition and personality give us a glimpse into what he was like and what it must have been like to associate with him. Those who knew him best, who had a fervent testimony of his principled character and prophetic mission, loved him and sustained him throughout their lives. Others, of course, through envy and resentment let enmity enter their hearts. One is struck with the Prophet's humanity, his down-to-earth temperament, his straightforwardness and cheerfulness. Some were disappointed as they expected a somber, kingly prophet who issued resonant pronouncements with the air of godly authority. So many others, impressed by his humanness and goodness, were drawn to him and stood with him all their lives. Although we know not the Prophet Joseph personally, we too can stand with him and sustain him today.

No month ever found me more busily engaged than November;
but as my life consisted of activity and unyielding exertions, I
made this my rule: When the Lord commands, do it.

JOSEPH SMITH
HISTORY OF THE CHURCH, 2:170

In November of 1834, twenty-eight-year-old Joseph Smith was leading the expanding Church and gathering the Saints in Kirtland, continuing to receive revelations, and building a temple wherein they would "be endowed with power from on high" (D&C 38:32). All this in addition to the personal challenges of striving to be a dedicated husband and father. It's difficult to imagine the countless pressures that the Prophet must have experienced throughout his life. The demands on his time and attention were relentless and never-ending. We can learn from his example: make every effort to put first things first, without hesitation obey the commands of God and walk humbly before Him, and be anxiously engaged in worthy causes (D&C 58:27). We will be blessed as we do what the Lord commands.

Salvation could not come to the world without the mediation of Jesus Christ.

JOSEPH SMITH
HISTORY OF THE CHURCH, 5:555

W hat are the fundamental principles of your religion?" To this question, Joseph answered: "The fundamental principles of our religion are the testimony of the Apostles and Prophets, concerning Jesus Christ, that He died, was buried, and rose again the third day, and ascended into heaven; and all other things which pertain to our religion are only appendages to it" (*Teachings*, 121). The Atonement is the most important event that has ever occurred: "For it is expedient that an atonement should be made; for according to the great plan of the Eternal God there must be an atonement made, or else all mankind must unavoidably perish; . . . yea, all are fallen and are lost, and must perish except it be through the atonement" (Alma 34:9). Jesus Christ "came into the world . . . to be crucified for the world, and to bear the sins of the world, and to sanctify the world, and to cleanse it from all unrighteousness; that through him all might be saved" (D&C 76:41–42).

*The history of Joseph Smith was written to share the story
of the Restoration of the Church in these latter days. The essence
of the story is a demonstration of trust in the promises of the Lord,
and a source of joy and certainty for all those who believe.*

CARLOS H. AMADO
LIAHONA, JULY 2002, 89

The history of Joseph Smith, as contained in The Pearl of Great Price, is a treasure worth reading and seriously pondering anew. Elder Carlos H. Amado of the Seventy said: "I have been able to read it many times and in different circumstances. It impressed me as a child; it was a guide and source of strength when I was a teenager; I shared it with courage and enthusiasm as a young missionary; and even now it continues to fill me with astonishment and a deep sense of gratitude. Since Joseph Smith first recorded it, it remains as a blessing and a gift of faith, a legacy, for the sincere believer; it is an open invitation for those who look for the truth, and a permanent challenge to the unbeliever. For those who are not yet members of the Church, I suggest you read the testimony of Joseph Smith with an open mind and real intent. You will feel his sincerity, and you will discover the establishment of the Church, restored in a miraculous way!" (*Liahona,* July 2002, 89).

*As a child I knew the Prophet Joseph Smith.
As a child I have listened to him preach the gospel that
God had committed to his charge and care.*

JOSEPH F. SMITH
GOSPEL DOCTRINE, 493

Joseph F. Smith, son of Hyrum, nephew of the Prophet Joseph, and sixth President of the Church, was born on this day in 1838 in Far West, Missouri. He was the last President of the Church who was personally acquainted with the Prophet. He said: "As a child I was [as] familiar in his home, in his household, as I was familiar under my own father's roof. I have retained the witness of the Spirit that I was imbued with, as a child, and that I received from my sainted mother, the firm belief that Joseph Smith was a prophet of God; that he was inspired as no other man in his generation, or for centuries before, had been inspired; that he had been chosen of God to lay the foundations of God's Kingdom" (*Gospel Doctrine*, 493). During his life and throughout the nations of the world, Joseph F. Smith bore strong testimony of the prophetic mission of Joseph Smith.

*Jesus Christ never did reveal to any man the precise time
that He would come. Go and read the Scriptures, and you cannot
find anything that specifies the exact hour He would come;
and all that say so are false teachers.*

JOSEPH SMITH
HISTORY OF THE CHURCH, 6:254

False teachers among us continue to calculate and proclaim the specified hour of the Lord's triumphant return. They do not know; their declarations are mistaken, and we cannot trust them. The Lord said, "I, the Lord God, have spoken it; but the hour and the day no man knoweth, neither the angels in heaven, nor shall they know until he comes" (D&C 49:7; see also Matthew 24:36, Mark 13:32), and "But of that day, and hour, no one knoweth; no, not the angels of God in heaven, but my Father only" (Joseph Smith—Matthew 1:40). Those who are wise will reject the false preachers and prognosticators, no matter how persuasive and compelling their arguments, and look only to the Lord, who said, "Watch therefore, for ye know neither the day nor the hour wherein the Son of man cometh" (Matthew 25:13; see also D&C 133:11). If we trust the Lord and follow His authorized apostles and prophets, we will stay the course and not be led astray.

*If I esteem mankind to be in error, shall I bear
them down? No. I will lift them up.*

JOSEPH SMITH
HISTORY OF THE CHURCH, 5:499

All about us are people in error. It may be the innocent error of misinformation or ignorance, or it may
be the error of sin and wickedness. Either way, all of
us—to one degree or another—walk in error. We have
a duty to reach out with a sincere and earnest regard
for all the sons and daughters of God to enlighten, lift,
and inspire them. If people are weighed down in erroneous notions and false ideas, do we just let them
alone because we don't want to get involved or it's not
worth the effort? Or do we have a genuine interest in
being an instrument in the hands of God to extend
helping and healing to others. So many are carrying
heavy burdens, overwhelmed with discouragement
and heartache—let us be among those who boost and
bless others with kindness and encouragement. The
world needs our light of truth, it needs the light of the
gospel, and it needs the light of love and
understanding.

NOVEMBER 16

Come, listen to a prophet's voice,
And hear the word of God,
And in the way of truth rejoice,
And sing for joy aloud.

JOSEPH S. MURDOCK
HYMNS, NO. 21

The beloved Latter-day Saint hymn "Come, Listen to a Prophet's Voice" is an invitation to seek truth. It was written by Joseph S. Murdock (1822–1899), who arrived in the Salt Lake Valley in 1847 with the pioneer exodus. He was a contemporary of Joseph Smith, and the hymn rings with a heartfelt expression of devotion and love for the Prophet:

We've found the way the prophets went
Who lived in days of yore.
Another prophet now is sent
This knowledge to restore. (Hymns, *no. 21*)

The first three verses of the hymn appeared in the 1843 Latter-day Saint periodical *Times and Seasons*, which was published in Nauvoo from 1840 to 1846. Joseph S. Murdock would go on to live a long life of great faithfulness to the restored gospel, including serving as the first bishop in Wasatch County, Utah.

Be aware of those prejudices which sometimes so strangely present themselves . . . against our friends . . . who choose to differ from us in opinion and in matters of faith. Our religion is between us and our God. Their religion is between them and their God.

JOSEPH SMITH
HISTORY OF THE CHURCH, 3:303–4

The Savior taught us a golden rule: "Therefore all things whatsoever ye would that men should do to you, do ye even so to them: for this is the law and the prophets" (Matthew 7:12). We must beware our prejudices and treat all people and their beliefs with the same respect we expect for ours. The Lord commanded the Prophet Joseph to "study and learn, and become acquainted with all good books, and with languages, tongues, and people" (D&C 90:15). We are to learn of other people, appreciate their viewpoints, and, at the same time, share gospel truth with the world: "[The Lord] inviteth them all to come unto him and partake of his goodness; and he denieth none that come unto him, black and white, bond and free, male and female; and he remembereth the heathen; and all are alike unto God, both Jew and Gentile" (2 Nephi 26:33; see also vv. 26–32). We must practice the Golden Rule in our attitudes and actions with all the children of God.

NOVEMBER 18

*No man is a minister of Jesus Christ without being a
Prophet. No man can be a minister of Jesus Christ except he has
the testimony of Jesus; and this is the spirit of prophecy.*

JOSEPH SMITH
HISTORY OF THE CHURCH, 3:389

The testimony of Jesus is the spirit of prophecy
(Revelation 19:10). Paul taught: "No man can say
that Jesus is the Lord, but by the Holy Ghost"
(1 Corinthians 12:3). The Prophet Joseph observed, "If
any person should ask me if I were a prophet, I should
not deny it, as that would give me the lie; for, according to John, the testimony of Jesus is the spirit of
prophecy; therefore, if I profess to be a witness or
teacher, and have not the spirit of prophecy, which is
the testimony of Jesus, I must be a false witness; but
if I be a true teacher and witness, I must possess the
spirit of prophecy, and that constitutes a prophet; and
any man who says he is a teacher or preacher of righteousness, and denies the spirit of prophecy, is a liar,
and the truth is not in him; and by this key false teachers and impostors may be detected" (*History of the
Church,* 5:215-16).

I beheld the celestial kingdom of God. . . . I saw the transcendent beauty of the gate through which the heirs of that kingdom will enter, which was like unto circling flames of fire; Also the blazing throne of God, whereon was seated the Father and the Son.

JOSEPH SMITH
DOCTRINE AND COVENANTS 137:1–3

Consisting of only ten verses, Doctrine and Covenants 137 is one of the most significant revelations in our scriptural canon. Joseph Smith's remarkable vision transcends normal mortal experience. In it is revealed the doctrinal foundation of vicarious work in behalf of our kindred dead. The Prophet was shown things as they yet would be in the celestial kingdom. He saw in the celestial kingdom his father and mother who were still alive in 1836 when he received the vision, he saw his beloved brother Alvin who had died on this day in 1823, and he learned the sacred truth: "All who have died without a knowledge of this gospel, who would have received it if they had been permitted to tarry, shall be heirs of the celestial kingdom of God; also all that shall die henceforth without a knowledge of it, who would have received it with all their hearts, shall be heirs of that kingdom; for I, the Lord, will judge all men according to their works, according to the desire of their hearts" (D&C 137:7–9).

Faith is not only the principle of action, but of power.

JOSEPH SMITH
LECTURES ON FAITH, 1:13

Faith is the first principle of the gospel, the moving cause of all action, and the great governing power of the universe. That's the macro level of faith. On the micro and personal level, faith is also the great principle of action and power. It is so much more than positive thinking. Miracles of peace and joy can be wrought if we center our faith in a correct belief in God and His Son. Joseph Smith instructed the School of the Elders that "three things are necessary in order that any rational and intelligent being may exercise faith in God unto life and salvation. First, the idea that he actually exists. Secondly, a *correct* idea of his character, perfections, and attributes. Thirdly, an actual knowledge that the course of life which he is pursuing is according to his will. For without an acquaintance with these three important facts, the faith of every rational being must be imperfect and unproductive; but with this understanding it can become perfect and fruitful" (*Lectures on Faith*, 3:2–5).

*Spent this day at home, endeavoring to treasure up knowledge
for the benefit of my calling. . . . At home. Continued my studies.
O may God give me learning, even language; and endue me with
qualifications to magnify His name while I live.*

JOSEPH SMITH
HISTORY OF THE CHURCH, 2:344

How many of us, overwhelmed with the challenges
and busyness of life, have felt ill-equipped to function
fully in a Church calling or fulfill our responsibilities as
parents. We're so busy living, running from one event or
activity to another, that we feel as if we seldom have
"downtime." But a lesson from the life of Joseph Smith is
instructive. The demands on his time and the unrelenting pressures and stresses must have been daunting—but
he still *made* time for pausing a while to ponder, read,
study, and pray. He knew that he wouldn't be able to fill
anyone else's well if he himself was empty; he would be
unable to enlighten others with knowledge and wisdom
if he had not paid the price to enlighten his own mind
and heart. We can give out only what we are filled with.
We need time to recharge our batteries and expand our
souls. A moment's pause from the hustle and bustle of
life can help us feel refreshed, rejuvenated, and more
determined to take on the challenges of the day.

*Men have to suffer that they may come upon Mount
Zion and be exalted above the heavens.*

JOSEPH SMITH
HISTORY OF THE CHURCH, 5:556

The Prophet Joseph wrote from the crucible of Liberty Jail after receiving letters from his loved ones: "We need not say to you that the floodgates of our hearts were lifted and our eyes were a fountain of tears, but those who have not been enclosed in the walls of prison without cause or provocation, can have but little idea how sweet the voice of a friend is; one token of friendship from any source whatever awakens and calls into action every sympathetic feeling . . . until finally all enmity, malice and hatred, and past differences, misunderstandings and mismanagements are slain victorious at the feet of hope; and when the heart is sufficiently contrite, then the voice of inspiration steals along and whispers, 'My son, peace be unto thy soul; thine adversity and thine afflictions shall be but a small moment; and then if thou endure it well, God shall exalt thee on high; thou shalt triumph over all thy foes'" (*History of the Church*, 3:293; last portion of paragraph later canonized in D&C 121:7–8).

*For it is necessary in the ushering in of the dispensation of
the fulness of times . . . that a whole and complete and perfect
union, and welding together of dispensations, and keys,
and powers, and glories should take place.*

DOCTRINE AND COVENANTS 128:18

This is the last and greatest of all dispensations of the gospel. The rivers of past dispensations flow into this final dispensation of the fulness of times. Elder Russell M. Nelson said, "Each prophet had a divine commission to teach of the divinity and the doctrine of the Lord Jesus Christ. In each age these teachings were meant to help the people. But their disobedience resulted in apostasy. Thus, all previous dispensations were limited in time and location. They were limited in time because each ended in apostasy. They were limited in location to a relatively small segment of planet earth. Thus a complete restoration was required. God the Father and Jesus Christ called upon the Prophet Joseph Smith to be the prophet of this dispensation. All divine powers of previous dispensations were to be restored through him. This dispensation of the fulness of times would not be limited in time or in location. It would not end in apostasy, and it would fill the world" (*Ensign,* November 2006, 79–80).

The earth will be smitten with a curse unless there is a welding link of some kind or other between the fathers and the children. . . . For we without them cannot be made perfect; neither can they without us be made perfect.

JOSEPH SMITH
DOCTRINE AND COVENANTS 128:18

Speaking of the great work of providing the saving ordinances for our kindred dead, President James E. Faust said: "Temple work is essential for both us and our kindred dead who are waiting for these saving ordinances. . . . They need the saving ordinances, and we need to be sealed to them. For this reason it is important that we trace our family lines so that no one is left out. Searching for our kindred dead isn't just a hobby. It is a fundamental responsibility for all members of the Church. . . . We believe that our deceased ancestors can . . . be eternally united with their families when we make covenants in their behalf in the temples. Our deceased forebears may accept these covenants, if they choose to do so, in the spirit world. . . . To turn our hearts to our fathers is to search out the names of our deceased ancestors and to perform the saving ordinances in the temple for them. This will forge a continuous chain between us" (*Ensign,* November 2003, 54–55).

When once our situation is compared with the
ancient Saints, as followers of the Lamb of God who has
taken away our sins by His own blood, we are bound
to rejoice and give thanks to Him always.

JOSEPH SMITH
HISTORY OF THE CHURCH, 2:22

So often we fail to be grateful for the present moments of life. We consume the joys of the here and now with a longing for something else. When we're on vacation, we may think of pressures mounting at home; and when we're at home, we long to be away on vacation. Happiness comes from feeling grateful, from rejoicing in the present and giving thanks to God. At the same time, grateful people are realists. They know that life has its challenges and heartaches, its satisfactions and joys. To be grateful doesn't mean we don't recognize the difficulties of life. Gratefulness flows from an abundant heart that delights in another day of life, for another opportunity to love and interact with God's creations. Thankfulness flows from eyes that see beauty even when they are surrounded by ugliness. It may be that our sorrows and trials become the very things that help gratitude grow in our hearts.

*In the evening went to see Brigham Young, in company
with Dr. Richards. He was suddenly and severely attacked by
disease, with strong symptoms of apoplexy. We immediately
administered to him by laying on of hands and prayer.*

JOSEPH SMITH
HISTORY OF THE CHURCH, 5:196

For several hours on this day in 1842, Joseph Smith
attended to Brigham Young, who was ill with a severe
fever. The Prophet recorded, "Although few so violently attacked ever survive long, yet the brethren were
united in faith, and we had firm hopes of his recovery"
(*History of the Church,* 5:196). The next day he visited
Brigham again, who remained sick for many days. We
learn from this account of the Prophet's abiding love
and concern for his people. We learn that healing
often takes time, and even a priesthood administration from the Lord's prophet depends on faith, and on
the Lord's desires, will, and timetable. There are lessons to be learned in suffering, and lessons to be
learned about faith and healing. We don't know the
details about all that was learned from this experience,
but we can have confidence that the Lord is ever
mindful of us and will tutor us if we are humble and
teachable.

As Adam and Noah and Abraham and Moses had been chosen
by God as his prophets in the respective dispensations in which
they lived, so was Joseph Smith chosen in these the latter days.
and called of God as his prophet, seer, and revelator.

N. ELDON TANNER
ENSIGN, NOVEMBER 1979, 53

N. Eldon Tanner, longtime apostle and counselor in the First Presidency, died on this day in 1982. He asked in general conference: "Of what great significance to the world are the contributions of Joseph Smith, the Prophet? . . . Perhaps most important is the concept of the Godhead. The New Testament clearly established that the Father, the Son, and the Holy Ghost are three separate and distinct beings. . . . The Father and the Son actually appeared personally to Joseph Smith to establish their personality and image. When the boy came out of that grove he knew the facts—that God is in form like a man. He speaks, he is considerate and kind, he answers prayer. He is a personal God for he called Joseph by name. His Son is a like and distinct person and is the Mediator between God and man. The occurrence in the grove was a flat contradiction that revelation had ceased, that God no longer communicated with man" (*Ensign,* November 1979, 52).

NOVEMBER 28

Being born again, comes by the Spirit of God through ordinances.

JOSEPH SMITH
HISTORY OF THE CHURCH, 3:392

We become born again through exercising faith in Jesus Christ, forsaking and repenting of our sins, and being baptized by immersion for the remission of sins by one having priesthood authority. Positive thinking doesn't do it—the ordinances of the priesthood and personal righteousness make becoming born again a reality. Alma declared: "Marvel not that all mankind, yea, men and women, all nations, kindreds, tongues and people, must be born again; yea, born of God, changed from their carnal and fallen state, to a state of righteousness, being redeemed of God, becoming his sons and daughters; and thus they become new creatures; and unless they do this, they can in nowise inherit the kingdom of God" (Mosiah 27:25–26). This process of being born again is a lifelong endeavor; it is gradual, little by little, almost imperceptible at times, but over a life course of overcoming the world we become new creatures and walk "in newness of life" (Romans 6:4).

Joseph Smith was a humble searcher after truth.
Therefore the Lord could use him. Truth must be placed
above all else, otherwise it cannot be found.

JOHN A. WIDTSOE
JOSEPH SMITH, 335

Elder John A. Widtsoe, who died on this day in 1952, spent his life in the quest for truth. He was a brilliant author, noted scientist and academician, and a member of the Quorum of the Twelve Apostles from 1921 to 1952. With all his intelligence and academic prominence, he maintained a burning testimony of the prophetic mission of the untutored plowboy Joseph Smith: "His life was a great contribution to human welfare. His teachings as accepted will in time make the earth a pleasant place in which to dwell. His career on earth lifts him to a towering place among men, second to none since the days of the Lord Jesus Christ. He stands on the pages of history a majestic figure. He sought truth; he found it. He used truth for man's eternal progressive welfare. Thus he won from God the prophetic title. Joseph Smith is himself the best evidence of the truth of his message to the world. Joseph Smith the truth seeker was a prophet of God" (*Joseph Smith*, 341–42).

Praise to the man who communed with Jehovah!
Jesus anointed that Prophet and Seer.
Blessed to open the last dispensation,
Kings shall extol him, and nations revere.

WILLIAM W. PHELPS
HYMNS, NO. 27

William W. Phelps (1792–1872) knew Joseph Smith well. He was baptized June 10, 1831, in Kirtland, Ohio, and worked closely with the leaders of the fledgling Church. He served as Joseph's clerk and scribe and was editor of the first Latter-day Saint hymnal. The Prophet inquired of the Lord for information concerning him, now found in Doctrine and Covenants 55. He was also the recipient of Joseph's forgiveness after his betrayal (*History of the Church*, 4:163–64). Soon after the Prophet's martyrdom, William W. Phelps expressed his heartfelt love and honor for the "man who communed with Jehovah":

Hail to the Prophet, ascended to heaven!
Traitors and tyrants now fight him in vain.
Mingling with Gods, he can plan for his brethren;
Death cannot conquer the hero again. (Hymns, *no. 27*)

William W. Phelps died a faithful member of the Church in 1872 in Salt Lake City.

DECEMBER

*Truth, virtue, and honor, combined
with energy and industry, pave the way to
exaltation, glory and bliss.*

JOSEPH SMITH

O God! where art thou? And where is the pavilion that covereth thy hiding place? How long shall thy hand be stayed, and thine eye . . . behold from the eternal heavens the wrongs of thy people and of thy servants, and thine ear be penetrated with their cries?

JOSEPH SMITH
DOCTRINE AND COVENANTS 121:1–2

While the Prophet Joseph was imprisoned with Hyrum Smith and four other companions in Liberty Jail, he expressed a heartfelt plea to the Lord (D&C 121, 123). They entered the jail, in Clay County, Missouri, on this day in 1838 and remained there awaiting trial until April 6, 1839. The conditions in the dark and dank dungeon-prison were horrendous. They were held in the cold prison by coarse and vulgar guards and under false charges. Some have called the Liberty Jail a prison-temple, for in it Joseph was instructed from on high and purified in the crucible of extreme suffering. On this occasion, and so many others, the Lord did not leave His prophet comfortless: "My son, peace be unto thy soul; thine adversity and thine afflictions shall be but a small moment; and then, if thou endure it well, God shall exalt thee on high; thou shalt triumph over all thy foes" (D&C 121:7–8). Joseph did endure it well and sits exalted on high.

Generations yet unborn will dwell with peculiar delight upon the scenes that we have passed through, the privations that we have endured; the untiring zeal that we have manifested; the all but insurmountable difficulties that we have overcome.

JOSEPH SMITH
HISTORY OF THE CHURCH, 4:610

All people from all generations past and future will look to this great latter-day work ushered in by the Prophet Joseph Smith and his faithful associates with deep gratitude, wonder, and respect. The Lord put the right people in the right place at the right time in order to lay the foundation of the work of gospel restoration. The Prophet Joseph said that this is "a work that is destined to bring about the destruction of the powers of darkness, the renovation of the earth, the glory of God, and the salvation of the human family" (*History of the Church*, 4:610). That bold promise uttered in the early days of the Church is being ful-filled today in a remarkable way. When one considers the sacred blessings for those on both sides of the veil, when one ponders the unnumbered rewards vouch-safed by the faithful who enter and keep their covenants, one is filled with ineffable joy and rejoicing.

Faith being the first principle in revealed religion, and the foundation of all righteousness, necessarily claims the first place in a course of lectures which are designed to unfold to the understanding the doctrine of Jesus Christ.

JOSEPH SMITH
LECTURES ON FAITH, 1:1

The *Lectures on Faith* were seven "Lectures on Theology" (*History of the Church,* 2:176) which were presented by Joseph Smith to the School of the Elders in the early winter of 1834 to 1835 in Kirtland, Ohio. The school was organized to help Church leaders and missionaries "[qualify] themselves as messengers of Jesus Christ, to be ready to do His will in carrying glad tidings to all that would open their eyes, ears and hearts," and to be "more perfectly instructed in the great things of God" (*History of the Church,* 2:176, 169). Lecture 1 concluded with a summary of the important subject to which they gave studious attention: "Faith, then, is the first great governing principle which has power, dominion, and authority over all things; by it they exist, by it they are upheld, by it they are changed, or by it they remain, agreeable to the will of God. Without it there is no power, and without power there could be no creation nor existence!" (*Lectures on Faith,* 1:24).

*The more I am with [Joseph], the more I love him; the more
I know of him, the more confidence I have in him.*

WILLIAM CLAYTON
IN JOSEPH SMITH, 499

William Clayton, an early British convert to the
Church, hymn composer, and close associate to Joseph
Smith, in a letter to Church members in Manchester,
England, wrote: "We have had the privilege of convers-
ing with Joseph Smith Jr. and we are delighted with his
company. . . . He is . . . a man of sound judgment and possessed of an abundance of intelligence, and whilst you listen to his conversation you receive intelligence which
expands your mind and causes your heart to rejoice. He is
very familiar and delights to instruct the poor saint. I can
converse with him just as easily as I can with you, and
with regard to being willing to communicate instruction
he says, 'I receive it freely and I will give it freely.' He is
willing to answer any question I have put to him and is
pleased when we ask him questions. . . . . . If I had come
from England purposely to converse with him a few days
I should have considered myself well paid for my trouble"
(in *Joseph Smith*, 501).

*In the cause of truth and righteousness—in all that would benefit
his fellow man, his integrity was as firm as the pillars of Heaven.
He knew that God had called him to the work, and all powers of
earth and hell combined failed either to deter or divert him.*

ELIZA R. SNOW
WOMAN'S EXPONENT, JANUARY 1, 1874, 117

Eliza R. Snow (1804–1887) was an author, poet,
teacher, women's leader, and second general president
of the Relief Society from 1867 until her death on this
day in 1887. She joined the Church in 1835 (her
younger brother Lorenzo would join a year later) and
gathered with the Saints in Kirtland, Ohio. She said of
the Prophet Joseph, whom she knew well: "With the
help of God and his brethren, he laid the foundation
of the greatest work ever established by man—a work
extending not only to all the living, and to all the generations to come, but also to the dead. He boldly and
bravely confronted the false traditions, superstitions,
religions, bigotry and ignorance of the world—proved
himself true to every heaven-revealed principle—true
to his brethren and true to God, then sealed his testimony with his blood" (*Woman's Exponent,* January 1,
1874, 117). The name of Eliza R. Snow holds an honored place in the history of the Latter-day Saints.

The truth is, simply, that he was a prophet of God—nothing more and not one whit less! The scriptures did not come so much from Joseph Smith as they did through him. He was a conduit through which the revelations were given.

BOYD K. PACKER
ENSIGN, MAY 1974, 94

President Boyd K. Packer told this story about a young man's courage: "A 15-year-old son of a mission president attended high school with very few members of the Church. One day the class was given a true-or-false test. Matthew was confident that he knew the answers to all except for question 15. It read, 'Joseph Smith, the alleged Mormon prophet, wrote the Book of Mormon. True or false?' He could not answer it either way, so being a clever teenager, he rewrote the question. He crossed out the word *alleged* and replaced the word *wrote* with *translated.* It then read, 'Joseph Smith, the Mormon prophet, translated the Book of Mormon.' He marked it true and handed it in. The next day the teacher sternly asked why he had changed the question. He smiled and said, 'Because Joseph Smith did not *write* the Book of Mormon, he *translated* it, and he was not an *alleged* prophet, he *was* a prophet.' He was then invited to tell the class how he knew that" (*Ensign,* November 2001, 63–64).

*I was seized upon by some power which entirely overcame me,
and had such an astonishing influence over me as to bind my
tongue so that I could not speak. Thick darkness gathered around
me, and it seemed . . . as if I were doomed to sudden destruction.*

JOSEPH SMITH–HISTORY 1:15

Elder Jeffrey R. Holland said: "There is a lesson in the
Prophet Joseph Smith's account of the First Vision which
virtually every Latter-day Saint has had occasion to experience, or one day soon will. . . . Before great moments,
certainly before great spiritual moments, there can come
adversity, opposition, and darkness. Life has some of
those moments for us, and occasionally they come just as
we are approaching an important decision or a significant
step in our lives. . . . Joseph said he had scarcely begun his
prayer when he felt a power of astonishing influence
come over him. 'Thick darkness,' as he described it, gathered around him and seemed bent on his utter destruction. But he exerted all his powers to call upon God to
deliver him out of the power of this enemy, and as he did
so a pillar of light brighter than the noonday sun
descended gradually until it rested upon him. . . . he found
himself delivered from the destructive power which had
held him bound" (*Ensign,* March 2000, 7).

When we rebuke, do it in all meekness.

JOSEPH SMITH
HISTORY OF THE CHURCH, 1:341

Rebukes help us to change and grow. For example, the Lord chastised Joseph Smith when he failed to teach his children (D&C 93:47–48). Always a rebuke must be given in the right spirit—a spirit of gentleness and meekness, love unfeigned and kindness, without hypocrisy and guile, as the Lord taught: "Reproving betimes with sharpness, when moved upon by the Holy Ghost; and then showing forth afterwards an increase of love toward him whom thou hast reproved, lest he esteem thee to be his enemy; that he may know that thy faithfulness is stronger than the cords of death. Let thy bowels also be full of charity towards all men, and to the household of faith" (D&C 121:43–45). The Prophet instructed the Saints while in Liberty Jail: "A frank and open rebuke provoketh a good man to emulation; and in the hour of trouble he will be your best friend; but on the other hand, it will draw out all the corruptions of corrupt hearts" (*History of the Church*, 3:295).

If we get puffed up by thinking that we have much knowledge,
we are apt to get a contentious spirit, and correct
knowledge is necessary to cast out that spirit.

JOSEPH SMITH
HISTORY OF THE CHURCH, 5:340

Intellectual snobbery is one of the clearest forms of pride. If we feel arrogant in thinking we are smarter, more knowledgeable, and better informed than others— even if it's true—we create in our hearts a feeling of superiority and condescension. Indeed, what does it profit a man if he has all the knowledge in the world and loses his own soul? What good does it do if a woman is brilliant as to the mind and dull as to righteousness. "The evil of being puffed up with correct (though useless) knowledge is not so great as the evil of contention," taught the Prophet Joseph. "Knowledge does away with darkness, suspense and doubt, for these cannot exist where knowledge is. . . . In knowledge there is power. God has more power than all other beings, because he has greater knowledge; and hence he knows how to subject all other beings to Him. He has power over all" (*History of the Church,* 5:340). True and pure knowledge will fill us with a spirit of humility and thanksgiving.

*We could not help beholding the exertions of Satan
to blind the eyes of the people, so as to hide the true light that
lights every man that comes into the world*

JOSEPH SMITH
HISTORY OF THE CHURCH, 1:206

The forces of evil are widespread and ever-increasing. The father of lies and his nefarious minions do not slumber or relax their efforts to distort, beguile, and deceive. Satan wants to blind our eyes and hide the light that emanates from God. But we are never alone. Thankfully, the marvelous gospel plan gives us the knowledge and reassurance that every person is given the gift of the Light of Christ to enlighten their understanding, to make decisions, to seek the good and shun the evil. This "Spirit giveth light to every man that cometh into the world" (D&C 84:46), it gives life to all things (D&C 88:11–13), and it fills the immensity of space. The Light of Christ becomes as a conscience, which equips all people with a basic discernment of good and evil (Moroni 7:16). Those who respond to this light are led to seek the further light of the Holy Ghost, for our aim in life is to receive more light—which for the faithful grows "brighter and brighter until the perfect day" (D&C 50:24).

In the celestial glory there are three heavens or degrees; And in order to obtain the highest, a man must enter into this order of the priesthood [meaning the new and everlasting covenant of marriage]; and if he does not, he cannot obtain it.

DOCTRINE AND COVENANTS 131:1–4

The greatest blessings of eternity come to us through the house of the Lord. Eternal life, God's greatest gift, comes only to a man and woman together; the fulness of the priesthood contained in the highest ordinances of the temple are received only by a man and woman together. All those who are worthy will someday have these transcendent blessings. In marriage, which is ordained of God, a husband and wife enter into an order of the priesthood called the new and everlasting covenant of marriage. This covenant includes a willingness to have children and to teach them the gospel. It includes a steadfast desire for righteousness and for keeping the marital covenant entered into in the house of the Lord. Indeed, we go to the temple to make covenants, but we go home to keep the covenants. Home is the proving ground and the place where we learn to overcome selfishness and be more like Jesus. Those who inherit the highest celestial heaven will have eternal increase.

Through his personal association with the Lord, his translation and publication of the Book of Mormon, and the sealing of his testimony with his martyr's blood, Joseph has become the preeminent revelator of Jesus Christ in His true character as divine Redeemer.

D. TODD CHRISTOFFERSON
ENSIGN, MAY 2008, 79

Because of Joseph Smith we know who God and His Son are, we know our divine nature and destiny, and we know the purpose of mortality. Because of Joseph Smith we know we can, through the atonement of Jesus Christ and by obedience to the laws and ordinances of the gospel, become new creatures in Christ. Because of Joseph Smith we know that revelation has not ceased, that the heavens may be opened and the mysteries of God unfolded to our understanding. Because of Joseph Smith we know that priesthood keys necessary to seal together families for eternity are once again upon the earth. The gospel light revealed by the Prophet gives meaning and purpose to life; it inspires hope, faith, and courage; it fills our hearts with humility and gratitude that we were brought forth in this day when the heavens were opened anew. Joseph Smith is the prophet, seer, and revelator of this final dispensation.

*To become a joint heir of the heirship of the Son,
one must put away all his false traditions.*

JOSEPH SMITH
HISTORY OF THE CHURCH, 5:554

The apostle Paul proclaimed, "The Spirit itself beareth witness with our spirit, that we are the children of God: And if children, then heirs; heirs of God, and joint-heirs with Christ" (Romans 8:16–17). To become a joint heir with Christ we must reject wickedness and put away false traditions. The Prophet Joseph said, "I have tried for a number of years to get the minds of the Saints prepared to receive the things of God; but we frequently see some of them, after suffering all they have for the work of God, will fly to pieces like glass as soon as anything comes that is contrary to their traditions: they cannot stand the fire at all. How many will be able to abide a celestial law, and go through and receive their exaltation, I am unable to say, as many are called, but few are chosen [see D&C 121:40]" (*History of the Church,* 6:185). False traditions are those things we hold onto that separate us from Christ. Gospel truth and Christlike behavior must be our traditions.

*One of the most important points in the faith
of the Church of the Latter-day Saints, through the fullness
of the everlasting Gospel, is the gathering of Israel.*

JOSEPH SMITH
TEACHINGS, 92

It was on this day in 1907 that the First Presidency for the first time urged European members not to immigrate to the United States. Before that time, converts from other countries had been encouraged to gather in Latter-day Saint communities in the western United States. We gather Israel anytime a person joins the Church and anytime temple work is done. The gathering of Israel is a two-part process: first spiritual, as people gather to Jesus Christ, to His living reality and gospel truth, to His church and kingdom; second temporal, as people gather to the lands of their inheritance or to the congregations of the faithful (2 Nephi 9:1–2). People gather as they receive the message of the restored gospel, exercise faith, repent, and are baptized into the Lord's church, and congregate with the Saints. The gathering takes place on both sides of the veil through missionary work and sharing the gospel.

A man of God should be endowed with wisdom, knowledge, and understanding, in order to teach and lead the people of God.

JOSEPH SMITH
HISTORY OF THE CHURCH, 5:426

One cannot authentically teach people concerning God or lead them to Him except one be endowed with wisdom from on high, inspired with knowledge of the things of godliness, and filled with the spirit of understanding and revelation. Such was the Prophet Joseph Smith and each of his successors. They are called to lead the Church because of their humility and righteousness, their meek and honest hearts, and their wise insight and good judgment, which come as an endowment from above but also as a result of diligence and faithfulness over a life of many years. Joseph Smith was hungry for knowledge; he was a lifelong learner who studied voraciously to expand his mind and gain understanding of everlasting things. Such is the case with all men and women of God—they read and study from the best sources; they take time to ponder and pray as they seek heaven's light; they keep the commandments and strive to live with charity and integrity, as did the Savior.

It is for the testimony of Jesus that we are in bonds and in prison. But we say unto you, that we consider that our condition is better (notwithstanding our sufferings) than that of those who have persecuted us, and smitten us, and borne false witness against us.

JOSEPH SMITH
HISTORY OF THE CHURCH, 3:226

While in Liberty Jail the Prophet Joseph wrote numerous letters of comfort and reassurance to members of the Church at home and abroad. On this day in 1838, he wrote: "May grace, mercy, and the peace of God be and abide with you; and notwithstanding all your sufferings, we assure you that you have our prayers and fervent desires for your welfare, day and night. We believe that that God who seeth us in this solitary place, will hear our prayers, and reward you openly" (*History of the Church,* 3:226). Five years earlier on this day in 1833, the Lord outlined some of the causes for the sufferings of the Missouri Saints and reassured them: "Therefore, let your hearts be comforted concerning Zion; for all flesh is in mine hands; be still and know that I am God" (D&C 101:16). Although our trials and difficulties can seem at times to be overwhelming, we can have confidence in the Lord and His promises—the Lord will always comfort and strengthen His faithful followers.

Truth, virtue, and honor, combined with energy and industry,
pave the way to exaltation, glory and bliss.

JOSEPH SMITH
HISTORY OF THE CHURCH, 6:425

As the Prophet stated in the Wentworth Letter: "We believe in being honest, true, chaste, benevolent, virtuous, and in doing good to all men; indeed, we may say that we follow the admonition of Paul—We believe all things, we hope all things, we have endured many things, and hope to be able to endure all things. If there is anything virtuous, lovely, or of good report or praiseworthy, we seek after these things" (Articles of Faith 1:13). Apostles and prophets of God teach the same truths as they guide our efforts to the everlasting things—these are the words of Paul the Prophet Joseph referred to: "Whatsoever things are true, whatsoever things are honest, whatsoever things are just, whatsoever things are pure, whatsoever things are lovely, whatsoever things are of good report; if there be any virtue, and if there be any praise, think on these things" (Philippians 4:8). Life is short and time is precious, so men and women of Christ center their energies on the things that matter most.

[Joseph Smith] was a meek, humble, sociable
and very affable man, as a citizen, and one of the most
intelligent of men, and a great Prophet.

DANIEL TYLER
IN WIDTSOE, *JOSEPH SMITH*, 354

Elder John A. Widtsoe, in his noteworthy biography
of Joseph Smith, included numerous eyewitness reports
of the character of the Prophet. Elder Widtsoe summa-
rized these statements from people who personally knew
the Prophet with the following: "Such was this man of
God to those who knew him personally. To those who
loved his memory and cherished his great life-work he is
truly a great and sincere seeker after truth. Indeed, he has
left us a great heritage of truth. Seekers for truth continue to marvel at his solutions of the many problems of
life. He kept close to the Lord. Revelations flowed to
him. Though but a man, he rose mightily above the men
of his generation. He had enough faith and humility to
be called by God to an office, transcending any other in
his day. As he died he exclaimed, 'O Lord, my God.' To
Him he had always gone for help and all his followers
must do likewise" (*Joseph Smith*, 354). We too can know
truth for ourselves.

There are two kinds of beings in heaven, namely: Angels,
who are resurrected personages, having bodies of flesh and bones.
. . . Secondly: the spirits of just men made perfect, they who are
not resurrected, but inherit the same glory.

DOCTRINE AND COVENANTS 129:1–3

The Prophet revealed several grand keys so we can know whether any visitation of ministering angels and spirits is from God: "When a messenger comes saying he has a message from God, offer him your hand and request him to shake hands with you. If he be an angel he will do so, and you will feel his hand. If he be the spirit of a just man made perfect he will come in his glory; for that is the only way he can appear—Ask him to shake hands with you, but he will not move, because it is contrary to the order of heaven for a just man to deceive; but he will still deliver his message. If it be the devil as an angel of light, when you ask him to shake hands he will offer you his hand, and you will not feel anything; you may therefore detect him" (D&C 129:4–8).

*Sunday, 20. —At home all day. Took solid comfort with
my family. Had many serious reflections.*

JOSEPH SMITH
HISTORY OF THE CHURCH, 2:344

We get a glimpse into the life of the Prophet with
these two entries in his journal: On December 20, 1835,
the Prophet Joseph expressed the comfort his family
brought him and wrote: "Brothers Palmer and Taylor
called to see me. I showed them the sacred records to
their joy and satisfaction. O! may God have mercy upon
these men, and keep them in the way of everlasting
life." The next day he wrote the following: "Spent this
day at home, endeavoring to treasure up knowledge for
the benefit of my calling. The day passed off very pleas-
antly. I thank the Lord for His blessings to my soul, His
great mercy over my family in sparing our lives. O continue Thy care over me and mine, for Christ's sake"
(*History of the Church*, 2:344). Joseph was passionate
about pondering the things of eternity. His soul was
filled with gratitude for a season of peace, for his dearly
loved family, for the progress of the work. And his heart
was ever drawn out in prayer for the welfare of others.

*The devil has no power over us only as we
permit him. The moment we revolt at anything which
comes from God, the devil takes power.*

JOSEPH SMITH
TEACHINGS, 181

The devil cannot compel us to do evil, just as the
Lord will not force us to do good. All is volitional—a
free choice as free agents. When we stumble and sin
we cannot excuse it away with "the devil made me do
it." We are permitted to act for ourselves, as taught by
Jacob: "Cheer up your hearts, and remember that ye
are free to act for yourselves—to choose the way of
everlasting death or the way of eternal life" (2 Nephi
10:23). The safeguard against this deception is to
beware of pride. Paul taught the Corinthians,
"Wherefore let him that thinketh he standeth take
heed lest he fall. There hath no temptation taken you
but such as is common to man: but God is faithful,
who will not suffer you to be tempted above that ye are
able; but will with the temptation also make a way to
escape, that ye may be able to bear it" (1 Corinthians
10:12–13). With humility and the Lord's tender mer-
cies, we can resist wickedness and reject the devil.

*I wish to correct an error among men that profess
to be learned, liberal and wise; . . . The error I speak of is
the definition of the word "Mormon."*

JOSEPH SMITH
HISTORY OF THE CHURCH, 5:399

Herewith we have another example of the Prophet
setting the record straight: "It has been stated that this
word was derived from the Greek word *mormo.* This is
not the case. There was no Greek or Latin upon the
plates from which I, through the grace of the Lord, translated the Book of Mormon. Let the language of the book
speak for itself. . . . I may safely say that the word
'Mormon' stands independent of the wisdom and learning of this generation. The word Mormon, means literally, more good" (*History of the Church,* 5:399–400). So
often critics and the so-called well-informed make statements about our beliefs that are erroneous or distorted.
Don't expect our detractors to present accurately our
beliefs; don't rely on enemies of the Church to speak with
pure hearts regarding our doctrines and practices. If you
want to know what Mormons believe, talk to a faithful
Latter-day Saint, study the words of our scriptures and
prophets, and pray about what you learn.

On December 23, 1805, Joseph Smith Jr. was born in Sharon,
Vermont. . . . On the day of his birth, as the proud parents looked
down upon this tiny baby, they could not have known what
a profound impact he would have upon the world.

THOMAS S. MONSON
ENSIGN, NOVEMBER 2005, 67

On this day, the birthdate of the great Prophet of the Restoration, we pause to reflect upon his life and teachings. He was unlike any other, called and ordained as a mighty messenger of the Lord, a preacher of righteousness, a revealer of God. He was larger than life, yet mortal, imperfect, and subject to the vicissitudes of life. He taught us by example many character traits worthy of emulation. From an excruciating leg operation as a young boy to his refining trial in Liberty Jail, he teaches us courage in the face of affliction. From his experience in the Sacred Grove to his willingness to return to Nauvoo to face certain martyrdom, he teaches us faith. From receiving news of the ancient record buried in the earth to waiting upon the revelatory timetable of the Lord, he teaches us patience. And from his ceaseless care and concern for his family and followers, he teaches us compassion. Let us follow his example and become people of courage, faith, and compassion.

This morning . . . I was aroused by . . . neighbors, singing, "Mortals, awake! with angels join," &c., which caused a thrill of pleasure to run through my soul. All of my family and boarders arose to hear the serenade, and I felt to thank my Heavenly Father for their visit.

JOSEPH SMITH
HISTORY OF THE CHURCH, 6:134

This was the Prophet's record of events on the last Christmas Eve of his life. What an image it creates to think of early morning carolers coming to serenade the Prophet they loved so much! Christmas was not yet a legal holiday in the state of Illinois, children went to school, and for many New Englanders, Thanksgiving was often more celebrated than Christmas. And while the Saints living in Nauvoo did not celebrate with all the same traditions to which we are accustomed, one thing remains the same: it is a time to give thanks, to express love, to celebrate the birth of the Son of God. Earlier, the Prophet had declared his testimony of the Christ: "And now, after the many testimonies which have been given of him, this is the testimony, last of all, which we give of him: That he lives! For we saw him, even on the right hand of God; and we heard the voice bearing record that he is the Only Begotten of the Father" (D&C 76:22–23).

*A large party supped at my house, and spent the evening in music,
dancing, &c., in a most cheerful and friendly manner.*

JOSEPH SMITH
HISTORY OF THE CHURCH, 6:134

Christmas Day 1843 was a day of rejoicing as about
fifty couples gathered in the Prophet's home for dinner.
Joseph Smith recounted a dramatic event: "During the
festivities, a man with his hair long and falling over his
shoulders . . . came in and acted like a Missourian. I
requested the captain of the police to put him out of
doors. A scuffle ensued, and I had an opportunity to look
him full in the face, when, to my great surprise and joy
untold, I discovered it was my long-tried, warm, but cru-
elly persecuted friend, Orrin Porter Rockwell, just
arrived from nearly a year's imprisonment, without conviction, in Missouri" (*History of the Church,* 6:134–35). The
next day the Prophet rejoiced that Rockwell had been
released and that "God had delivered him out of [his cap-
tors'] hands" (*History of the Church,* 6:143). We get a sense
of the Prophet's heart from this Christmas Day occurrence: his goodness and generosity, his love and loyalty,
his gratitude for good friends.

*It is in vain to try to hide a bad spirit from the eyes
of them who are spiritual, for it will show itself in speaking
and in writing, as well as in all our other conduct.*

JOSEPH SMITH
HISTORY OF THE CHURCH, 1:317

We cannot hide for long who we really are. The soul—who we really are, not what we appear to be—is reflected in our thoughts and attitudes, in our speaking and writing, in our actions and interactions with others. Joseph Smith said, "It is also needless to make great pretensions when the heart is not right; the Lord will expose it to the view of His faithful Saints" (*History of the Church,* 1:317). We may be able to fake it for a while, we may even be able to fool others, but sooner or later our true character is revealed. Although we're all less than perfect, hypocrisy, duplicity, and pretentiousness always lead to anxiety and discontent. Our lives are more peaceful and secure when we live with inside-out congruency. Character and authenticity are essential. If we are worthy and sensitive to the whisperings of the Spirit, we can enjoy the gift of discernment that will protect us from deceivers. If our hearts are honest and humble we will have the Spirit to guide us, correct us, and bless us.

I send you the "olive leaf" which we have plucked from the
Tree of Paradise, the Lord's message of peace to us.

JOSEPH SMITH
HISTORY OF THE CHURCH, 1:316

Doctrine and Covenants section 88 is a revelatory gem that contains the Lord's message of peace to those who desire to know His will. This remarkable revelation, which Joseph Smith began to receive on this day in 1832, commands the Saints to build a temple in Kirtland and offers insights associated with the Light of Christ and the law governing the celestial, terrestrial, and telestial kingdoms. The Lord gives specific direction for us today: "Cast away your idle thoughts and your excess of laughter" (D&C 88:69); "seek ye diligently and teach one another words of wisdom; yea, seek ye out of the best books words of wisdom; seek learning, even by study and also by faith" (D&C 88:118); "love one another; cease to be covetous" (D&C 88:123); "cease to find fault one with another; cease to sleep longer than is needful" (D&C 88:124); and "clothe yourselves with the bond of charity, as with a mantle, which is the bond of perfectness and peace" (D&C 88:125).

Joseph Smith, the Mormon Prophet . . . born in the lowest ranks of poverty, without book learning and with the homeliest of all human names . . . made himself at the age of thirty-nine a power upon earth . . . his influence . . . is potent today and the end is not yet.

JOSIAH QUINCY
IN SWINTON, *AMERICAN PROPHET,* 153

Shortly before his death, the Prophet Joseph was visited by Josiah Quincy, a Harvard graduate, lawyer, and future mayor of Boston, Massachusetts. Years later, in his book *Figures of the Past,* Quincy wrote of his impressions of the Prophet: "It is by no means improbable that some future textbook, for the use of generations yet unborn, will contain a question something like this: What historical American of the nineteenth century has exerted the most powerful influence upon the destinies of his countrymen? And it is by no means impossible that the answer to that interrogatory may be thus written: Joseph Smith, the Mormon Prophet. And the reply, absurd as it doubtless seems to most men now living, may be an obvious commonplace to their descendants. History deals in surprises and paradoxes quite as startling as this" (in Gibbons, *Joseph Smith,* 361).

I read [your letter] over and over again; it was a sweet morsel to me. O God, grant that I may have the privilege of seeing once more my lovely family. . . . To press them to my bosom and kiss their lovely cheeks would fill my heart with unspeakable gratitude.

JOSEPH SMITH
JOSEPH SMITH, 241

The letters Joseph wrote to his beloved Emma while imprisoned in Missouri reflect faith and courage, love and longing: "My dear Emma, I very well know your toils and sympathize with you. If God will spare my life once more to have the privilege of taking care of you, I will ease your care and endeavor to comfort your heart. I want you to take the best care of the family you can. I believe you will do all you can. . . . Tell [the children] I am in prison that their lives might be saved. . . . God ruleth all things after the counsel of his own will. My trust is in him. The salvation of my soul is of the most importance to me forasmuch as I know for a certainty of eternal things. If the heavens linger, it is nothing to me. I must steer my [ship] safe, which I intend to do. I want you to do the same. Yours forever" (*Joseph Smith,* 245).

DECEMBER 30

We were now confirmed in the opinion that God was
about to bring to light something upon which we could stay our
minds, or that would give us a more perfect knowledge of the plan
of salvation and the redemption of the human family.

LUCY MACK SMITH
HISTORY OF JOSEPH SMITH BY HIS MOTHER, 82–83

The Smith family, from generations back, were seekers after righteousness and humble followers of the Lord.
With great conviction and rejoicing, they believed their
son and brother and wanted to know the marvelous
things God had revealed to him. Joseph's mother
recalled: "During our evening conversations, Joseph
would occasionally give us some of the most amusing
recitals that could be imagined. He would describe the
ancient inhabitants of this continent, their dress, mode
of traveling, and the animals upon which they rode; their
cities, their buildings, with every particular; their mode
of warfare; and also their religious worship. This he
would do with as much ease, seemingly as if he had spent
his whole life among them" (*History of Joseph Smith by His
Mother*, 83). How could a teenager, untutored in the ways
of the world, fabricate such an elaborate scheme? They
who knew Joseph best knew of his integrity and believed
him with heart and soul.

Sunday, 31ˢᵗ. — At home.
At early candle-light, went to prayer-meeting; administered the
sacrament; after which I retired. At midnight, about fifty musicians
and singers sang Phelps' New Year's Hymn under my window.

JOSEPH SMITH
HISTORY OF THE CHURCH, 6:153

On the closing day of 1843, the Prophet Joseph recorded in his journal the events of his last New Year's Eve in mortality. It reflects the simplicity of the day, the sacredness of the Sabbath, and the warmth of beloved friends who came to ring in the New Year with him. Also on this "warm and rainy" day, he included a list of "a few of the publications for and against the Saints during the year" (*History of the Church*, 6:154). Indeed, the end of the year is a good time to look back and reflect upon the events of the year. It is a time to evaluate what can be improved upon and what can be learned. It is also a time of resolution, a time to begin anew our efforts to become our best selves and reach out more fully to others in love and service. We have our problems and our worries, but all things will work together for good if we hold on to hope, stay with the Savior, and strive to be humble and obedient.

SOURCES

Cannon, George Q. *Life of Joseph Smith, the Prophet.* Salt Lake City: Deseret Book, 1986.

Conference Reports. Salt Lake City: The Church of Jesus Christ of Latter-day Saints, 1880–2008.

Cowley and Whitney on Doctrine. Compiled by Forace Green. Salt Lake City: Bookcraft, 1963.

Davidson, Karen Lynn. *Our Latter-day Hymns: The Stories and the Messages.* Salt Lake City: Deseret Book, 1988.

Encyclopedia of Latter-day Saint History. Edited by Arnold K. Garr, Donald Q. Cannon, and Richard O. Cowan. Salt Lake City: Deseret Book, 2000.

Ensign. Salt Lake City: The Church of Jesus Christ of Latter-day Saints, 1971–2008.

Evans, Richard L. *Richard L. Evans Quote Book.* Salt Lake City: Publishers Press, 1971.

"Family, The: A Proclamation to the World." *Ensign,* November 1995, 102.

Gibbons, Francis M. *Joseph Smith, Martyr, Prophet of God.* Salt Lake City: Deseret Book, 1977.

Heroes of the Restoration. Salt Lake City: Bookcraft, 1997.

Holzapfel, Richard Neitzel, Alexander L. Baugh, Robert

C. Freeman, and Andrew H. Hedges. *On This Day in the Church: An Illustrated Almanac of the Latter-day Saints.* Salt Lake City: Deseret Book, 2000.

Hymns of The Church of Jesus Christ of Latter-day Saints. Salt Lake City: The Church of Jesus Christ of Latter-day Saints, 1985.

Improvement Era. Salt Lake City: The Church of Jesus Christ of Latter-day Saints, 1897–1970.

Journal History of The Church of Jesus Christ of Latter-day Saints, February 23, 1847. Compiled by Andrew Jenson et al. Salt Lake City: Historical Department of The Church of Jesus Christ of Latter-day Saints, 1906.

Journal of Discourses. 26 vols. London: Latter-day Saints' Book Depot, 1854–86.

Lee, Harold B. *The Teachings of Harold B. Lee.* Edited by Clyde J. Williams. Salt Lake City: Bookcraft, 1996.

McConkie, Bruce R. *Doctrinal New Testament Commentary, Volume III Colossians-Revelation.* Salt Lake City: Bookcraft, 1973.

Peterson, Janet, and LaRene Gaunt. *Elect Ladies.* Salt Lake City: Deseret Book, 1990.

Praise to the Man: Fifteen Classic Brigham Young University Devotionals about the Prophet Joseph Smith, 1995–2005. Provo, Utah: Brigham Young University, 2005.

Pratt, Parley P. *Autobiography of Parley P. Pratt.* Revised and enhanced edition. Edited by Scot Facer Proctor and Maurine Jensen Proctor. Salt Lake City: Deseret Book, 2000.

Roberts, B. H. *A Comprehensive History of The Church of Jesus Christ of Latter-day Saints, Century I, Volume II.* Salt Lake City: Church Deseret News Press, 1930.

Smith, Joseph. *History of The Church of Jesus Christ of Latter-day Saints.* Edited by B. H. Roberts, 2d ed. rev., 7 vols. Salt Lake City: The Church of Jesus Christ of Latter-day Saints, 1932–51.

———. *Joseph Smith.* A volume in *Teachings of Presidents of the Church* series. Salt Lake City: The Church of Jesus Christ of Latter-day Saints, 2007.

———. *Lectures on Faith,* Salt Lake City: Deseret Book, 1985.

———. *Teachings of the Prophet Joseph Smith.* Selected by Joseph Fielding Smith. Salt Lake City: Deseret Book, 1976.

Smith, Joseph F. *Gospel Doctrine.* 5th ed. Salt Lake City: Deseret Book, 1939.

Smith, Joseph Fielding. *Essentials in Church History.* Salt Lake City: Deseret Book, 1950.

Smith, Lucy Mack. *History of Joseph Smith by His Mother.* Salt Lake City: Bookcraft, 1958.

Snow, Eliza R. *Women's Exponent,* January 1874, 117.

Swinton, Heidi S. *American Prophet: The Story of Joseph Smith.* Salt Lake City: Shadow Mountain, 1999.

Taylor, John. *The Gospel Kingdom: Writings and Discourses of John Taylor.* Edited by G. Homer Durham. Salt Lake City: Bookcraft, 1987.

Widtsoe, John A. *Joseph Smith: Seeker After Truth, Prophet of God.* Salt Lake City: Bookcraft, 1951.

Young, Brigham. *Brigham Young.* A volume in *Teachings of Presidents of the Church* series. Salt Lake City: The Church of Jesus Christ of Latter-day Saints, 1997.
———. *Discourses of Brigham Young.* Selected by John A. Widtsoe. Salt Lake City: Deseret Book, 1954.

About the Author

Lloyd D. Newell holds a Ph.D. from Brigham Young University, where he serves on the faculties of Religious Education and the School of Family Life. He has addressed audiences in forty-five states and more than a dozen countries through his seminars and keynote-speaking engagements and has worked as a television news anchor and news magazine host. He has served as announcer and writer for the Mormon Tabernacle Choir broadcast *Music and the Spoken Word* since 1990. The author of several books, he co-authored, with Robert L. Millet, four previous daily devotional books: *Jesus, the Very Thought of Thee, When Ye Shall Receive These Things, Draw Near Unto Me,* and *A Lamp Unto My Feet.* Lloyd is the author of the most recent book in that series: *Come, Listen to a Prophet's Voice.* He and his wife, Karmel, are the parents of four children.